For

Hillel Black

1930-2016

Editor of my first four books, and a mentor to many writers.

For Katherine Harrington

Halcyon, Mississippi

Death Under Live Oaks

Scott Faragher

When windblown myrtles litter
desolate streets, wraiths and
specters through the darkness
creep, once cherished voices
haunt my troubled sleep, and
as the Spanish moss weeps,
I remember.

Felicia Labatut, Halcyon 1847

Halcyon, Mississippi

Death Under Live Oaks

(ScottFaragher.com)

ISBN : 978-1-7344528-5-3

Published by Deathcat Media 2026
Po Box 50292
Nashville, TN. 37205
Website : DeathCatmedia.com
Email : **deathcatmedia@gmail.com**

This book is a work of fiction, loosely based upon the famous Natchez `Goat Castle Murder of 1932.' While that case was fairly quickly resolved then, there are still many people even today, both Natchezians and others, who still, believe it or not, maintain differing opinions regarding what actually happened then, nearly a century ago. As an author with longstanding roots in both Natchez, Coffeeville, and Holly Springs, Mississippi, I've often wondered how this scenario might have played out had it happened today given the current advances in modern forensics. With the exception of the two defendants, the characters herein are based upon actual persons I know now or have known. You know who you are..

CONTENTS

1.

Home

Los Angeles talent agent Tom Roberts took a shot of last night's coffee and wiped the sleep from his eyes. It was great to have a day off, several days, in fact. He'd certainly earned them. `That kid in the basement,' as he'd been called, wasting time with acts nobody's ever heard of, had somehow managed to pay his way, taking chances and developing new acts that only he'd believed in. Eventually he'd been moved upstairs with the other agents and had progressed rapidly from that point, developing a reputation as a risk taker and a problem solver. His risks paid off, and now, after ten years, he'd just made one of the biggest deals in film history.

He absent mindedly cast his glance upon last Friday's edition of *The Hollywood Reporter* and thought about all he'd gone through to get to this point. It all seems so glamorous to everybody on the outside, the red carpets, flashing cameras, television and print exposure, but the reality is hard work, most of which is done behind the scenes by people nobody's ever heard of. Long hours of mostly unheralded day to day grunt work: prop department, wardrobe, makeup, cameras, catering, set design, construction, transportation, writing, editing; dozens of people in various locations scurrying around like ants on and off the actual set. The actor, the star, is just the visible tip of a very large iceberg.

Roberts plopped down in the desk chair, facing several sleeping computer screens. The phone message light flashed, alerting him to a message received. Two a.m. call, 601 area code. "Home," he muttered to himself automatically as he looked at its screen. Freudian slip. L.A. was home now, not Halcyon, Mississippi. He'd been born in Halcyon but left more than ten years ago after an unfortunate love affair, unfortunate for him,that is, or was. But that was ten years ago, and he'd moved on. He pushed the blinking red light on his answering machine, and got the news.

"Tom, Dad died this morning. Funeral arrangements are incomplete. You never answer your phone, so I hope you get this message. I expect you to be here, it's the least you can do." Click. His Brother Bill's voice. That was just like Bill, the often disapproving tone, the latent hostility and the unspoken implication that Tom had somehow left the family to starve to death by seeking a career in an actual city.

He found his favorite travel site, typed in `Baton Rouge from Burbank,'and `Baton Rouge from LAX.' 1:00 p.m. from Burbank. Click, that's the one. Next, rental car. Lincoln sedan, Baton Rouge. Click and done. A look at the clock confirmed that it was already 10:30 a.m. L.A. time. He'd better get moving. He also needed a place to stay tonight in Halcyon: Moro Hotel. Richlife/hotels.com. Done. Travel arrangements. New York, London, Paris, whenever, wherever, all in a day's work.

Tom Roberts had no way of knowing that this time, his hastily made travel arrangements to a family funeral in Halcyon, Mississippi were about to unexpectedly transport him beyond the security of his everyday world into the realm of synchronicity and place him right in the middle of what would soon become one of the most sensational murders of this century.

Hopefully there were no terrorists on the plane, although the `authorities' had dutifully checked, patted down, and felt up all of the children and crippled elderly white women they could find, further delaying departure.But he'd made it on board in time, and the plane was in the air.So the old man had died. Well, he was old, but they weren't close, they'd never been. Tom's older brother Bill had been the `good son.' Every family has one. You know, first born, named after the father and grandfather, the favored child who becomes an Eagle Scout, captain and quarterback of the football team, the one programmed for success from birth. He couldn't fault Bill, at least not for failure to achieve, the one unpardonable sin for any member of the Roberts clan, whose family tree, if it were to be believed, predated the Mayflower. Not really, but their mother and grandmother, and beyond, far back into the dim mists of antiquity had been D.A.R., United Daughters of the Confederacy, and every other thing which could be recognized with a certificate on the wall. Same for the old man: Society of the Cincinnati, Sons of the Confederate Veterans, Sigma Chi, Ole Miss, Harvard Law School, Governor's Staff in every state in the south. Tom's older brother Bill, was also the superman on the family tree. He'd graduated at the top of his class at LSU, led the Tigers to an S.E.C. championship, nearly won the Heisman Trophy, studied law at Vanderbilt, and become the District Attorney of Black County, a job which he would probably hold until he, in due time, became either a district federal judge or Mississippi Supreme Court justice. The perfect son.

And then there was Tom's sister Sarah, the apple of their father's eye, the high school cheerleader, beautiful debutante, Chi Omega at Ole Miss, Homecoming Queen, who never got knocked up, married a doctor, and in due time produced three beautiful blonde grandchildren. She'd performed as programmed, and was nice enough. Tom genuinely liked her, although she had absolutely no idea what the world was like beyond Black County, and very little personal depth. She `didn't do that much thinking' as their former yardman had once observed in regard to his own wife, but at least his sister wasn't any kind of trouble maker, like some women.

Tom sighed, shifted uncomfortably in his seat, and raked his fingers through his unruly dark brown hair, the `mark of Cain,' his father used to joke, dark like his mother's, from an ancient mixture of French and Spanish blood. "And then there's me," Tom reflected somberly, the third child, like most third or later arrivals, an accident, an afterthought, a mistake, an inconvenience, the bottom of the family gene pool. Tom's relationship with his father had been an open wound covered with a woven grass mat, like something in an old Tarzan movie, a deep hole, a dangerous place to be avoided, but something you could fall into if you weren't vigilant. A trapwhere you were alone in a dark place, with time to reflect upon yourshortcomings, your failure to live up to your rich potential, in other words, your failure to live up to the expectations of others.

His father had probably loved him, Tom reflected, but the fact was, there'd been no place for Tom, no preordained perch on any branch of the family tree. Most young people left Halcyon and seldom returned, generally making a life in Jackson, Mississippi, Baton Rouge, or some other nearby metropolitan area. Some stayed though, their parents holding them close by doling out just enough money to keep them dependent, but never enough to allow them to break free. It's probably a southern thing, but maybe not. Maybe it's that way anywhere and everywhere there is money which can be used to control one's offspring.

The plane hit an air pocket and dropped several feet, breaking Tom free from his musings just as a passing stewardess grabbed his arm involuntarily, in a successful attempt to keep from falling. "Turbulence," she stated factly. "May I get you anything?"

"Sure get me one of those Mr. T Bloody Mary mixes and a small bottle of Smirnoff, or whatever vodka you have. Thanks." He would drink the spicy Bloody Mary mix now, and stick the miniature bottle of vodka in his pocket for later. There was no doubt he'd need a drink sooner than later, but as a rule, he didn't drink on any plane. If he were to die in a plane crash he wanted to be fully aware of what was happening, he didn't want to die drunk. The `Tibetan Book of the Dead' said that it was important to die in full consciousness. Tom still didn't like flying, but in his line of work, it was a necessary evil, an acceptable risk. But an airport was now basically a very large bus station, and the flights were always overbooked, usually crowded, and overweight, and the planes were probably poorly maintained by ground crews on anti-depressants with hangovers. It was a good thing that there weren't many people on this plane since it was more maneuverable with less weight, and probably faster. The downside was that it was more subject to bouncing around and was probably a bit less stable in the air. But at least the wings weren't flapping like they do when the plane is completely full. Just now, Tom reflected, if the plane went down, he wouldn't care that much. He wasn't depressed or anything. It just didn't matter too much to him one way or the other at this particular moment, whether or not he lived or died.

"Good afternoon, this is the Captain Thompson, and we are concluding flight 147 to Baton Rouge. If you would, please hand your drink glasses toyour flight attendant, and return your seats and trays to their full, upright and locked positions. We'll be on the ground shortly. We hope you've enjoyed your flight with us today and that you will have a safe journey after you leave this plane. It has been our pleasure to serve you today and we hope that you will continue to make us your first choice in the air. Thanks again."

"On the ground," Tom laughed, looking at the man in the aisle seat across from him. "The term `landing' would seem more comforting than `on the ground.' It's kind of like when you order something from McDonald's and they say your food will be `up' in just a minute. Your food will be `ready' in just a moment sounds much better."

"You're right about that," the stranger said. "Have you got business in Baton Rouge?"

"No, I'm renting a car there and driving over to Halcyon."

"I've always heard that Halcyon is one of the most beautiful places in America, though I've never been there. Business or pleasure?"

"It's an oil man's convention," Tom lied, not wanting to cast a pall upon the stranger's day by saying he's going to Halcyon to attend a funeral.

"Well, have fun."

"Thanks, you too."

The plane landed on schedule and Tom retrieved his overnight bag and aluminum Halliburton case from the overhead bin. This was a funeral, and he didn't intend to stay long. He picked up the rental car, threw his stuff in the trunk and soon was on his way up Highway 61 through St. Francisville, Woodville, and a detour west to Halcyon. One thing was certain, nobody who was not going specifically to Halcyon ever ended up there, unless they were lost. In other words, it wasn't positioned in such a way that anybody could ever accidentally stumble upon it en route to somewhere else. If you were going to Halcyon, it was because that was your destination. No interstate, no passenger trains, no real airport, just a two lane Highway 61 North or South, and then more miles west. The closest fairly large city was Vicksburg, to the north of Natchez, or Baton Rouge, to the east but there weren't any direct flights from Los Angeles, London, or New York to Vicksburg, and Vicksburg was out of the way.

The scenery isn't particularly breathtaking from Baton Rouge northwest, until one crosses the state line into Mississippi. Before that it's flat, nondescript, and covered with gas stations, oil storage tanks, new and used car dealerships, convenience stores, low end chain restaurants, strip malls, generic cement block hotels, and individual vendors situated in the abandoned parking lots of closed businesses, trying to sell discarded crap that nobody wants.

Just south of Woodville, however, right below the Mississippi state line, things start looking better, especially in St. Francisville, Louisiana. The giant live oaks of Louisiana are now in a more natural setting, punctuated by dripping Spanish moss and surrounded by blooming magnolias, their waxy white flowers permeating the air with an incomparably thick and fragrant sweetness that seems to say `Welcome Home.' St. Francisville has many beautiful antebellum plantation homes still surviving and open to the public. Among them are the magnificent Greek Revival mansion Greenwood, located several miles to the west off of Highway 61 North, and, of course,The Myrtles, allegedly the `most haunted' house in America. There are also the ruins of the gothic Afton Villa destroyed in a 1947 fire, which are now a beautiful series of gardens which are open to the public. And then there is Asphodel, the house wherein lived the `mama's boy' who wouldn't propose to Joanne Woodward in the classic 1953 southern movie `The Long Hot Summer.'

The further north Tom drove,the more tense he became. This was probably going to be unpleasant, his brother Bill sulking around, playing the put upon martyr, dutifully acting in his role as the good son, implying if not actually stating, and probably in front of everyone present, how Tom had never done anything to help the family, and had been such a disappointment to the decedent. Their sister Sarah would probably be buzzing around like the devoted daughter she was, chatting endlessly and high as a kite on some combination of anti-depressants and other unspecified prescription drugs, each tugging her mind in a different direction, and wires not connected toanything, just sparking away inside that beautiful empty blonde head of hers.

At length, the presence of the magnificent moss-draped oaks began to produce a soothing effect on Tom, reminding him of the real reason for his dread at the thought of returning to Halcyon, the reason he'd left in the first place, Leah. Sure, Tom had been the red - headed stepchild, the black sheep, of the family, and he could live with it. That was the hand he'd been dealt. He couldn't live with the knowledge that the one he'd loved with his heart and soul, his other half, his best friend from childhood, had at the last moment chosen someone else over him, someone `with better prospects for the future.' That's what she'd told him. A dentist, for God's sake. It had been a financial decision after all. That's why women are more practical than men, he reflected. They're always looking for a better deal, `Window Shopping,' as country great Hank Williams had put it. Love is fine, but `show me the money.' He thought he'd known her and he hadn't known anything. Men are the true romantics, just big-hearted stupid, fumbling dogs. Women are like cats, cold, calculating, surreptitious and covert. Nothing is ever actually what it seems.

But that's not really fair either, and Tom knew it. A man is likely to select a beautiful woman with a shapely body over a pretty girl with a kind heart, for the same reason a woman chooses a man with money, because we are all programmed that way by nature. A man is unconsciously selecting a good breeder, while a woman is seeking a good provider, one who will be more able to protect her offspring. It's all unconscious and pre-programmed. Still, she'd broken his heart, and the bottom line is that he couldn't live in the same small town with `them,' her husband's smirking, victorious, artificially white smile, and her pervasive presence, a constant reminder of his betrayal at her hands. Both of them deserved each other.

It had been ten years and he still hurt for her, but how could this be? How could he have any feelings but contempt for this woman who'd basically chosen someone else due to purely financial considerations? Who'd chosen money over love, and besides, who was it he really carried this torch for? Someone who'd betrayed him, cheated and lied? He hadn't seen her in all of this time and hadn't asked about her. He didn't know and didn't want to know. Probably, by now she was old and ugly with three or four howling brats clinging to her. Hopefully, she wasn't still as he remembered her, naked in the diffused moonlight of the garconniere, her skin luminescent as if lit from within. The very thought of her tortured him even now, ten years later. Still, he'd see her at the funeral, and she would speak to him, offering genuine sympathy for the loss of his father. There was no way around it, and he must prepare himself. He'd have to see and speak to her.

The good thing, is that scorned by his true love in favor of someone with `better prospects,' someone who `knew what he wanted to do with his life,' Tom had ventured to Los Angeles arriving in town a decade ago at age twenty-five in a beat-up Cadillac convertible, with his tail between his legs and a couple of hundred dollars his mother had given him to help him out. He'd been just another nobody in a town full of nobody want-to-bees. Leah's rejection had fueled in him an intense desire to succeed financially. He would be somebody, he would have more money than that goofy yuppie dentist husband of hers, and more money that his own father had probably left his brother, Bill, the `good' son. And he'd succeeded. He'd waited outside the Fire Intergalactic Entertainment Agency office everyday all day long for almost three weeks talking to nearly everyone who came in or out, asking for a job. Finally he was given a job as a gofer, solely due to his tenacity and his refusal to take no for an answer. But he hadn't remained long in that capacity, and was finally hired as an apprentice agent. His casual southern style and warm accent effectively masked his dominant `Type A' business personality and won him many loyal clients. Within five years he was well established, having taken chances on some unknowns who'd subsequently become very famous, and he'd been granted that rarest of commodities in the entertainment world, loyalty. Now he was the responsible agent for some of the most important entertainers in the world and indispensable to the agency. Somewhere along the way though, he'd lost his need to prove anything to anybody, especially his judgmental brother, and even to `her,' his lost love. As far as his family, or anybody else in Halcyon knew, he'd become `a mailman out in California,' but the fact was that he could now afford any house in Black County's Halcyon, and pay cash for it. The thought was comforting, but somehow, none of that mattered anymore. Halcyon was just an early scene in an ongoing, unfinished screenplay whose location had shifted.

Tom stopped briefly in St. Francisville and ate a late dinner at a local favorite called The Magnolia Cafe. It was situated just off 61 in a gravel parking lot, surrounded by giant live oaks, and a few small rental cottages with motorcycles sporting out of state tags parked in front. The familiar was comforting, even in what was otherwise, a very uncomfortable situation. By the time Tom had driven through Woodville and checked into the Moro Hotel in Halcyon, it was just after 10:00 p.m. He dreaded making the call but dialed his brother's number.His sister in law Nancy answered."Oh Tom, it's you. Where are you? Are you in town?"

"Yes, I'm at the Moro. I just checked in."

"You can't stay there. I insist you come over right now and stay here. It's your house, after all. Bill's still at the police station, but I expect him any moment. Visitation isn't until tomorrow afternoon, Bill's already made the arrangements. Should I come pick you up? Are you sure? You know your mom's here. I'll tell her. Fifteen minutes? OK, see you then."

His house? Tom was amused. He'd grown up in the house all right, Forsythe, it was called, the huge but graceful antebellum monstrosity that it was. Almost all of the grand houses in Halcyon had names, which were every bit as significant as the family names of those who'd built them. Forsythe had never been his though, his brother Bill had planned on owning the house since he was a child, and had been living there almost nonstop all of his life. Bill had squatter's rights if nothing else, and now that the old man had gone to glory, it was a certainty. It wasn't that Tom wanted the house, Bill could have the damn thing and everything in it as far as he was concerned. Bill had worked hard all of his life, so good for him. He'd known what he wantedand gone after it. That was worthy of respect. The only thing that bothered Tom was that he'd been so blatant about it, as if somehow there wasn't enough of everything for everybody. That was probably the supreme irony. Tom was now rich, not well off, but rich, likely more so than anyone currently living in Halcyon, other than the spinster Jeannie Murdock and her cousin/boyfriend, Mark Delgado, that is, if either of them were still alive.

Tom kept up with the upper end of L.A. entertainment society, as expected of someone in his position, but didn't attempt to live ostentatiously. His name and reputation were universally known among the movers and shakers in Hollywood, but as a rule, he avoided the public spotlight except for that required by work. A certain extravagance was expected and delivered. Tom drove a 1964 Lincoln convertible as a daily driver, though there was also new black Rolls-Royce Phantom in the other side of his garage for formal occasions.

God, it had been a long day and was about to get longer. Tom swallowed hard and turned the rented Lincoln through the open iron gates of Forsythe, and followed the long winding driveway toward the 1850s mansion into another era, another dimension, actually, its lights sparkling in the distance like diamonds through the gently waving Spanish moss overhanging the brown gravel,which crunched beneath the tires as he drove. The air was thick and warm, and the expression `velvet night' came to mind. That's what it was like, velvet, warm, soft, and inviting, a comforting heat which soothed and caressed. The summer heat of Los Angeles was somehow different, oppressive, for lack of a better description. The summer heat in Halcyon is pervasive and all-encompassing, a part of who you are. It felt good now.

By the time Tom reached the house he realized that his brother

Bill had returned from the police station. A bright black Dodge Charger with alloy wheels, darkened windows, a battering ram on the front, a black search light next to the outside mirrors on each side of the car, and twin exhaust pipes indicated his presence. Bill's royal chariot. Bill stepped through the open door and down the front stairs of Forsythe and greeted Tom warmly, an unexpected surprise.

"I'm glad you got my message. You know how hard it is to get you on the phone." It was both a statement and a question at the same time. "Do they not let you carry a cell phone on your mail truck?"

"I came as fast as I could. I had a couple of days off so I slept in this morning. It was after ten when I checked my phone today. You know, I'musually at work at 5:00 a.m., and sometimes before that." If Bill intended to be cordial, this was a good start, but he was volatile and could turn on a dime without notice. Still, an extended hand was certainly a welcome one. Better an olive branch than a club. Maybe this wouldn't be so bad after all. In the wink of an eye, Tom quickly sized up his brother's appearance, and noted some changes. The slender six-foot former athlete was now on the backside of forty, a little heavier, with slightly graying hair around the edges of his face. He looked distinguished, but it was more than that, `settled,' for lack of a better word. People who are settled cause less problems. Bill also looked more like their father now, and his dark rumpled Brooks Brothers suit and blue pinpoint oxford shirt further confirmed the family resemblance to the old man.

"Bill, it's nice to see you," Tom said, extending his hand. "I mean it. You look good."

"Thanks. I've been working out at the gym regularly, and have just started running again. I've dropped eight pounds so far. You look good too. I'm glad you haven't gotten fat out there. You must still be running."

"About three days a week, depending on the smog situation, but what happened to Dad?"

"Heart attack...on the golf course, yesterday afternoon. He was playing with Judge Angelicola, like they had nearly every Thursday for the last forty years. He just grabbed his chest and fell onto the fairway. He died early this morning. You were the first person I called. Want a drink?" Bill asked his brother, before taking a sip of his usual gin and tonic from a large delicately filigreed sterling silver chalice. "Do you still drink Schlitz? I remembered and got you some this morning, although I don't know why anybody would drink that stuff."

"Hell yes, I'll have a Schlitz. It's the beer that made Milwaukee famous. I can't get that in L.A., at least not in my part of town."

"What part of town do you live in?"

"North of Hollywood," he said without thinking, not that he actually livedthere, and not that it mattered. His brother had never been to California and didn't intend to set foot in the place, referring to it upon occasion as the `real Garden State,' a title owned in actuality by the state of New Jersey. OK, why is California the real Garden State? Answer: Its population consists mainly of `greens, nuts, and fruits.' Tom had laughed in spite of himself.

"Do you like it out there? Well, you must. You've been there for what, ten years now?"

"Yeah, just about. It's all right, you know, except for the crime, mudslides, wildfires, violent street gangs, crooked politicians, insane taxes, bankrupthospitals, homicidal maniacs, and weirdos," he laughed.

"Do you have a girlfriend out there, I mean anyone special?"

"No, not anybody in particular."

"Well," Bill observed, "that's too bad. You're old enough now that you should be thinking about settling down. It's the best thing I ever did."

"I know," Tom answered, not wanting to start an argument, "and

Nancy's been good for you, but to me, given the way the world is today, no man should even think about getting married until age thirty-five at the minimum. But I'm glad that things have worked out for you, Bill. I really am. Women were different when you got married."

"That's true," he said, "and I'm genuinely thankful for that. Let's go see Mom. Let me caution you to keep it simple. Daddy, well, you know he'd been seeing his secretary Suzy Bennington all of these years. You knew that didn't you? Oh, you didn't. I'm sorry, that is one of the most widely unkept secrets in Halcyon. He'd bought her a 1840s cottage on Washington St. I'm sorry, I thought you knew that."

"Well, I didn't, but I don't think any less of him. Living in California, one gets used to pretty much anything as `normal.' We don't have any siblings I need to know about, do we?"

"Not that I know of yet," Bill laughed, "but then, hell, this is Halcyon, anything is possible. Let's go, everybody's been waiting to see you."

The magnificent Forsythe loomed in the background, its lights shining through the lace curtains of the front parlors. Tom had forgotten how big the house actually was. At around 8,000 square feet in size, it wasn't any larger than any average mansion in Los Angeles, but much more imposing visually. Its four huge, round fluted stone columns at the front extended upward toward the sky, almost converging and disappearing into the darkness above them, punctuated only by a second story gallery. The steps which the pair ascended to the front porch were of single pieces of cut stone, each of inestimable weight. There were once cut stone blocks on both sides of the stairs, each about six feet tall and topped by ornate large cast iron planters. Except for their absence, nothing had changed, but the house somehow seemed much taller than Tom remembered.

His brother held one of the pair of front doors for Tom as he stepped through the opening into another world. He was immediately assailed by the smell of decay, not the decay of something rotten, but rather of something rotting, wood, bricks, mortar, stoneand iron, nearly two centuries old, settling gently into the rich soil from which they'd sprung. He'd forgotten the smell, but it came back to him now, unforgettable, and strangely comforting. All of these magnificent old houses smelled the same: Waverly, Lady of the Lake,Tomachichi, Windy Hill, Halcyon, Marble Hall, Ivory, Concordia, Longview, Eldorado, Twelve Oaks, Sheraton Hall, and yes, Forsythe. And there was his mother sitting in a gilded French chair in the ladies' parlor, with an iced tea, or possibly bourbon, the heavy crystal glass sweating profusely in the humidity next to her on a mahogany table, wet condensation running down the sides of the vessel and forming a pool of water on the table's brightly polished surface, despite the presence of a coaster.

"Darling," she smiled, starting to rise to greet her youngest child. "I'm so glad you could make it. Bill said that he'd left you a message but wasn't sure whether you got it or not, but I was certain you'd be here. I'm so happy to see you."

"Don't, no Mom, don't get up," Tom said quickly stepping across a large nearly threadbare Persian rug. "I'm so sorry," he said. "I thought Dad was in perfect health. This is a shock."

"Well, of course it is, but you know he was seventy-eight. When you get beyond age fifty, people start dropping like flies. You're only thirty-five, but you'll see, and when they do, you won't believe it. Now it's just us old ladies."

"You're anything but an old lady, Mom," he said, but she actuallylooked frail for the first time in his life. Time had been kind to her and she was still beautiful, only now beautiful for her age rather than in general.

"Well, your father had five years on me, but I'm not that far behind him. It's just the cycle of life, and you might as well accept it as you have no choice in the matter anyway."

"You look great, Mom, I mean considering the circumstances. You seem to be holding up well."

"Your father married me because he always respected my independence. He could've had anybody he wanted. He was rich, handsome, and well-bred. There were plenty of Halcyon debutantes who'd set their caps for him, but he chose me, I think probably in some measure, because I could take him or leave him. He wasn't used to that. Anyway, I'm still standing, just the way he would've wanted me to, expected me to. But the biggest part of my life is over now. He cut a wide path, that father of yours. I know that he's already well on the way to whatever's next, if anything. He wasn't the type of person to wait around to see what would happen here after he left. He's already moved on to somewhere else. But I'll miss him. I'm still too upset to talk about it. I'm sure we'll have some time for reminiscing later. The funeral is at Mon Reve at two, the day after tomorrow. Did you bring a tie? You know your father would want you to wear a tie."

"No Mom, I didn't bring a tie. It was all I could do to get here."

"Well, no matter, your brother can lend you one. I want you to look nice, and you know how formal your father is...was. By the way, and speaking of formality, Miss Murdock wants you to stop by to see her. I would appreciate it if you'd do that for me, since she's become even more reclusive and seldom leaves the house anymore, at least not socially. She still lives at Eldorado,so you go and see her in the morning. I told her to be expecting you at around ten."

"I wish you hadn't done that. I really don't know what to say to her. I haven't seen her in years. Do I have to?"

"Yes dear, I told her you were coming in for the funeral and that I would send you over for a visit, now that's all there is to it. You be there in the morning at 10:00 o'clock."

For a moment, Tom felt like he was ten years old again and taking orders from his mother. It seemed like nothing had really changed, but it had. Sure, he'd go see Miss Murdock if that made his mother happy. What difference did it make? "Is she still as eccentric?"

"Yes, even more so, but she's so rich that it doesn't matter. She always liked you, though. Do you remember that $1000 I sent you eight or nine years ago? Well, that came from her. She said, and I quote, that `a young man should get the hell out of this dying river city.' She told me not to tell you that the money came from her. I still see her, but not often, though I speak with her on the phone generally, once or twice a week. She seldom goes outside, except to work in her garden, and she no longer bothers to dress to go out. She rides that old Schwinn bicycle of hers every once in a while, only nearly every inch of it is covered with bailing wire and grocery sacks. I asked her about it and she said that she wanted to protect the paint, as if it mattered one way or the other. Meanwhile, that expensive foreign car of hers rots away in her garage, and her side yard is all grown up to the point that you can barely see the house. She's only in her sixties, too young to be acting crazy, but not too young to be eccentric. Just go see her. She's expecting you."

"But what about the visitation?"

"It's not until tomorrow afternoon, I believe. And besides, your father isn't going anywhere anytime soon, at least I hope not. And oh yes, it was his wish to be cremated before burial. He didn't want a bunch of `imbeciles gawking at him' so it will be a closed casket. I hope that suits you, it's what he wanted."

"Yes, of course, I fully understand that. I don't want people looking atme either, if I can't look back."

"Did you say something about Miss Murdock?" Bill asked his mother.

"Yes, she said she wanted your brother to visit her tomorrow. You know Tom used to cut her yard," she smiled. "I think he had a crush on her, if I'm not mistaken. Why?"

Tom blushed, “Look…”

“No,” Bill replied. “I’m just curious because there was an altercation over there the day before yesterday, at her house. Apparently, she shot a neighbor’s goat that had wandered into her yard and was tearing up her garden. The neighbor had threatened to kill her over the matter and she, that is, Miss Murdock, called the sheriff’s office. He sent a deputy over and he calmed things down, but tempers flared over the situation.”

“What neighbor?” their mother asked.

“I don’t know. Jim told them both that he would take them in for disturbing the peace if they didn’t quiet down.”

“Well, she didn’t say anything about it to me,” Mrs. Roberts observed, “not that it matters. Tom you just make sure you’re over there at around 10:00.”

“I’m glad it’s you and not me,” Bill laughed.

“What do you mean?” Tom asked.

“That place gives me the creeps,” Bill laughed. “Hell, I’m just kidding.”

Tom’s welcome, wayward son that he was, had been warmer than he’d anticipated, despite his brother’s chilly phone message, so that was a plus. Still, he didn’t want to hang out in Halcyon any longer than necessary. It brought back too many memories. Most of them had been pleasant enough, but the biggest, most important one had not been pleasant, not at all. And Miss Murdock? Why did she want to see him? He could hardly imagine that she even remembered him, although he’d been secretly in love with her in his preteen years and even beyond. And who wasn’t? She was really, at that time, the most elegant and beautiful woman he’d ever seen. And she was rich, really rich, with a Newport, Rhode Island mansion which dwarfed anything in Halcyon. She also owned two plantations in south Louisiana, each consisting of several thousand acres of sugar cane and cotton. Her father had been the Russian ambassador, and she’d been the toast of the European continent in her day. But she'd never married, and now she was in her sixties. That would have put her in her late thirties, back when he was cutting the yard. She'd always invited him into that elegant house of hers for lemonade when he finished the yard. It had been so hot outside, even for him, who loved heat. As much as he'd needed money then, he would've probably paid to cut the yard, just to be near her. He'd fantasized about her before he even knew what that meant, dreaming of her coming through his bedroom window and kissing his face while he slept. She had the form and face of an angel, and that long, flowing sandy brown hair of hers, and such graceful movements. She literally couldn't go into town without people stopping in their tracks just to look at her. Her every movement, gesture, and facial expression were commanding, as if she contained some hidden power somewhere inside of her which radiated through her skin. It was the power conferred by pure physical beauty. To look directly at her was almost painful, as if she caught you looking at her she would be able to read your thoughts and would know that you were in love with her. She'd really been that beautiful. In fact, she was probably the standard against which every woman he'd ever known had been unconsciously measured, now that he thought about it. Everyone in Halcyon assumed that she would marry one of the many rich international suitors who would come to town, stay at the Moro Hotel for a few days, and then leave alone, their hearts broken by her refusal of marriage. But she'd never married. After a while, speculation had become rampant. Some said that she'd had an unfortunate love affair in Europe which had scarred her for life. At length, as she remained unmarried, it was conjectured that she thought herself to be above, that is, better than anyone in Halcyon. And when she would drive to town in that car of hers, she'd pull in front of a store and honk the horn until someone came out to see what she wanted. That attitude didn't win her any friends, but what did she care about so-called Halcyon society and its once patrician families whose fortunes had faded like the Old South? She knew who she was, and her sense of self-worth wasn't subject to the whims of people who meant nothing to her. As the years passed speculation ceased, and she became just another curious and anachronistic part of the Halcyon landscape.

But even Tom knew the basic rudiments of her family history. Hell, everybody in Halcyon did. When her father had become ill he'd resigned as the Russian Ambassador and along withJeannie, returned to Halcyon, to Marble Hall, one of Halcyon's largest houses, a massive two-story with a full cast iron gallery and additional one- story wings that extendedprobably sixty feet or more from each side of the front gallery. For some reason, the rest of her family remained in Newport, and New York, not caring to return to Halcyon, even for a visit. For a season, Marble Hall had been the social center of Halcyon society, with frequent visits from European royalty, and lavish parties which lasted all night, hosted upon the beautiful lawn, the air heavy with the fragrance of magnolias and mimosa blossoms wafting through the undulating Spanish moss adorning the giant live oaks. After her father's unfortunate death, however, she moved from Marble Hall, which she sold to a former Halcyon mayor, to nearby Twelve Oaks, another giant antebellum mansion, and finally to the smaller Eldoradowhich she acquired with around forty-five acres, and where she resided at present.

2.

Jeannie Murdock

Tom was up by eight a.m. the next morning, later than usual, but early enough to eat a delicious breakfast of pancakes and bacon at the Moro before driving to visit Miss Murdock at her house, Eldorado. In a way, he looked forward to the visit, now that he'd had time to think about it. He was somewhat embarrassed at the thought that she might still remember that he'd once upon a time written her anonymous love letters which he'd placed in her mailbox at night upon occasion. She was probably old and haggard by now, he reflected, as he drove down the winding, oak-canopied road which led to her house. His thoughts of her were suddenly stopped cold by the sight of Cypress Hill, one of the most elegant antebellum mansions in Halcyon. My God, he thought, slowing his car quickly, what could have happened here? He paused in front of the house long enough to see a man and a woman, dressed in rags sitting on the front porch in the distance. They noticed the car and waved pleasantly, obviously unconcerned by the decay and filth around them. The elegant front doors of the house opened into the darkness of a large central hallway, through which he could glimpse but vaguely the grandeur of the massive spiral stairway situated against the far wall, illuminated partially by light from the open door of the room behind, the dining room, as he remembered. The light passing from the rear gallery through the dining room's ruby glass panels, one of the house's most noted and distinctive features, partially bathed the staircase in an eerie crimson light, transforming it from the elegant architectural element that it was, into a fitting palette for a Bosch painting. Cypress Hill was a typical Greek revivalmansion with a large central hallway with two large rooms on either side.

The second floor was a repetition of the same plan, and also had large front doors which opened outward onto the upstairs front gallery. Like the main entrance below, the second story doors were bordered on each side with a vertical row of leaded glass windows, and topped by an elaborate elliptical fanlight transom, which was simply not there. All that remained was the dark outline of where it had once been. There were six large round columns positioned across the front of the house. A second-floor gallery was located above the first with identical columns placed directly above those of the first floor and supporting the second story gallery, but two of those columns, on the left side of the upper gallery, were missing altogether, and large sections of the upstairs gallery rail were gone, while other parts of the railing dangled precariously over the side. It had been the home of Bill Toma. He must'vedied sometime within the past decade and the house was now probably inhabited by squatters, as there were no heirs that he knew of. But that wasn't possible either. Vagrants would never have been allowed to take over the house. Tom had also cut the grass at Cypress Hill each time he'd mowed Miss Murdock's yard. Mr. Toma had been very nice, and the house had been one of the grandest in Halcyon. How could it possibly have come to this in a mere ten years? Something was out of place here, and the thought of it actually made him dizzy. He didn't want to appear rude by staring any longer, so he waved and drove on, quickly covering the remaining short distance to Miss Murdock's house.

Tom pulled his car around to the front of Eldorado, past the side which faced Cypress Hill. That side had become overgrown to the point that it resembled a jungle. This, also was strangely out of character for this small, exclusive, and very private street in a neighborhood of the really wealthy. As he parked his car in the circular brown gravel driveway at the front of the house, he noticed a 1980s Aston-Martin Lagonda, parked in a darkened shed, illuminated by light through a dilapidated door and the shed's missing side window sash. The car appeared to have originally been a royal blue, but it was so covered with dirt that it was impossible to say for certain. It also seemed that its two back tires were flat. Again, he couldn't be sure. It was a strangely exotic car for the era, and reportedly expensive and difficult to maintain. Very few of the wedge-shaped sedans were made, and few, if any, remained on the streets now, even in L.A.

Eldorado was a crisp, white, one-story raised cottage with two adjacent covered galleries configured in an `L' shape which ran across the front and down the full length of the side of the house facing what was left of Cypress Hill, about two hundred yards away. It was an earlier house than the larger, now dilapidated Cypress Hill, having been constructed in the early 1830s, while Cypress Hill had been built in 1841. It was not unusual that Tom would know the names or dates of these two houses, since he'd mowed both of their lawns. He'd also had to work the annual Halcyon Pilgrimages as a Boy Scout, so he knew about most of the houses in this town where nearly every house had a name, and he also knew the people who inhabited them. Tom climbed the short set of stairs to the front door of Eldorado and rang the bell. The cool morning mist over the Mississippi River had already been eclipsed by the rising summer heat which was now enveloping him like a hot bath. As he stood there he noticed a white wooden sign affixed to the wall beside the front door. `No Admittance,' it read in black letters, each about three inches high. Beneath that in larger upper case black letters, `MURDOCK.' A third line read `Inquire Elsewhere for Persons of Other Names.' In a moment the door opened and he was face to face with Jeannie Murdock, still every bit as beautiful as she'd been, only now older, and if possible, even more elegant and graceful than he'd remembered her. She smiled, held out her hand, and beckoned him into the front parlor, a room which brought back fond memories. "Don't mind the sign," she said, "I simply grew weary of people, mostly Yankee pilgrimage tourists, dropping by unknown and uninvited, banging on my door and generally wanting to `have a look around the place,' if you can imagine anyone actually thatlacking in even the most basic manners." Eldorado had the same characteristic and decadent fragrance that graced his parents' house, giving it an immediate familiarity, which made him feel a bit less uncomfortable.

The formal front parlor was exquisitely furnished, just as he remembered, dominated by a beautiful rosewood 1850s Knabe square grand piano, and a large rosewood dining suite, surrounded by eight elegant side chairs. Nearly every antebellum house in the south had a square grand piano, and many of them were Knabes. Mr. Knabe had personally come down south from Baltimore and sold a number of his pianos before `the war,' which in the deep-south meant the Civil War, even now. There were still the same ancestral paintings he remembered adorning the large room, each surrounded by massive gold leaf frames. The rosewood Belter chairs and settee were still arranged exactly as they had been, and the same leaded crystal decanters rested upon the same silver tray placed atop an 1820s pier table with a black marble top and gold stenciling. The house seemed comfortably familiar even though he hadn't been here in years, and its familiarity was refreshing on this hot morning. His thoughts were distracted by her soft voice. "I was sorry to hear about your father. He was someone whose company I really enjoyed. Both he and your mother are from backgrounds not dissimilar to my own. Today, breeding and accomplishment count for so little, and art and music, what have they become? But tell me about yourself, I'm sure that you've taken over Hollywood by now," she smiled.

"Well, Miss Murdock, actually I'm a letter carrier, a mailman, if you prefer, although that term is for some reason generally considered demeaning in postal circles."

"Your secret is safe with me," she smiled again, while pouring lemonade from a sterling silver pitcher into a cut glass goblet. "I've got friends in high places," she said offhandedly, "and I've kept up with your progress over the years at the agency. Your success hasn't been surprising to me. I expected no less. You might have met John Blumenthal," she noted. "He's an old family friend. He tells me that you've become quite successful."

How could she possibly know anything about his life in L.A. he wondered, as he attempted to maintain his composure? "Well, I've met Mr. Blumenthal on several occasions in social settings," he replied, dropping the pretense, "but he's at the top of the Hollywood food chain. He is Hollywood, that is, everything it represents in its current iteration. I couldn't honestly say that I know him that well, though we've met professionally upon several occasions, but he's in a higher stratum than I am."

"Don't be so certain of that," she smiled. "There are always things in play in each of our lives, people, circumstances, and events, which might strongly influence us for better or worse, of which we know nothing, and suspect even less. Let's just say that your progress has been `helped along' to some degree, but then you've earned your excellent reputation."

This conversation was making him almost dizzy. How could this woman in Halcyon, Mississippi know anything about him, his work, or especially about John Blumenthal? He was certain that Blumenthal lived between New York, Connecticut, Miami, and L.A. Period. He was one of the most important figures in the entertainment business worldwide, but Tom doubted that he'd ever as much as set foot in the state of Mississippi, let alone Halcyon. Miss Murdock was old money and really rich, he knew that much, and she'd traveled all around the world in the highest international circles, but it still didn't make any sense. As if sensing his perplexity, she cautioned him, "Sometimes it's best to just accept that things may have been working in one's favor and not look too deeply at the reasons why."

"This isn't quite what I expected to hear from you today," Tom said, still perplexed over her meaning, but her manner was so warm and friendly that he felt sufficiently at ease to address what had once been a very sensitive subject, and one which had been on his mind since his mother had mentioned her last night. "May I tell you something?" he asked, suddenly feeling bolder and less inhibited, finally able to look directly into her eyes for the first time in his life without turning away. "You know I had a big crush on you when I was fifteen," he said, not waiting for her permission to continue.

"I know," she smiled, "I was very much aware of that, and flattered. I hope I treated you kindly."

"Well, yes, you did," he blushed, "and I'm thankful for that. Young hearts are easily broken, and I'm thankful you didn't break mine, it would have been such an easy thing for you to have done, even if unintentionally. I hung on your every word. I literally lived to cut your yard, and every time somebody famous came to town to see you I was afraid you would marry him and leave Halcyon forever. You were so beautiful that I could barely look at you. I mean you are still, I just…I mean…" as his face turned crimson.

"It's all right," she smiled, "what you mean is that I'm older now, sad but true. I'm happy with my life though, and as you see, I never married. I think now, in looking back, that I valued my freedom too much to let anybody else ever determine what I should,could, or could not do. My fortunate circumstances financially, provided me the ability to come and go as I pleased without the inconvenience of ever having to answer to anyone, ask for anything, or be subjected to the necessity of having to explain myself. Anyway, I appreciated your infatuation at the time, and your kind words are welcome now. Like I said, though, my life is happy now, even if much less interesting. The only thorn in my side is that riff-raff next door at Cypress Hill. Those people are from a background which rivals my own, and yet they live like the very animals that inhabit their so-called house."

"I passed that place a few minutes ago on the way over here. There was a man who waved at me, and some woman. Who are they, and what have they done to that house? It was in perfect shape the last time I saw it. It's been ten years since I've seen the place, I know, but still, it shouldn't be that bad in a decade, despite the ravages of this climate. I used to mow the lawn there too."

"Yes, I remember, but those two are now the bane of my existence. The house is literally falling down around them, but that's the least horrifying aspect of the matter. They actually have goats running through the house, sleeping on, and literally eating the furniture out from under them. And there are chickens, and hogs as well, which roam the halls at will, and even cattle, freely using the entire house as their bathroom. Ted Parker, the editor at *The Halcyon Democrat* renamed Cypress Hill as the `Animal House,'and the name has stuck. Not only were they not offended by that appellation, but they embraced it proudly. The place has become a public nuisance, to put it mildly. To make matters worse, if that's even possible, those two slaughter animals on the front porch in broad daylight. You can hear the animals' horrible cries as they are being most brutally murdered with crude kitchen implements. They butcher them on the premises and cook the meat over smudge pots placed in the upstairs fireplaces, you know, smudge pots, like the highway department used to put out on the highways years ago. They smell like kerosene, the entire neighborhood does. God knows what sort of toxins enter the meat from those things, not that it would matter to either of them, one way or the other. And the city will do nothing to stop them. This past April, the two of them advertised by illegally nailing posters on utility poles all over

Halcyon inviting visitors to the pilgrimage to come visit them and tour the famous `Animal House' as Toma entertains them with Negro spirituals and hillbilly music on that ancient piano of his. This is how they support themselves now. Would you believe that nearly six hundred people paid $8.00 each to walk through that flea and disease infested hovel? There were tour buses lining the street and Yankees and foreigners taking pictures, and probably returning to wherever they're actually from, saying that this is how `they really live down south.'"

"You mean Mr. Toma still lives there?"

"Yes, that was him."

"It can't be. I've been inside that house before on many occasions," Tom remembered, "since I generally cut their lawn at the same time I did yours. Mr. Toma seemed nice enough, and he always paid me well. As I recollect, the house was beautiful. It might have needed a coat of paint, or a plank replaced on the gallery here or there, but as I remember, it was as nice as any house in Halcyon."

"It was, but that was a long time ago. I think that they just ran out of money," she said. "But that doesn't explain anything, and it's no excuse. They're plenty of people living in big houses in Halcyon whose family fortunes are gone. Poverty is seldom the problem, it's generally symptomatic of something worse, lassitude and indolence perhaps, a misplaced sense of entitlement, an outgrowth of insanity, or in this instance, possibly some desire for revenge against me personally, for some imagined slight, or even against the population of Halcyon altogether. Who knows? But the idea of coat-tailing the pilgrimage with a detour to the lunatic asylum they inhabit cannot be considered to be anything other than an intentional affront to everyone who lives here. They actually placed posters throughout the city shamelessly referring to Cypress Hill as `The Animal House,' seeking to capitalize on their reckless insanity, exhorting people to pay to see them as if they were part of some decadent aristocratic carnival sideshow, and Cypress Hill, nothing but a large, rotting circus tent."

An elderly black maid suddenly and silently appeared in the room, as if having materialized out of nowhere. Her crisp white apron, collar, and hat seemed like something from the movie `Gone with the Wind,' and yet this was nothing remotely out of the ordinary in Halcyon, even now. Roberts rose from his seat, affording the same courtesy to her that he extended to any woman entering his presence from elsewhere. "Excuse me, Miss Jeannie, I didn't mean to interrupt you, but I was about to head to the store to get the groceries and I wondered, did you want me to take a check?"

"Can't you see that I have company? You know better than that Hattie, but since you've already interrupted us, you know where the jar is. Take a hundred dollar bill out of there and get everything on the list. Are you cooking today?"

"I'll be cooking dinner this `eenin' before I go, but you said you wanted me to fetch you lunch from somewhere, while I was out, you just didn't say where."

"Oh, very well. Just pick up something for me at the Carnival House, and remember, cornbread. Cornbread. I don't want any rolls Hattie. Last time, you brought me rolls."

"Yes `em," she said, bowing slightly before backing out of the room. "And please bring me my change Hattie," she shouted as the maid left and Roberts returned to his seat. "This time, I want my change," she shouted toward Hattie. "I hope that she can stay focused long enough to complete the simple tasks which I've assigned her. The truth is, it's difficult finding anyone to work around here at all. You can't get a Negro to perform domestic work anymore. The government pays them to stay home and watch television. As a result, the Mexicans have taken all of the jobs they used to have."

"Mexicans?" Tom asked. "In Halcyon? Really?"

"Yes, Mexicans. Mexicans in Halcyon, Mississippi. Can you believe that?"

"No," Tom replied, "but then, there are so many Mexicans in L.A. that I don't even notice them. They're just part of the landscape, and for the most part, very productive."

"Well, they don't belong here. Hattie's fairly useless, but she's familiar. I've been around Negroes all of my life, and I understand them. These Mexicans don't belong here, but where were we? Yes, Cypress Hill."

Tom was uncomfortable with Miss Murdock's reference to `Negroes,' not that he held it against her. Halcyon was still the old south, cut off and isolated as it was from the rest of the world, it just made him uncomfortable, and he changed the subject. "Well, Mr. Toma always seemed to me to be `patrician' for lack of a better word," Tom observed.

"Yes, he is, or rather was, and so is his step mother."

"Step mother?"

"Yes. His `woman' Olivia Dautery, for lack of a better word, adopted him as a technicality. But then you wouldn't have known that. Well Bill Toma's real name is of course, William Henry Clay Toma. His father and grandfather were both famous Episcopal ministers, and one of them was the rector at the Episcopal Church here. Toma's great, great, great grandfather presented Robert E. Lee for confirmation in Alexandria, Virginia. In fact the great, great grandfather and General Lee were fast friends, so much so, that Lee gave him many family heirlooms and hundreds of leather bound books from his own library at Arlington. The house, Cypress Hill, I mean, is furnished almost entirely with goods formerly at Lee's house, `Arlington,' in Virginia. Not the Arlington to the north in Natchez, which burned, as you've probably heard. Arlington in Virginia, of course, was confiscated by the Yankees after the war and used as the national cemetery, mainly as a permanent insult to the Lees of Virginia. That illegal government land grab ensured that no descendent of Robert E. Lee would ever be able to return to Arlington other than as a tourist. But back to Cypress Hill. You probably remember the large marble bust of Robert E. Lee in the front parlor. That was given to Toma's great, great grandfather personally by General Lee, and there was, or is still, a cradle upstairs, in which General Lee was rocked as a child. It was also used by Toma as an infant. And one of Toma's ancestors wrote `Twenty Years at Sea.' Another one was Abraham Lincoln's Under Secretary of the Treasury. Toma's father died when Toma was two years old, I think, and his mother died when he was fourteen or fifteen. Toma attended Chamberlain-Hunt Military Academy in Port Gibson, just as you did. Then he took a degree from Vanderbilt University in Nashville before moving to New York to study music.

"He returned to Halcyon for good after an accident which crushed part of his hand and left him mildly disfigured. You've most likely noticed his left hand. In any case, that was probably the defining moment of his life, since it brought an end to any plans he had of becoming a concert pianist. He returned to Cypress Hill, which he'd inherited, in good condition, I might add. We traveled in the same circles socially, of course I was still living at Marble Hall then, and he was older than me, but he was a frequent guest there. He cut quite a figure then and was considered one of the most eligible bachelors in the state of Mississippi. Rich, attractive, accomplished, and from a distinguished family, he was the ideal marriage candidate for every debutante in Mississippi, Louisiana, or anywhere else, for that matter.

"His alleged `step mother,' or `woman,' if that's what one would call her, Olivia Dautery, is equally well-pedigreed. She was born at Le Mamarte Plantation in Arkansas and was a direct descendant of Cato Walker, who served as the Mississippi Territorial governor for a short while, I think around 1800, or thereabouts. Her great, great grandfather was Confederate Brigadier General Thomas Paine Dautery, commander of some Arkansas regiment in the War Between the States. As I recollect, he'd been captured at Vicksburg and subsequently released by General Grant, who of course, later became President Grant. Grant and Dautery had become very close friends despite their having been on opposite sides during the war. Olivia and her sister Lydia both attended school in New York, where the family had moved after the war due to the friendship which existed between her great, great grandfather and President Grant. Olivia's sister Lydia, later married Richard Forman, a great, great nephew of Varina Howell Davis, wife of former president Jefferson Davis. Apparently, Olivia had moved in with the sister and her late husband, Forman, a cotton planter from Jefferson County...Fayette, I think.For awhile, they had lived the rich life of delta cotton royalty, attending the most important events in Halcyon, Vicksburg, New Orleans, and of course, New York, where she'd become a successful journalist in her own right. But she never married, though she could have. She was certainly pretty enough, then, but she'd become tired of the social life and returned to Fayette, permanently.

"After Lydia's husband died, Olivia continued living with her sister, but they had fallen on hard times as so many agrarians had. Lydia and Olivia, born to the purple, had no idea how to run a cotton plantation. As Lydia lay dying she prevailed upon Toma to take Olivia in, at Cypress Hill. I think that Olivia, was, is, a bit older than Toma. So, in she came to Cypress Hill, bringing with her most of the furniture and personal items which had passed down to her from Varina and Jefferson Davis. Of course, Varina Davis, Varina Howell...Howell was her maiden name, had been born and raised in Natchez and was married to President Davis there, but you know all about that. I'm sure you remember Miss Dautery."

"Well, I remember her, now that you mention it, but I didn't see her often, as she generally remained upstairs."

"Now Toma has no money left, nothing but his good breeding, formerly genteel manners, and his education. Where has all of the money gone? Who knows? It's just gone. Like so many of the fallen aristocracy, he'd inherited land and property, but couldn't actually `do anything' which would provide him an income. And of course, there isn't much to do in Halcyon anyway. That's why most young people leave as soon as they can jump out of the nest. Toma no longer cared for the high life, or could no longer afford it, and began retreating socially, first by refusing invitations, and then by basically becoming a recluse, leaving the house, if at all, almost under duress, and then only when unavoidable. Meanwhile, sometime after you left, Olivia came up with the idea of starting some sort of chicken farm or ranch, God knows why, though ridiculous ideas like that frequently pop up in the minds of the over-bred. But she didn't limit herself to chickens, no, she also acquired cows, ducks, hogs, and goats. Over the last six or seven years the place has become a zoo.

"Do you see this?" she asked, suddenly producing a .45 caliber Colt automatic, seemingly out of thin air, "It was my father's `service revolver.' That's just an expression I saw in a movie once, probably in reference to some British military officer stationed in India during the colonial period. Of course, I know it's really an automatic pistol, and not a revolver, but believe me, I do know how to use it. I've shot and killed three of their goats in the past year alone. In fact, I dispatched one of those gnawing vagrant animals just the day before yesterday. I'm sure it will be in the paper next week. It's probably the talk of the town already, as if I cared. They refuse to keep their animals on their own property. The goats roam over here uninvited, eating everything in sight, going into the garage and jumping up and down on my car, excreting nasty little pellets everywhere, trampling my flowers, and digging up my garden. Yet those people have the audacity to get angry every time I shoot one of their marauding animals, as if they're the injured parties. The solution is simple enough. They should keep their vile, wretched animals on their own property. Both of them have sufficient breeding to understand that. The municipal ordinance which prohibits the keeping of livestock within the city limits doesn't apply in this instance due to some long-standing technicality, because the amount of land which they own removes this restriction. In other words, technically, Cypress Hill was…is considered a farm.

"I have great personal sympathy for eccentric members of the former aristocracy, since I'm regarded that way myself, even now, by the so-called `people' of this town. Eccentricity is in my estimation a virtue, insanity is not, other than to the degree which it succeeds in maintaining privacy. That crazy harpy Olivia actually threatened me the day before yesterday, the last time she and Toma came over to retrieve one of the goats I'd shot. She told me that if she had to come over here again, to my house, to retrieve another dead goat, that she'd be coming after me as well. I told her to wait a minute…that I had to run in the house and get something that I wanted to show her. I went inside and returned with my .45, cocked the hammer, pointed it directly at her and told her that if she wanted to escalate matters to the next level that she should prepare herself for the inevitable consequences of her actions. Do you know what she said in response?"

"No, I can't imagine," Tom replied, seemingly spellbound.

"She looked at me with those wild eyes of hers moving from side to side rapidly, and that uncontrolled mass of gray thatch which covers her head waving with the breeze like Spanish moss, and told me, and I quote, 'I'll blow your head clean off.' It was as if she were the one with the pistol, rather than me. I just looked at her there dressed in rags with the ruins of Cypress Hill standing majestically in the background, and despaired that this is what our great culture has finally become. I didn't know what to say. The once exquisitely beautiful Olivia Dautery had been transformed into some hideous wretch of a creature, a wizened sea-hag, displaying not even a trace of who, or what she'd once been, not a trace. Things have been quiet for a day or so over there, at least more so than usual, yet I can't help but think that the two of them are up to something nefarious, quietly plotting some new mischief. They're shrewd and calculating, even if insane. Just because someone is crazy doesn't necessarily mean that they're stupid, so I wouldn't be surprised if they attempt to burn my house down, at some point, or even kill me. I mean it. In their irrational minds, that would probably solve everything. I'm genuinely afraid of them."

"Neighbors can pose a big problem. I'll speak to Bill and see if there's something that can be done to rein them in."

"It's no use, I've already spoken with your brother about it, and he told me that inasmuch as they've not actually violated anything other than a misdemeanor nuisance law, there's not really anything he can do about it. `You can't prosecute someone for what they might do,' he told me. And somehow, they actually pay their property taxes, so they manage to skate just along the edge of the law."

"Well," Tom said thoughtfully, "that's one of the loopholes in our legal system. Have you considered a restraining order?"

"No, I want them to be able to come and collect the body of the next goat, cow, hog, or chicken that I kill, and that's inevitable, just a matter of time. Also, she'd probably consider that sort of action as a declaration of war onmy part, and might react with some sort of preemptive act of violence. Oh well, I'm sorry for boring you with all of this about the `Animal house.' I'm sure it'll all take care of itself, one way or the other. I just wanted to express my sympathy for the loss of your father, and as I don't intend to come to the funeral, I wanted to tell you in person. Also, I wanted to see how you were doing in California."

"One other thing, before I go," Tom said. "I was wondering about your cousin, Mr. Delgado. How's he doing?"

"Mark's fine, and thank you for asking, I'll tell him I saw you when he arrives for dinner tonight. I'm sure he'll be pleased to know that you're doing well."

"Well, you know, I idolized him when I was fifteen, that is, I wanted to be just like him. He was handsome and elegant, so tall and slim, and was always treated with such courtesy by everyone in town, as if nobody wanted to ruffle his feathers. I always thought that he looked a lot like Errol Flynn, well, he reminded me of him. I always had the feeling that if anyone ever said anything which he found offensive, he would have challenged him to a duel on the spot. He literally radiated both power and prestige."

"I'll tell him you said that," she smiled. "That will make his day, I promise you. Thanks again for coming by, it's been such a pleasure seeing you again."

Tom stood to leave, sensing correctly that he'd been dismissed, took her hand briefly, bid her farewell and stepped back into the bright sunlight. He could see Cypress Hill, in the distance, a looming, dark and sinister shadow, and was seized by a sudden chill which he shook off with a shrug of his shoulders. As he drove past it on the way out, he noticed chickens, goats, and cattle roaming the premises, with a large jersey cow standing comfortably in the doorway swishing flies with its tail. He didn't see either of Cypress Hill's human inhabitants, which was probably for the best, as it also meant that they hadn't seen him. There was somebody else there though, standing next to the front door. No, apparently at second glance, it was a wool blanket, or perhaps an old overcoat or raincoat, which had been draped over one of the coach lights on either side of the doorway. The elegant window casements with their wavy hand-blown glass panels were simply gone, and where they'd once been, were now merely several tall frightening rectangles of darkness. A large owl, nearly two feet tall, peered at him unnoticed from the high bough of a giant live oak, its head turning to follow the car as it drove away.

Tom stopped by the only Thai joint in town and ate lunch while he read the *Wall Street Journal,* not that he would ever put a dime in the stock market personally, but it was one of the better daily papers still in print. He also knew that when he arrived at the funeral home he'd be there all afternoon as expected, so he elected to eat now. There would probably be food at the funeral home but it would be a very cold day in an extremely hot hell before he ever ate even a bite of food at any funeral home. The very idea was ghastly. After lunch Tom stopped by the Moro Hotel and made phone calls to his office in L.A. and elsewhere, and then went for a drive. The town had changed little in the past ten years, and this was somehow comforting. Tubby Turetha's, a tamale place and a local hangout famous for its `F You Up' gin coctails and famous secret recipe `Yello Jack,' a Galliano based concotion known to frequently incite nakedness among its imbibers, had moved across and down the street to a larger place, and there was a new, modern hotel downtown situated on a bluff dontown overlooking the Mississipi River. After an hour's run, he returned to the hotel to shower and freshen up, reluctantly donning his sport coat, and the tie his brother had loaned him. Ten minutes later found him approaching the funeral home where a fairly large crowd had already arrived, as he'd anticipated.

Tom's father had been born and raised in Halcyon and had been well liked. Under his jurisdiction, the family home, Forsythe, had been a lively place and the scene of many gatherings of the local bon-ton. It was a new era now, however, and the upper crust of Halcyon was not as large as it had been a hundred years ago, or even twenty years ago, and the lavish parties and a specific social season, were mostly a thing of the past. It was no longer the era of extravagance, and many of those who still had money were anything but ostentatious, preferring to fly under the radar unnoticed, rather than draw attention to themselves.

The funeral home was an old mansion, on Highway 61 North, just outside of town past the remaining ruins of Halcyon Plantation. `Mon Reve,' as it was called, literally meaning `My Dream,' was the former home of Confederate General J.B. Walker who'd died in the siege of Vicksburg. It was located now on several acres, all that remained of the original thousand-acre Spanish land grant. General Walker had only occupied the house for two years before the War Between the States, as it is called in Halcyon, rather than the Civil War, a minor point in the vast expanse of time, to be sure, but one of significant distinction to the descendants of the former Confederate aristocracy. Mon Reve was true to the original concept of the funeral home as a home, rather than as a new and modern corporately owned structure, which seemed to be the current trend. It was large and stately and could accommodate several funeral services at one time. Its name seemed strangely appropriate, Tom reflected, for those who repose there briefly before continuing their journey into the eternal `land of dreams.'

Tom recognized some of the cars parked outside, including several newer Lincolns and Cadillacs, as well as old Mrs. Wentworth's 1976 shiny royal blue Cadillac Fleetwood. A life-size cast iron Negro lawn jockey dressed in rags greeted him silently as he stepped through the open double doors and into the main hallway, its face frozen in a perpetual smile. The pervasive atmosphere was for the most part predictably jovial, as expected. If this were a black funeral, Tom reflected, there would be weeping, moaning, and wailing with people draping themselves across the casket, shouting lamentations and wringing their hands in despair. Nothing like that here, as excessive emotional displays in public are frowned upon in polite Halcyon social circles. The solid rosewood casket containing his father's body, or rather ashes, rested comfortably enough on a gilded, but somber looking wooden bier, itself a relic of the mid-nineteenth century, an era father away in reality than merely the span of years the interval encompassed. Tom recognized many familiar faces although he wasn't generally noticed at first. For a few moments it seemed that he might be invisible. Who were these people? Surely he knew everyone in Halcyon, and yet many of these faces were unfamiliar. It had been a nearly a decade since he'd been back to Halcyon for more than a day or so, and that had been only at Christmas. In and out. He'd not stayed long enough to visit anybody and had been happy to return to L.A., well, actually more relieved than happy. He'd been scared to death of seeing Leah. He was strong enough now to face the fact that she'd chosen someone else over him, but it was easier to accept from somewhere else, a place where there were no reminders of their time together, or of his loss.

His ruminations were interrupted by a tap on the shoulder and the sound of a vaguely familiar voice which he almost recognized before completely comprehending that it came from Bernice Conley, a girl, who at seventeen, had bestowed her considerable favors upon himself and two of his grateful friends one warm spring Sunday afternoon upon the widow's walk at Longview, back when the house had been in private hands. "How are you doing Tom? I'm truly sorry about your father, I lost mine last summer, so I know what it's like, but I'm so glad to see you. You still look great. This is my husband, Captain Bob."

"A navy man?" Tom asked, genuinely impressed by any naval officer of that rank.

"No, silly," she laughed. "He's `the' Captain Bob. He hosts a children's show on cable television out of Jackson. It's on in three hundred plus cities. Certainly you've heard of it, of him?"

"Of course I have," he lied. She was obviously proud of him. "I've seen you myself on television. I guess I just wasn't expecting to see a celebrity of any kind in Halcyon, especially at a funeral. Nice to meet you," he said.

"Isn't he well mannered?" she asked, obviously seeking an `amen' from Captain Bob.

"Yes, yes he is. I'm sorry about your father," her husband said, attempting to appear appropriately sympathetic.

"Yes, well thank you both for coming."

"How long are you planning to be in town?" she asked. "Perhaps we could get together for lunch. Or a drink...or something," she winked, out of sight of her husband.

"I sincerely appreciate the thought, but I'm planning to leave the day after tomorrow, after the funeral."

"Well, it's been so nice seeing you again," she gushed. "And don't be a stranger to your home town. I expect you to call me...us, the very next time you're in town, and I won't take no for an answer."

As it turned out, there was to be a receiving line and he'd arrived just in time. He positioned himself in front of the closed casket to the left of his mother, brother, and sister, and stood there for the next several hours as well wishers and sympathizers from across the broad spectrum of the Halcyon social order stopped by to pay their condolences. It would've been a tiresome ordeal except for the fact that Tom saw several of his former friends and schoolmates. Of course, many more, like himself, had left the city in search of greener pastures, and were absent.

Suddenly, there she was, Leah, the one who'd broken his heart a decade ago. She was in the line and would be standing in front of him at any moment. Damn, she was every bit as beautiful as she'd been then, only now somehow less of a girl and more of a woman. Sadly, he reflected, she looked even better than she did the last time he saw her, hardly what he'd hoped for, not that he wished her ill. She was dressed in a close fitting somber beige linen skirt and a crisp white blouse with her brown hair pulled back tightly, and her neck adorned with a simple string of pearls. He'd moved on, but in the back of his mind, he knew that it would be easier to face her if she'd lost some of her beauty. Perhaps then, he reasoned, his sense of loss wouldn't seem so great. His heart raced as she moved closer and his breathing became faster and shallower, just like it always had. "Damn you, Tom," he said to himself angrily, "remember who you are, remember your success, your power, your accomplishments, your paid for house, your many women. Remember how she treated you, as if you didn't matter, as if your love had meant nothing." He had no idea what he was saying now to the people who stopped in front of him to express their sympathies. He just shook their hands and smiled, thanking them for coming. Suddenly she was there beside him, in front of his sister. They were speaking and then, just now, she was standing here in front of him, her two hands in his. There was so much he'd planned on saying to her if he ever saw her again, and how he'd rehearsed the lines. He'd tell her that, if she could've just waited, he would've given her anything she wanted. He'd berate her for her shallowness and cruelty. He'd tell her how he hated her for selling out, for becoming everything she professed to despise. He'd condemn her for expecting any man to have his entire life planned at age twenty-five. Eventually he'd decided that if he ever saw her again he'd walk on by as if she didn't exist, as if she didn't even deserve his contempt. And now, here she was standing directly in front of him, and strangely, none of that mattered any longer. For the moment, at least, it was enough to be looking at her.

"I'm sorry about your father," she said, looking directly into his eyes, "he was a great man who did a lot for Halcyon." Then a long pause. "You're looking good," she said. "You look healthy. Life must be treating you well in sunny California."

"Thank you. You too," he fumbled, "Time has been kind. You…I mean. It's nice to see you…I…Dad always liked you."

"How long are you going to be in town?" she asked.

"Well, I'm planning to leave the day after tomorrow, that is, the day after Dad's funeral, `labor me vocat,' as they say. `Duty calls.'"

"Well, perhaps I'll see you before you leave," she said calmly. "There are people in line behind me waiting, so I'd better be going. It was nice seeing you again. I'm sorry about your father."

It was as if time had simply stood still. She was basically unchanged, except now, even more beautiful. Damn, why did he have to see her? Leah. His life was working. He'd told Reynaldo, his gay hairdresser in L.A. all about her. Reynaldo had instructed him to just `put the bitch in a box on the top shelf in a closet somewhere deep in the back of an empty room in a dark corner of your mind, and never open that box again.' And that's what he'd done. But it was like having a box with a rattlesnake in the closet. He'd always been aware that the box was there. It was something that he didn't approach, something whose contents terrified him, literally. Every woman he'd met and bedded had pushed the memory a bit farther back, but never far enough. Her memory was ever present, threatening, and always there. Now, through no fault of his own, this box had been opened and there was no good which could come from it, none at all, just more searing pain and the knowledge that he somehow just hadn't been `good enough.' Suddenly the recollection of his success, of his many accomplishments meant absolutely nothing. He felt like a child who hadn't been chosen to play some game at third grade school recess.

The visitation was over by five-thirty, and only the family and the attendants still remained at the funeral home. If there hadn't been a funeral service already publicly announced for the next day, they'd have held the service privately, right then, and been done with the matter. Mrs. Roberts was tired, and the weight of her seventy-three years was wearing her down, especially under the circumstances. She just wanted to go home. Nancy agreed to take her, since Bill needed to run by the police station.

Tom had accepted an invitation to a gathering at Queen's Court Tavern, one of the oldest buildings in Halcyon. The two-story 1790s wooden structure was fairly small with greatly weathered cypress boards outside, and relatively low ceilings indoors. The old tavern allegedly had a haunted room upstairs, and it did too, he'd seen the ghost of the woman with his own two eyes, though she didn't present herself to everyone. `She' had shown herself to Tom and had startled him, but he'd sensed no evil emanating from whoever or whatever she was. Supposedly she'd been murdered and was buried in the place somewhere. Ghosts were a very real part of life in Halcyon, and nearly everyone who'd grown up here had some ghostly experience of one sort or another. They generally consisted of sightings of disembodied spirits which were for the most part benign, or indecipherable whisperings, moved objects, etc. The `presence' in Queen's Court Tavern was openly hostile to most, though it reacted differently from one manifestation to the next, that is, it had `moods,' for lack of a better word. In high school and college, the place had been, for the most part, a hangout of the local gentry, except during pilgrimage, when it was abandoned in favor of the country club or the bar at Waverly, which with its majestic surrounding columns, was perhaps the most representative of all the great houses of Halcyon. Tom could use a drink, and it would be nice to catch up with some old friends. Things were supposed to be cranking up at six-thirty. That would give him time to visit with the family for a bit and perhaps make some more phone calls. He paused for a moment, trying to remember whether or not he'd thought to bring his cell phone, or had left it at the hotel.

As he drove back to Forsythe he recollected what it had been like growing up in Halcyon. Everyone had known each other, and the racial shadow which always hangs like a dark cloud everywhere else had been pretty much absent in Halcyon. Things had always been the same, and upper class white children had generally been raised by black maids. He remembered swimming down by the waterfront, riding his bike around town, the Confederate Ball, and Sunday lunches with his family at The Kitchen behind Lady of the Lake. Halcyon had existed apart from anywhere else in Mississippi, or the entire south, for that matter. To the north was Adams County's Natchez, and further north, Claiborne County's Port Gibson, a beautiful antebellum town which had been spared by General Grant because it had been the birthplace of Confederate General Van Dorn, who'd shown Grant's wife great courtesy in Holly Springs, Mississippi during the winter of 1862. Now, Port Gibson was reminiscent of Port Au Prince, Haiti, prior to the 2010 earthquake, full of beautiful but empty buildings, abandoned houses, and a total absence of commerce and culture. North of that is Vicksburg,

Mississippi, one of the major river cities of the south, and the one which had suffered most from Union bombardment and occupation during `the late unpleasantness.'

To the southeast of Halcyon, down 61 was Woodville, another small antebellum southern city which, until recently, still had commercial buildings with rusting Falstaff and Jax beer signs hanging from them. Unlike Port Gibson to the north of Halcyon, Woodville had been undergoing a transformation of sorts with a growth in new housing, but an adherence to maintaining the historic integrity of the original town square, and the area's significant residential and commercial architecture.

After a brief visit to Forsythe, Tom aimed his rented silver Lincoln to the right, pulling off of Hwy. 61 South down Jefferson Street to Queen's Court Tavern. He entered the weathered wooden structure through the door facing the street and was pleased to see several familiar faces stationed at the bar. It was in a way, reminiscent of both high school and college. Here were some well-known Halcyon natives who, like himself, had left town seeking their fortune elsewhere, but who'd decided, unlike him, that what they'd sought was to be found in their own backyards after all. Dr. Bob Wilson, 34 years old, married, and now on the staff at Halcyon Regional Medical Center. Tom remembered him hugging the commode, sick and drunk, at age 17 in the filthy restroom of some beer joint outside Woodville, almost seventeen years earlier. There was Mike Purefoy, one of Tom's best friends at Chamberlain-Hunt prepschool who'd turned out to be gay, and now owned a high-end antiques store in town on the upper end of Jackson Street. There was redhead Kaye Wyklor, a high school cheerleader, back in the day. She still looked good. And there was the now balding Mike Hunt, former all state quarterback who'd become the golf pro at the country club. They all smiled and held their glasses aloft as Tom ducked slightly to enter.

3.

Eldorado

Thursday evening at 8:30 p.m. found District Attorney Bill Roberts sitting at the police station with the chief of police, Gary Bowman, and several deputies. It had been a hot day in Halcyon and Roberts had had an overdose of his friends and neighbors at the funeral home. Although he sincerely appreciated their sympathetic condolences, it had just been more input than he could process. The visitation had lasted several hours, and now there were still more people at his house. He'd invoked the `executive privilege' option afforded him as district attorney to temporarily escape the madness of everything associated with the funeral, at least for a couple of hours. The actual service was tomorrow, and he would once again serve as family spokesman, and become the rock upon which family members would lean in this time of darkness. But for a couple of hours tonight, at least, he was free.

He'd invited his brother Tom over to tour the police station and the jail, all part of the new Criminal Justice Center compound. Tom had joined some friends for a drink earlier at Queen's Court Tavern, but Bill expected him momentarily. As a rule, Halcyon closed early on weeknights in the summer, and Queen's Court Tavern quit serving dinner at 8:00, though the bar generally remained open as long as anyone was there.

The conversation at the police station was, for the most part, routine surface level chatter, as nothing of any significance of a criminal nature had happened in Black County in quite a while. There were always the D.U.I.s, infrequent domestic disturbance calls, and an occasional armed robbery, stabbing, or shooting somewhere in the north end of town, but no bank robberies or grand crimes. In other words, a typical Halcyon summer night.

Tom entered through the front door of the police station followed by a visible swarm of mosquitoes, most of which entered with him before he could close the door. "Hello my Christian friends," Tom shouted, waving his hand casually. It was a radio greeting used by a fiery preacher out of Jackson, Mississippi who Halcyonians frequently listened to,both for amusement and inspiration. His famous sermon on the `Towel of Babel' was well remembered even now by Tom and his high school friends.

"Everybody, you remember my brother Tom," the district attorney said, standing to greet him. "He's in town from California, Hollywood, to be precise, `swimming pools, movie stars,'" he joked. Most of those gathered in the room had probably never been any farther from Halcyon than eastern Texas, or New Orleans.

"Are there really movie stars just walking around everywhere out there?" one of the deputies asked.

"Well, yes and no," Tom answered. "There are plenty of them who live out there, and you run into one of them at a restaurant, Starbucks, or a book store from time to time. It's not like I see somebody famous every time I leave my house, but yes, a lot of them do live in Los Angeles and surrounding areas."

"Are you in the entertainment business?" a deputy asked.

"I wish," Tom laughed, "but no, not unless you happen to consider delivering mail to be particularly entertaining. I'm a letter carrier."

"You mean a mailman?"

"Yes, I'm a mailman," Tom smiled.

"Is there anybody famous on your route?" the same deputy asked, apparently awed by being able to talk to someone who actually lived in Los Angeles.

"Well, no. My route is downtown. I do have the courthouse

though, you know, the one pictured on Sgt. Friday's badge on the old TV show `Dragnet. Not gthat anybody remembers it now.'"

"Man, how cool is that?"

"I don't know about that, but I enjoy my work. It's never cold in L.A., I mean not like it gets here. It does get hot though, and the smog hangs around sometimes for days. You'd think that the winds from the ocean would keep it cleared out, but for some reason that really just doesn't happen. Maybe it's the Hollywood hills."

"I'll bet the place is just crawling with beautiful women who've moved there to become actresses."

"Well, yes, that's true, but regrettably we generally travel in different circles," Tom said.

"What's the best thing about your job?"

"I like getting paid regularly for steady work," he laughed. "Everybody thinks all movie or television stars are rich, and plenty certainly are, but with the majority of them, it's feast or famine. You can probably easily think of some actors who were really hot a couple of years ago, whom you haven't seen or heard from lately. I think it's a rough business, probably like the music business, though I can't say for sure. I'm told the big money is usually to be found in whoever's going to be the next big star, not who was big last year, or even who's big now. The money has already been made on who's big now, I mean, everybody who is likely to make some money off of them has already staked a claim. You know, managers, agents, accountants, lawyers, publicists, wives or husbands. Some famous actors, that is, the most successful, move from acting to directing after their acting careers slow down. Like they say out there, `all directors want to be actors, and all actors want to be directors.'

"Well, who do you think is the best director in Hollywood?"

"It's a subjective thing, but many of the mainstream directors of the past two decades are retired now, and some of them may have already said everything they had to say, from a creative standpoint.

When that happens, some of them take chances and relinquish some artistic and personal integrity in a misguided need `to feel loved.' The need to be appreciated is the death of art as art. True art and the need for approval are incompatible."

"What do you mean?"

"While everybody wants their work to be appreciated, I think some of the older directors take on projects outside their normal range in a need to feel current, contemporary. I understand the need to be relevant, though. It's basic human nature. On the other hand, there are a whole new group of younger directors doing made for TV series for HBO, Showtime, and others, who are already at the top of their game and may, in time, evolve into front line movie directors, not that they all necessarily need the money. It's an exciting time."

"You seem to know a lot about the way things work out there for someone who's just a mailman."

"I read *Variety* and *The Hollywood Reporter* frequently, and who knows? Maybe some important somebody will discover me one day walking around in my shorts, mailbag over my arm, and make me rich and famous. In the meantime though, I'm not holding my breath."

"Excuse me Chief," interrupted Sgt. Taylor as he stepped through the door, "I've got Rabbit in the squad car and some other subject from Port Gibson. They were in an altercation behind Fat's Chicken Shack. Now, of course, they're best friends."

"I think their only best friends are Mr. Boston and Ole Grandad," the Chief laughed. "Are they behaving now?"

"Yes, they're fine now," the sergeant answered. "What do you want me to do with them?"

"I'm feeling generous tonight. Take Rabbit home, and when you get to the door turn on the siren so that his wife knows that the police are bringing him back. I don't want him slipping in the back door unnoticed. She'll work him over with that rolling pin of hers, like she does every time he comes home drunk and cursing. Tell him I said this is his third episode in the past three weeks. There'd better not be a fourth."

"Is that Rabbit Poteet?" Tom asked, amused but not surprised.

"Hell yes," Bill replied, "as you can see not much has changed in your absence. Rabbit and the rest of them still drink behind Fat's Chicken Shack, you know the drill. They start out as best friends, but then as that cheap swill they imbibe begins to circulate through their already greatly diminished neurological circuits, they start getting mad at each other, and one of two things happens. Either they start cursing each other and a fight, if you could call it that, breaks out, a `scuffilation,' as they say in Ferriday, or they curse each other mightily, but then, recognizing the absurdity of the situation, just start laughing. But there's seldom anything more than that. Hell, Rabbit's got to be almost seventy-five."

Their speculations were suddenly interrupted by a loudly ringing telephone which was answered by the duty officer, Farrel. "What? You what? Where? What do you mean `not there'?" he asked excitedly. "Just a minute, yes, he's right here. And don't touch anything," he said excitedly, handing the phone to Chief Bowman.

"I'll be right there," Bowman said quickly, hanging up the phone. "There's been a murder at Eldorado, I think. Bill, you better ride with me. Bob you take your car and park at the street entrance. And get another car down at the other end of that street and block it off. I don't want anybody coming in there from either end. Let's roll."

"Eldorado?" Tom asked in stark disbelief. "There's been a murder at Eldorado." It was more of a statement than a question. "Was it Miss Murdock?" he asked, hoping the answer was no.

"I don't know," the chief answered, grabbing his keys off the desk. "There's no body, just blood."

"Can I come along?" Tom asked.

“Yeah, I guess,” the chief replied, looking at the district attorney for approval. “Just stay out of the way and don’t touch anything, don’t move anything and don’t ask any questions. You can ride with us. Now let’s move it.”

The sleek black Dodge Charger with its siren blasting and flashers spinning, raced through the downtown streets of Halcyon, reflections from the overhead street lights bouncing off of its glistening black surface, sending shafts of light darting in different directions. In less than five minutes it was speeding past a dark and ominous looking Cypress Hill, its monstrous outline barely visible and threatening against the dark night sky. Chief Bowman slowed the police cruiser as he approached the brown gravel driveway leading up to Eldorado, not wishing to disturb any possible evidence. He stopped fifty feet or so from the house, stepped out of the car and handed each of its occupants a large police issue Maglite. “Follow me,” he instructed as they proceeded single file toward the front porch gallery, the gravel crunching beneath their feet as they walked. They could clearly discern the silhouette of the elegant and most imperially slim Mark Delgado, cousin of Jeannie Murdock, standing under the porch light by the open front door, smoking a cigarette.

“I’ve disturbed nothing,” he said as the trio approached, not bothering to address any of the men by name, though all three were known to him. “Miss Murdock is not in the house. I’ve searched and she’s not inside. I did not go outside, that is, beyond the driveway’s outer edge, inasmuch as I don’t have a flashlight, although I did call loudly for her. It’s very dark tonight.”

“When did you get here?” Chief Bowman asked.

“Precisely at 9:00 p.m. The door was unlocked, which is irregular. I entered the house and there was nobody here. All of the usual lights were on, and then I discovered blood on the dining room floor. I searched the house, calling for her, but there was no answer.

That's when I called you.I thought the first thing to do would be to try and locate her. Obviously, she needs help. There's a blood trail to the back door which was also unlocked, and a larger pool of blood on the side gallery steps. I cannot help but suspect that it belongs to her. There is also a very distinct and pervasive odor of gunpowder."

"The first thing we need to do is find her, so let's scour the property and see what we come up with," Chief Bowman suggested. "Walter, call for back-up, but keep it low key. I don't want a big scene and I don't want to destroy any evidence trail, but we've got a lot of land to cover and time is critical. She may possibly still be alive, but it's going to take more than the two of us to find her, considering how dark it is. Go to my car and get the yellow crime scene tape and let's secure the perimeter of the house. I don't want anyone in or out, at least, not yet. Mr. Delgado, show me what you've been able to find. Tom, you can come with me and your brother if you like. And let's all keep our eyes open for anything out of the ordinary."

The three of them followed Mr. Delgado, and the trail of blood through the back door and onto the side porch gallery. There wasn't that much blood, scarcely enough to be called a trail, that is, until they reached the bottom stairs of the side porch gallery where a larger pool of blood was found at the base of the first step.

"It would appear," Mr. Delgado observed, "that the blood stops here."

Tom couldn't help but suspect that enough blood had already been spilled that when, that is, if, Miss Murdock is found, she'll already be dead. He kept his opinion to himself, however, since both his brother and the police chief had instructed him to keep quiet.

It was very dark outside, and there was too much land to search, much of it wooded with tall brush, weeds and blackberry bushes bristling with razor sharp thorns. Chief Bowman decided to immediately call in some specialists, in the off chance that Miss Murdock might still be alive. It was a tough call, whether to risk her life any further by delaying an immediate blanket search of the area, in favor of waiting for the bloodhounds of George Wilson up in Vicksburg. Chief Bowman already knew from his own experience that no adult, man or woman could lose that much blood and still be alive. Yet, if there was any possibility she might be alive...in the meantime it was important to process the facts at hand. In less than ten minutes he'd analyzed the present situation thoroughly, having studied the scene quickly and reached preliminary conclusions based upon his past experience. Turning to the district attorney, he assessed the situation, "What we have here is blood spatter consistent with gunshots, but no victim, a bullet hole in the bedroom wall, and what appears to be a .32 caliber bullet lodged in the window frame. In the dining room there is more blood, a heavy brown overcoat which obviously doesn't belong here, a bloodstained bedroom slipper, a blood trail from the dining room to a bedroom, through a side door, across the outside gallery, and down the steps in the direction of Cypress Hill. Another bloodstained slipper, presumably belonging to Miss Murdock is at the bottom of the steps. A bloody comb was found approximately 30 feet from the house in the driveway, and a pool of blood approximately 40 feet from the house in the driveway. But the body is nowhere to be found. What happened here is clear enough, at least the basics. There is no sign of forced entry."

"That's true enough," Delgado observed, "which would seem to indicate that she knew her assailant or assailants. She always locked her doors, especially at night, and, if you were to ask me, I would suggest that you begin your investigation next door at Cypress Hill. In all probability that's where you'll find her, assuming they haven't already butchered her. There existed an ongoing enmity between the denizens of that `rotting shack' and herself. Anyone who knows

Jeannie is certainly very much aware of that. I want her found. Now. You need to go over there right this minute, surround that house, bring in some flood lights, and find her before it's too late."

"You were here this morning, Tom. Did she say anything about that to you?" the district attorney asked.

"Actually, she seemed certain that her neighbors were going to do something to her house. She thought that they'd probably try to burn it down, Eldorado, I mean. She also told me that Olivia Dautery, the companion of Mr. Toma, had threatened to, and I quote, `blow her head clean off.'"

"Gentlemen, you're wasting valuable time," Delgado stated with mounting irritation. "I suggest you save your speculations for later. Right now, it's imperative that she's found."

"Walter, you stay here at the house and don't let anybody else on the property except the photographer. I don't want anything disturbed," Chief Bowman ordered. "Bill, why don't you come with me over to Cypress Hill, in case there are any legal issues. I want to run this by the book. Let's drive over there rather than walk. If we just knock on the door in the dark, those people are likely to take a shot at us. I assume they're probably well, if primitively armed, and they're indeed feral. If they see the police car's lights they're more likely to come out of the house on their own. I don't want to have to go into that place in the dark. There's no telling what we might step in, or on. Tom, you should probably wait here. Too many people showing up unannounced might spook them. Let's go."

The Darkness was almost total, given the tiniest sliver of a crescent moon mostly obscured by black, heavy, clouds. The distance between Eldorado and Cypress Hill seemed much further at night than it actually was, Bill Roberts reflected. Perhaps it was the absence of any point of visual reference. Chief Bowman brought the car to a stop in front of Cypress Hill, hoping one or more of his tires wouldn't be punctured by the board he'd unintentionally run over as he pulled around the circular driveway near the front door. After he'd stopped, Bowman activated the siren briefly and turned on the car's light bar, so that the house's inhabitants would realize that this was indeed an official visit.

The sudden and not unexpected presence of the police car was acknowledged by Olivia Dautery, who immediately turned on a pair of large gilded bronze porch lanterns from a wall switch somewhere inside the main hallway, sending several roosting chickens scurrying off the front porch into the surrounding darkness. "I've been expecting you," she said, casually, stepping through from the dim shadows of the hallway into the light of the front porch lanterns.

"You have, and why's that Miss Dautery?" Chief Bowman asked.

"I heard the commotion, what's going on over there, anyway?"

"You don't know?" Bowman asked.

"Hmph! How would I know?" she asked indignantly. "I don't have anything to do with that woman over there."

"What woman?"

"That Murdock woman and her cousin of course. Again, what's going on over there?" she asked.

The dim light from the two front porch lanterns cast an eerie glow upon the scene which the D.A. and the Chief of Police beheld. A sleeping goat, a broken chair, positioned on its side, broken window glass, piles of rotting fabric, a couple of old wagon wheels, and the spectacle of Olivia Dautery dressed in the filthy rags of a peasant from a Charles Dickens tale. The absurdity of her physical circumstances was heightened rather than diminished by her haughty attitude and the vexation she seemed to radiate as a result of having had her sleep interrupted by a policeman, despite the fact that it was barely 9:30 p.m.

"Where is Mr. Toma?" Bowman asked, ignoring her question for the second time.

"He's upstairs, of course. Where do you think he'd be at this hour?" she replied, incensed at the direction she perceived the conversation to be taking.

"Would you ask him to come down here?" the chief asked.

"Ask him yourself," she replied. "He's upstairs. No, wait just a minute. Why don't you tell me what you want with him?"

"Well," District Attorney Roberts answered, "Miss Murdock is missing."

"What would that have to do with either of us? I don't see that…."

"Just get him, Miss Dautery, if you would be so kind, I'd just like to ask both of you some routine questions, if you saw or heard anything unusual, that sort of thing, but I'd prefer to only have to do it once, so would you please ask him to come down?" The fact of the matter was that Chief Bowman had no desire to enter that house at night given the potential dangers it posed. He automatically slapped his own face, crushing a mosquito.

Olivia Dautery turned without reply and stepped into the darkness, her path through the debris dimly lit by a flashlight which illuminated large hanging sheets of water-stained, peeling wallpaper, which hung like sails from the Flying Dutchman, moving slightly as she passed. She disappeared into the darkness while Chief Bowman, and the district attorney speculated as to the increasing likelihood of the pair's involvement in Miss Murdock's disappearance and probable murder.

"I'd been to Miss Murdock's house, and she'd been to my office in regard to the differences between herself and these two, here at Cypress Hill, and she'd expressed her concerns to me," the district attorney observed, "but still, it seems unlikely that Toma and Dautery would actually murder her over a couple of goats. And yet, her fears seemed real enough to her, and apparently weren't unfounded, given the present circumstances. Perhaps you should take them in for questioning, hold them as long as you can without charging them with anything, get a search warrant, and then come back here and crawl over every inch of this place like a fly."

"One of many," Chief Bowman laughed.

"You've got that right. Flies, ticks, ants, fleas, roaches, mice mosquitoes, rats, and God knows what else," Roberts speculated.For the most part, he'd stood by idly, just observing, intending to let the police chief conduct the investigation as he saw fit.

Upstairs, Olivia Dautery found Toma in his bedroom lying on his mattress reading by candle light. "Something's going on `over there'" she said, derisively waving her flashlight in the direction of Eldorado. "The police are downstairs and want to ask us some questions, you know, if we saw or heard anything, so you'd better come on downstairs to the front porch."

"Well, why didn't you invite them in?" Toma asked.

"As far as I'm concerned, they're illegally trespassing on private property," she answered, "and we don't know anything about anything having to do with that Murdock woman anyway. We mind our own business and don't owe the police anything."

"Well, Olivia, we'd probably better answer their questions, so they will go away and leave us alone."

"I suppose you're right," Dautery answered, "but still, their presence, however minimal, is an annoyance nonetheless. As far as I'm concerned, let's hope Jeannie Murdock's disappearance is permanent, and I have no use for anybody from any branch of the government, but I suppose you're right."

In a few moments the pair emerged from the darkness of the house onto the front porch. "I apologize for disturbing you," Chief Bowman said, "but Miss Murdock next door has disappeared, and I want to know if you noticed anything suspicious or unusual tonight."

"Well," Bill Toma replied, "We heard three short, loud bangs, like a car backfiring."

"Or gunshots?" Chief Bowman offered.

"I didn't say that, but I suppose it could have been," Toma answered. "Yes, it could have been that."

"What time would you say that you heard that?" D.A. Roberts asked.

"I can't say since I don't wear a watch and have no need for a clock. I'm generally not particularly concerned with either time, or its passage, if you know what I mean. One day here is pretty much like the day before, or the next day, for that matter. I seldom leave the house."

"Well when did you hear the noise, whatever it may have been, the gunshots or car backfiring?"

"I really don't know," Toma answered.

"Well, was it five hours ago, or half an hour ago?" Bowman asked.

Olivia Dautery answered for him. "It was probably half an hour or so ago, maybe an hour. I don't know for certain."

"Did either of you leave the house tonight?" Chief Bowman asked, attempting to get to the point.

"No, we've been here all day and all night," Dautery replied. "We haven't left the house."

"What's that on your shirt?" Chief Bowman asked, pointing his flashlight at Toma's filthy shirt, which despite its overall condition appeared to have several large dark, and probably recent stains. "That looks like blood."

"Well…I…I…." Toma replied, as he avoided the chief's eyes, looking down shyly at his feet, and then at Olivia Dautery.

"He killed a hog this morning," Dautery interrupted. "So what! It's nothing."

Chief Bowman recognized a recent blood stain when he saw it. "I think, if you don't mind, I'd like to take you to the police station and ask you some additional questions," Bowman told the pair.

“We don’t have to go anywhere with you, and I do very much mind,” Olivia Dautery stated flatly.

“It’s merely a formality,” Chief Bowman replied casually, “but the sooner we can get you down there, the sooner we can get you home.”

“Well then, let’s go right now. I don’t want to waste all night with this crap.” She looked at Toma and said, “It’s o.k. Bill, we’ll be back soon enough. They’ve got nothing, and they can’t hold us.”

Chief Bowman opened the door of the police cruiser and held it for them as they both slid across the seat. “Watch your heads, that’s a low roof.” The Chief, and D.A. Roberts slid onto the front seat of the car and the four returned to Eldorado.

“I’m getting someone to take you to the station,” Chief Bowman said, looking through the heavy steel mesh grill which confined the two passengers in the back seat. “I’ll leave the car running so that it stays cool in here. I’ll be right back.”

As the chief and District Attorney Roberts walked through the gravel and ascended the front porch stairs to Eldorado, the chief expressed his concerns regarding the residents of Cypress Hill. “I’m suspicious of those two, both for their lack of concern over the report that Murdock is missing, and by the fact that Toma’s clothes, his shirt in particular, appear to be covered with blood.Well, we’ll know soon enough one way or the other from the lab report.If that’s her blood then we know who killed her, and I do imagine that she’s dead. Even if the blood on his shirt isn’t Miss Murdock’s, I would still consider them prime suspects, given their history of mutual animosity. I can hold them at the Black County Jail up to 48 hours legally without charging them, not that they won’t be charged earlier, if necessary.”

“In the meantime, you don’t have a body,” the D.A. observed.

4.

First Evidence

Inside Eldorado, Mark Delgado rested casually on a laminated ornately carved Belter rosewood armchair, a cigarette gently clasped between the thumb and second finger of his left hand. He sat there, his face tilted slightly upward, and his legs crossed at the knee, as if he were upon a throne, but surveying the scene before him as if he were somewhere else. Tom remembered Delgado from back when he used to mow the yard at this house. Delgado had been a frequent guest at Eldorado back then, and Tom remembered being somewhat jealous of him at the time, given the obvious attraction and ease of interaction between Delgado and Miss Murdock. Delgado was handsome by anyone's standards, tall, slim, and always well-dressed. He was the type of man who dressed elegantly if for no other reason than that it was expected, not from any outside source, but because anything less would be disrespectful to his own high opinion of himself. He could be said to have resembled Clark Gable in Gable's `Gone with the Wind' period, as both were tall and thin and had dark wavy hair and a moustache. Delgado's face was thinner now, almost gaunt, and his hair more grey than brown, yet the passage of time had not diminished his commanding presence, although it now seemed more latent than actual. Tom recalled that Delgado had been generally disliked by nearly everyone in Halcyon, given his arrogant attitude, short temper, and biting sarcasm. Delgado's wealth and aristocratic pedigree exceeded that of anyone else in Halcyon, with the sole possible exception of Miss Murdock's. He was the living embodiment of the expression `old money,' in a place where former but long lost great wealth conferred a much higher social status than current prosperity. This is not to say that Delgado's fortunes had waned, for he was even now, considered to be one of the richest men in the state of Mississippi.

What Tom knew of Delgado's personal history wasn't much except what he'd learned from his history books back at Chamberlain-Hunt, specifically that Halcyon native Mark Delgado was the direct descendent of Stephen `Don Estevan' Delgado, an enormously wealthy aristocrat who'd sold the Spanish government the very land on which the city of Halcyon had subsequently been built, in 1792. Don Estevan Delgado had later been the Governor General of Halcyon after that. Mark Delgado was now basically the end of the line and had inherited the wealth of nearly two centuries of increase through acquisition, and inheritance, having lived with his mother until her death in the house which he now inhabited, Oakmont, an 1835 one-story raised cottage not far away. The Delgados' great ancestral home, Live Oaks (1788), had been one of the earliest, if not the first of the grand mansions of Halcyon. It had been built completely on the ground with no foundation other than a herringbone patterned brick floor which surrounded the base of the first story. A two-story portico topped by a large pediment was supported by four large columns with simple round capitals at one end of the house. A large open dog trot approximately ten feet tall and eight feet wide ran unobstructed through the first floor from front to back, all the way through the house, essentially dissecting the first story longitudinally into two separate sections, a right and a left. This open hallway which lacked both front and rear doors was surrounded by dual external spiral staircases, one on each side, at the front, which curved gracefully to the residence and columned gallery on the second story. Except for the decidedly Greek Revival side porch, the house would have to have been considered Spanish, given its exterior stairways, and its second-floor gallery, which extended across the entire front of the house and down both sides to the rear. Tom remembered Live Oaks now, as he looked at Mark Delgado, although it had burned to the ground some time ago, and now nothing remained but the massive stone double spiral stairways curving still,but reaching now only toward an open sky. Tom also remembered that Mark Delgado had long been rumored to have been the secret lover of the now missing Miss Murdock, Delgado's cousin. It was said that neither had married due to their lifelong love for each other. It was a fact that neither had married, whatever the real reason, or reasons.

Miss Murdock's roots were nearly as deep and significant as Delgado's, Tom reflected, and she was extremely rich in her own right, again, old money, the most desirable type of money in Halcyon. The two of them, Miss Murdock and Mark Delgado, considered themselves so far above even the upper end of Halcyon society that they seldom had any interaction socially with anyone, and confined any commerce with the locals to mundane affairs only, an occasional trip to the market, the bank, or the post office. Their greatest crime, and the one unforgivable thing for which they were most despised, was that they did not want or need the approval of Halcyon society. They inhabited their own world, protected from the necessity of working for a living, so secure in their wealth and sense of self-worth that they neither sought, needed, nor even accepted the approval of anyone. The current owners of the grand mansions of Halcyon were no more significant to them than the formerly poor blacks who lived in sharecropper's shacks in the cotton fields of the Mississippi delta.

"What did you ascertain?" Delgado, asked pointedly, tipping the long ash from his gold tipped Sobranie Black Russian cigarette into a sterling silver ashtray.

"The neighbors claim to have heard what sounded like either gunshots or a car backfiring earlier in the evening, but didn't think anything of it one way or the other. They're being taken in for questioning," Chief Bowman replied.

"Given the fact that the blood trail stops out in the driveway, I suspect that she's been taken elsewhere," Delgado observed.

"Yeah," Chief Bowman answered his phone. It was a deputy from one of the other police cars at the end of the street. A crowd had gathered, having heard the police scanner, and sought permission to aid in the search for Miss Murdock. "How many of them are there anyway? OK. Let fifteen of the men in. I think it's more important at this point to find her than to worry about disrupting any possible evidence. Men only, I don't want this to turn into some sort of gala. And don't admit anybody who doesn't already have a flashlight in hand. It was wise of you to use your phone. I don't want any further calls pertaining to the situation here going over police radio. Believe it or not, there are people who have nothing else to do but sit around and listen to the police scanner all night."

"What about fingerprints?" Delgado asked.

"I'm calling in J.E. Kroeger, the fingerprint expert from Jackson," Chief Bowman said. "Everybody in professional law enforcement knows him. His testimony as an expert witness in the Caleb Paris case over in Vidalia got an innocent man acquitted of a murder charge. He knows what he's doing."

"But don't you have your own man here, in Halcyon?"

"Yes, we do" Chief Bowman answered, "and he's good, but I don't want any mistakes, so even though Jack is adequate, I'd feel more comfortable, given the high-profile crime that this is certain to be, having an expert from the state forensics lab rather than someone local."

"I suppose you're right," Delgado agreed, "but I'm infinitely more concerned at this moment with finding Miss Murdock, than I am with the rather remote possibility of your aggregation solving any crime of this magnitude at some point in the distant future."

Chief Bowman let Delgado's remarks pass unchallenged.

Inside Eldorado, the police photographer continued his work, documenting everything and placing markers beside certain objects and photographing them again. There was plenty of evidence, Tom surmised, if an abundance ofblood could be considered evidence. "The blood tells a tale," his brother had told him. In other words, a pattern of spatter could indicate the direction and proximity of a bullet. Was it fired at close range, or from across the room? Was it a large caliber round? Did it come from a pistol or a rifle, or even a shotgun? A revolver or an automatic? It was likely that more than one shot had been fired, Tom surmised, given the amount of blood present. The weapon was most likely a revolver inasmuch as no spent shell casings were found despite an extensive search. An automatic pistol could have been the weapon used, and the assailant could have picked up and removed the empty shells from the crime scene. This, however, was unlikely. Pistols eject spent shell casings differently, depending upon a number of factors, such as the caliber of the round, the amount of powder propelling the bullet, the size and manufacture of the pistol, etc. Although no spent shells had been found at the scene, at least as of yet, what appeared to be a .32 caliber bullet had been found partially imbedded in the side of an interior window frame. There was also a bullet hole in the bedroom wall. The murder weapon, if that was what it turned out to be, did not appear to be in the house, but that did not mean that it wasn't here, it merely meant that it hadn't been found yet. Miss Murdock's .45 pistol hadn't been located at the site either. The killer could've taken either or both weapons, thrown them as far as he could into the brush, or, he could have simply kept them. Period. He also could have thrown them into the Mississippi River. Tom reflected that if it were his own intention to dispose of a murder weapon, he would disassemble it, and toss its parts into different places in the Mississippi, way downriver from the bridge. This would make the weapon impossible to find.

"Cigarette?" Delgado asked casually, extending an open and extremely ornate sterling silver case to Tom Roberts.

"No thanks," Tom replied, not that he wouldn't enjoy a cigarette. He just knew that his brother wouldn't approve. Bill didn't care whether or not Tom smoked, he just didn't want him altering the crime scene in any way. However, even the chief of police and the district attorney lacked the audacity to tell Mark Delgado not to smoke. Tom remained seated on the dark laminated rosewood sofa, also a creation of John Henry Belter, careful not to make any sudden moves, given the inherent fragility of the furniture, a condition which had only increased with the passage of time. Such furniture was common in Halcyon, New Orleans, and in the remaining plantations along River Road, from Baton Rouge, southeast to New Orleans. German born (1804) Belter had migrated to New York and set up shop in 1844, soon replacing Duncan Phyfe as New York's most important furniture maker. Belter made a few exotic and extremely ornate beds, but was most known for his delicate and elaborate laminated rosewood settees and chairs, most with smooth backs which raked gently upward, away from the upholstered seat cushions. The chairs were generally small, elegant, and uncomfortable, befitting the small size of the people they were originally intended for, primarily the moneyed class of the antebellum era.

People had been much smaller then, Tom reflected, probably due to poor nutrition. That's the reason that the door knobs were so close to the floor in most of the antebellum mansions. Miss Murdock's house could be considered `cluttered' by conventional standards elsewhere, Tom Roberts reflected, but not by those of Halcyon. While in many cases the money had run out for the once wealthy owners of the great houses of Halcyon, there were always the trappings of the former aristocracy, large paintings, sterling silver, exquisite china sets, gilded French clocks on stands under glass domes, Persian rugs, massive mahogany and Rosewood beds by Prudent Mallard, Charles Lee, and others, and the ever present gold-leaf French parlor sets, and gigantic pier mirrors of the 1840s, which seemed to increase in number over time rather than diminish. Such was the case here, in Eldorado, which represented the distillation of the contents of Marble Hall, Serenity, and the Newport, Rhode Island, and New York City mansions.

Tom sat there quietly absorbed for the moment within the familiar and comforting ambience of his surroundings, but at the same time inevitably contrasting its anachronism and what it represented, that is, his former life, with his own current lifestyle in L.A. Nothing ever happened in Halcyon, he reflected suddenly and with a trace of contempt. That was a fact, and the loss of his false love ten years ago, here in his own home town had been the fortunate catalyst which had propelled him halfway across the continent, basically as far away as he could get. And yet just now, at least for the moment, that is, he felt that he belonged here, in Halcyon, in its warm, quiet, graceful, and elegant embrace. In his soul there was Halcyon, his first real love, his true love. The feeling was more nostalgic than actual, and passed quickly. His disappointing `relationship' here had somewhat hardened him to the degree that nearly everything for him now was all about the bottom line. Halcyon was a nice place to have been a child, to have grown up, but it was no place for anyone who had grander ambitions.

His California lifestyle was something those who'd remained here couldn't even begin to imagine. He'd told them, his family, that is, that he was a mailman because his brother had some Freudian need to feel like the patriarch of the family, and if Tom were perceived as too successful, his brother would be openly resentful. Why rock the boat, not that it really mattered one way or the other? Fimily, family, fumily. So far, this trip, at least, his brother had acted decently, friendly even. But still, nobody in his family could even imagine life in L.A. In Los Angeles, one could have literally anything he wanted at any hour, anything. Take restaurants, for example, he reflected. Numerous five-star French restaurants, the exquisite cuisine of northern India, spicy traditional Thai, Japanese Kobi or sushi, real Chinese food, not that deep fried crap, but real Chinese, Kosher, Mediterranean, anything. Any type of food he wanted, anytime, literally. In contrast, the most exotic restaurant in Halcyon was some Mexican joint on the South 61 strip toward Woodville, and Tex-Mex at that. Sure, there was horrible traffic in L.A. but he seldom had to fool with it as he had a company limo and driver for meetings, an errand boy, known as an intern, and his own secretary and assistant. And his love of cars was tweaked everyday by exotics which he could enjoy without having to own. Lamborghinis, Ferraris, Aston Martins, Maybachs, and Bentleys, were common street scenery in Beverly Hills, Santa Monica and along Wilshire, Sunset, Hollywood Boulevards, and Rodeo Drive. There were probably more Rolls-Royces in L.A. than in London. And the women, certainly the most beautiful in the world. He was always in their company at meetings, parties, movie premiers, concerts at the Greek, the Hollywood Bowl, or hip clubs with both famous and soon to be famous rock bands. They were always available and willing. And then there were the places he particularly enjoyed, The Beverly Hills Hotel, The Polo Lounge, Jerry's Deli on Ventura. And there was always the great personal satisfaction offered by his work, the backdrop against which everything else in his life took place. He represented some of the most famous actors, actresses, and musicians in the world, and had the continuous satisfaction of making deals, and the sense of accomplishment that can only be achieved by constantly being fed on a diet of business completed, contracts signed, and work played and paid. Thank God he'd gotten out of here. He'd have died in Halcyon, literally. Emotionally, mentally, and spiritually. A man has to do something, he has to produce something. It's part of a built in genetic code. To be truly happy, a man must set goals and strive to reach them. It doesn't matter what the goals are, it's this constant striving which hones one's instincts to a sharp, hardened edge. Even his early defeats and disappointments had been instructive and worked toward a greater end. Losses, he reflected, are lessons learned. They show you what you did wrong so that your intuition and instincts are sharpened even further.

There was nothing here. Halcyon was just another dying river city, as Jeannie Murdock had said, like so many others in Mississippi and Louisiana which had been left behind by the passage of time. Elegant, but empty buildings and vacant lots in the downtown commercial district indicated that once, Halcyon had been a vibrant, prosperous place, but that was a long time ago, and even the presence of a riverboat casino wasn't going to resurrect the city's former grandeur. There were casinos all the way down the Mississippi River from Minnesota to New Orleans. Big deal. In fact that pie had been sliced so many times that many had closed, starting north in Tunica. A lot of investors got left holding the bag. Fortunately, he wasn't one of them.

Tom's reflections were interrupted by the voice of the police photographer. "What's this?" he asked lifting the corner of a large Persian rug, withdrawing an 8"x10" photograph, holding it aloft and examining it with a gloved hand. "I saw the corner sticking out from under this rug. It looks like a head shot of a woman, but the eyes, nose, and mouth have been blackened by some kind of magic marker and sewn shut with coarse string or thread."

"Let me see that," Chief Bowman said, reaching for the photo and taking it with his handkerchief. "What the hell is it?"

"It looks like a photograph of Miss Murdock from here," Delgado said. "May I see it?"

"Here," Bowman said, handing the item to Delgado. "Don't touch it.Use the handkerchief, it's clean. This might be significant, but I don't know what it is."

"I know precisely what it is," Delgado said, "and I can well imagine its intended purpose, and from whence it came."

"What is it?" Tom asked.

"It's obviously a Voodoo charm of some sort," Delgado observed, "a primitive, and juvenile attempt to injure Miss Murdock. See, it's her photo. That photograph has been missing for about a year or so. The eyes and mouth have obviously been sewn shut and blackened in an attempt to `silence' Miss Murdock. It was intentionally placed face down under a rug so that Miss Murdock would be `stepped on' by anyone walking across the room. Given its presence, I suspect that there are probably other similar items elsewhere in the house. This is most likely the work of Miss Murdock's maid, Hattie, who probably considers Miss Murdock to be `uppity.' They argue with each other constantly."

"If that's what it is, it shows a decidedly hostile intent, regardless of its effectiveness, or lack of it" Chief Bowman speculated, retrieving the photograph and placing it in an evidence bag.

"I'm sure it's the work of Hattie," Delgado observed coolly. "You know how they are. You can ask them point blank what they want but you can't get a straight answer, ever. Instead, if they feel somehow wronged they'll harbor a secret resentment for years, rather than just be clear, succinct, and open. You never know what they're thinking. I suspect that this is some sort of infantile attempt at retribution for some fancied insult. You need look no further than Hattie."

"Do you mean Voodoo?" Chief Bowman asked.

"Of course," Delgado answered. "While what presumably happened to Miss Murdock tonight has no relation to that `doctored' photograph, you can bet that a causal relationship between that photograph and the disappearance of Miss Murdock will be established in the minds of Hattie and her associates. She will now feel vindicated for whatever minor slight she might have imagined herself to have received at the hands of Miss Murdock. Of course it's illogical, but that's the way they think."

Tom Roberts found the frequent use of the term `they' in reference to black peoplesomewhat offensive, but realized that's just the way it is in Halcyon. Any racial bias was unintended and even unnoticed by the people in the room, yet still, Tom reflected, what we regard as our southern culture, wouldn't exist at all without the black population. We were raised by `them.'

"I've heard of this all of my life," Chief Bowman said, addressing Delgado, "but this is the first actual evidence I've seen personally. Can you tell me if you've noticed anything out of the ordinary here, in the house?"

"Be specific sir. Do you mean, is there anything missing?"

"Yes, is anything missing?"

"There could be. She had quite a bit of jewelry, and all of it was valuable, but I can't say with certainty, that is, in regard to personal items, jewelry, money, or anything like that. Let me just say that there doesn't appear to be anything obviously missing. I haven't looked, since I'm more concerned with finding her. On the other hand, the `elephant in the room,' as they say, is that brown overcoat, yes, that one thrown across the chair in the corner. That is conspicuously present. I've never seen it before, and it doesn't belong here. I would consider that to be `Exhibit A.'"

"You've never seen it before?" Chief Bowman asked.

"No, it obviously doesn't belong here, and it doesn't belong either to myself, or Miss Murdock," Delgado stated flatly.

"I may have seen that coat before," Tom interrupted. "It was, that is, it looks like a coat which was hanging on a chair or lantern on the porch of Cypress Hill when I passed it this morning. I mean, it caught my eye as I drove by. At first, I thought there was somebody standing on the front porch, but then I realized it wasn't anyone, and wondered why there would be a heavy overcoat on the front porch in this kind of heat. It seemed strange to me. That looks like the coat I saw, but I can't swear to it. I just thought it was unusual, that's all."

Chief Bowman placed a disposable latex glove over his hand and held the coat aloft. "Is this it?" he asked.

"That looks like it, but I can't be sure," Tom answered.

"If Mr. Delgado says that it doesn't belong here then it doesn't. Let's bag it as evidence." Chief Bowman withdrew the cell phone from his pocket and called the patrol car at the front end of the street. "Sgt. Williams, can you come down to the house here and secure some evidence for me? Yes, thanks."

"We have a blood trail from the dining room to the bedroom, a solitary bloodstained house slipper in the dining room, the mysterious heavy brown overcoat, a bullet lodged in the window frame of the dining room, and evidence that a second bullet was fired in the form of a bullet hole in the bedroom wall. The blood trail continues along the porch around the side, and down the front steps. Approximately forty to fifty feet down the driveway there is a second bloody house slipper, another bloody comb, and a pool of blood. The trail stops there, indicating that Miss Murdock was moved, that is, transported somewhere else from that point. The absence of blood after that would seem to indicate that she had been placed into a vehicle of some sort, or physically moved by some other means to a different location."

"Personally, I don't think she's on the property," Delgado observed coolly, "but given the amount of blood present, there would be no reason to suspect that she could possibly still be alive. And then, if she were no longer alive, what would be the point of moving her? To cover the crime? Only a moron, or morons would conceive of such a stupid plan, which of course, returns me to my original theory," he said, holding his hand rigidly aloft and pointing angrily in the direction of Cypress Hill.

"We're on that now," Chief Bowman replied. "Toma and Dautery are both already at the station by now, and will be questioned as soon as I arrive. In the meantime they're together at a table in an interview room behind a two-way mirror. They're being both filmed and recorded, so anything they say will be admissible as evidence. They've been Mirandized already."

"Well, I have no doubt that those two can lead you to the body."

"It's nearly midnight, Mr. Delgado. It's time for you to leave so we can secure the property for the night," Chief Bowman said.

"Very well, please keep me apprised of any developments," he said, rising to leave. "I trust you have my number?"

"Yes I do," Bowman said, "I'll notify you when we find her."

Delgado turned and left through the front door without saying anything further.

"That Mark Delgado is as cool as a cucumber," Chief Bowman said to District Attorney Roberts on the drive back to the police station. "He'sdisplayed very little emotion about any of this."

"Well, what's he supposed to say?" Roberts asked. "I'm sure he knows that she's already dead, even though her body hasn't been found. Wait…surely you don't consider him to be a suspect?"

"Not at all. There's absolutely no motive. They're both rich, both lifelong best friends. No, there's no motive at all and Delgado's not even remotely a suspect, at least not to me. I just think that it's peculiar that he doesn't seem more `emotional'for lack of a better word. And he's very strange, more than merely unusual."

"What do you mean?"

"Well, it's long been rumored that Delgado and Murdock were secretly married. You know Halcyon as well as I do. I'm sure you've heard that yourself at some point," Bowman replied. "Nobody ever bothered to check it out. I never did. It wasn't any of my business, and what difference would it have made anyway?"

"Of course everybody in town has heard the rumor at least once, but those two ceased being of any interest to anybody a long time ago, and the younger generation doesn't know who they are, and couldn't care less one way or the other," Roberts observed, "but I think you should check it out when you get time. Obviously, there are more pressing matters at the present."

"Yes, but my point is, that given the closeness of their relationship, Delgado should have seemed a little something…a little less `aloof,' for lack of a better word. She was, is, as far as I know, his only friend in Halcyon."

"That does seem strange," the D.A. conceded, "but the rich really are different, and the really rich, even more so, especially the few surviving aristocrats. They're very different from us, and Delgado decidedly falls into that category. He doesn't seem the type to get upset enough about anything to display common emotions, apart from general annoyance and irritation, but still, he didn't seem particularly upset that Miss Murdock is probably dead, and by violence at that. He's every bit as eccentric as he's reputed to be."

"Well, a fart at one end of Jackson Street is a tornado by the time it reaches Jefferson Street" Chief Bowman observed, "and people talk, you know what I mean. Supposedly Miss Murdock ordered him around like a dog, the same way she treats her maid, Hattie. Apparently, from what I've been told, he just took it. But he's a strange one for sure. Bob at the hardware store told me that Mark Delgado was so cheap that he won't even repair his own house. He bought enough shingles to replace the roof at Oakmont, which actually has gaping holes into which the water pours unchecked every time it rains. That was three years ago. The shingles are still sitting in a pile in the back yard."

"Why's that?" asked Tom.

"Bob said that after the shingles had been paid for and delivered from Jackson, that Delgado came in to buy some roofing nails but left in a huff because he said they were `too expensive.' I have no idea what he intended to do with the roofing shingles, but he sure can't put them up without nails, and somehow, I don't see Mr. Delgado climbing the roof with a square of roofing shingles on his back and a hammer in one hand, getting baked in the hot sun under any circumstances. I doubt he's ever done a day's worth of hard physical labor in his life. I still don't know what his intentions may have been, regarding the roof. He paid cash for the shingles but wouldn't buy the nails. If it was his intention to make some kind of point or statement, he succeeded, whatever his point may have been, but he still doesn't have a roof."

"Maybe he's fallen on hard times," Tom speculated.

"No, he's rich," Tom's brother Bill replied. "I know that for a fact. We have the same accountant here. Delgado uses somebody in New York, some big firm that takes care of his business interests there. Somebody up there needed some information to do something, I think it was five or six years ago, right before his mother died. Delgado told whoever it was to call Sally Wilson, you know, the C.P.A. on Franklin Street, and have her give him whatever he wanted. Mom, Dad, and I have used her for years. She apparently had some information that Delgado had given her a couple of years earlier about a several hundred-acre sugar plantation he owns, or owned, in Sunset, Louisiana. He's just cheap, that's all. His maid, Chantelle, told Mom that she has to cook his dinner standing under an umbrella in his kitchen when it rains. The inside stairway to the second story actually collapsed due to water intrusion. He literally gets to his bedroom by climbing a wooden fireman's ladder to the second story. The ladder is actually in the main hall, inside the house. And Chantelle's husband is his yardman, off and on. He told me himself, that Mr. Delgado had him move his bed twice to other upstairs rooms to escape the leaking roof. How strange is that?"

"I don't understand that," Tom said. "Actually, it's insane. But you hear stuff like that all the time. You guys remember old Mrs. Moore. She lived like she didn't have a penny to her name. After she died and her daughters from Baton Rouge came over to get the place ready to sell…you remember that when they had to do some remodeling, they found more than $20,000 in small bills stuffed in the walls. God knows why."

"Yeah," the chief said, "That type of thing is not uncommon."

"Like that person who lived on the streets in New York City like some bum. When he died, it turned out that he had more than $350,000 squirreled away in some bank somewhere. It's a form of insanity."

"I remember that," the chief said. "That was crazy. The guy lived in a cardboard box over some sewer exhaust vent, or something like that, eating out of garbage cans, with all of that money resting comfortably in the bank. That doesn't make any sense."

"For me, something has to make sense," Tom said, "or I can't understand it. I mean it has to be logical, linear. Is Mark Delgado crazy?"

"What do you think? Did he seem crazy to you?" the district attorney asked.

"No, that's what's so puzzling. He seems perfectly normal."

"That's one of the things I have to deal with, being the Chief of Police here," Bowman interjected. "Somebody or something might seem irrational or illogical to me, or to any other normal person. But that's because we're normal. Being able to temporarily enter the mind of someone irrational and pursue his sense of logic from his own viewpoint is an art which I seek to cultivate. However stupid or deranged someone may be, his actions seem logical from his own point of view, but back to Delgado. He's not stupid, or irrational, but obviously something isn't right somewhere."

"The chief's right," the district attorney replied to his brother Tom. "I suggest that you take a ride down there, by his house, Oakmont, tomorrow in the daylight, and see for yourself. Pieces of the front porch rail are just plain gone, and the facing board along the front of the house is missing several feet of wood. You can see indentations in the roof at the front of the house where it's literally rotting from beneath. In the meantime, you should probably go back to the Moro and get some sleep. It's been a long day, and whatever happens with this, we still have Dad's funeral tomorrow. Chief Bowman intends to interview Toma and Dautery, and I want to be behind the mirror for that. After that, I'm going home to bed. It's been a long day and a long night, and I doubt that things will let up any tomorrow."

"Yeah," Bowman said, "I want to interview those two thoroughly, then I'm going back over to Cypress Hill. By now I'm sure I have a search warrant. Judge King has already been called."

"I'd really like to hang around, that is, if you don't mind," Tom said, "since I know the people involved. I mean nothing like this has ever happened in Halcyon in my lifetime. I've never seen anything like it."

"I've never seen anything like it either," Bowman replied. "Most of the homicides I've worked here, and believe me, they're very rare, generally involve either domestic disputes, or are the result of misunderstandings over gambling, or women, and happen in the north end of town. But if you want to hang around, I guess it wouldn't hurt anything. Again, I need you to stay out of the way and to keep quiet."

"Tom, you should probably stay out of Chief Bowman's way," D.A. Roberts interrupted.

"No, Bill, I don't mind, Tom's welcome to come along. He might actually be helpful," Chief Bowman said, "since he was one of the last people to have seen her alive. He won't be in the way."

"Well, if you're sure Gary, but send him to the hotel if you need to."

"Do you really need a search warrant to go inside Cypress Hill? Didn't they invite you inside already?" Tom asked.

"Yes they did," Chief Bowman replied, "but your brother here, the district attorney, would consider me remiss if I failed to follow the proper procedure, and believe it or not, those people, Toma and Dautery, are well-liked in town. They're considered eccentric and amusing. When they're charged with murder, and I believe they will be, probably before the night is over, they're going to get some big time lawyer in from Jackson, Baton Rouge, or New Orleans."

"But they obviously don't have any money, how can they afford anybody like that?"

"It won't cost them anything. It'll be some hot shot with a big reputation, and an even bigger ego. He'll work pro bono, that is, `free,' just to garner publicity, and there'll be plenty of it. You can bet on that. Bill will have his work cut out for him."

"But this is Halcyon," Tom said, "not New York or L.A. These are not famous people. Nobody outside of Halcyon has ever heard of them, and to tell you the truth, nobody cares about Halcyon one way or the other, except the people who live here."

"Just because you don't care about this place doesn't mean that nobody else does," Bill answered curtly. "Halcyon has always been good to you. You could've been happy here, and you should've stayed. Dad missed you, and we all have. You should just move back and pick up where you left off. The post office would probably let you transfer."

"Come on, Bill, you know why I left."

"Leah? Please, come on, you've got to be kidding. There are too many fish in the sea for me to believe that. You need to get over that crap. That was ten years ago, and, besides, she's divorced now. She caught that dentist husband of hers with one of his hygienists. Her mouth was open, but he wasn't examining her teeth, if you get my drift.It was a big scandal here, for about a week. Anyway, that was last year. I thought you knew all that."

"No, I didn't" Tom said. "How would I know?"

"And you're wrong about nobody outside of Black County caring about Halcyon. The south is the only place left in America that isn't absolutely generic. We still have a culture here and those Yankees are jealous of us, still. You see how we're depicted on TV and in the movies. We're portrayed as backwoods hicks and racists. The fact is that most southern cities have black mayors and councilmen. We have much better race relations than any of those squalid urban cesspools up north. I mean it. Most of the people who write about us have never even been in the south."

"Amen," Chief Bowman chimed in.

"I should think that you're joking, but somehow, I suspect that you're not," Tom replied, "but really, you can't be serious."

"Think about it. Nobody ever talks about `northern cooking', `northern hospitality,' or `northern style.' It's all generic urban crap up there. The north is boring in its sameness. If you think that there won't be reporters and camera crews from literally all over the world descending upon this place, you're greatly mistaken. We're the only interesting part of America left. They'll be landing on us down here like flies. `Look at those poor, decadent southerners. We always knew that they probably had goats and chickens in their houses, and this proves it.' They probably think that we all have animals running around everywhere, and that we sit barefoot on hay bales on the front porch smoking corn cob pipes. The fact is that we need a few more movies like `Deliverance' or `Mississippi Burning.' Those two movies alone kept Yankees out of the South for an extra ten years."

"I've always been treated well when I'm in New York," Tom replied. "They may seem to hate each other in Manhattan, but they find us, southerners, that is, quaint, colorful, and amusing. And it's called `Southern Hospitality' for a reason."

"When have you ever been to New York?" Bill asked. "You've never been to New York in your life."

"I went as a member of the Postal Workers Union to a meeting up there last year," Tom said, neglecting to mention that he was generally in Manhattan at least once or twice a month on business.

"Well, anyway," his brother continued, "you just wait and see. Another thing is that Jeannie Murdock had big time connections in New York. She still owns, or did own a building in downtown Manhattan, believe it or not, and even Olivia Dautery spent time in the city. She wrote for both *Newsweek* and *Atlantic.* I'll bet you didn't know that. No? I didn't think so."

"Olivia Dautery lived in New York?" Tom asked.

"Hell yes, and she traveled in the highest social circles there. She returned home to care for her sister. There's a lot you don't know about, Tom."

"Obviously, but still, I just don't…."

"I'm telling you Tom, you just wait. You're going to see this story all over the world. Just wait. Well, here we are," Bill said, pulling his car into a reserved spot in front of the Black County Criminal Justice Center. "Let's go in and check the traps."

After checking in, giving some instructions and answering some questions from deputies and coworkers, Chief Bowman proceeded to the interrogation room. "Tom, you can come into this adjoining room over here and look through the two-way mirror, if you want. That way you can see and hear what's going on. Yeah, this way, through here. This is detective Butler. He'll be here with you, observing the interview, along with your brother."

Chief Bowman walked into the interrogation room and took a seat across from Dautery and Toma. "I apologize for keeping you here as long as I have, and it's late," he began, "but, the fact is, Miss

Murdock is still missing and presumed dead."

"Dead? She's dead?" Olivia Dautery asked.

"We don't know that yet for a fact, but a large amount of blood was found at her house," Bowman said, "but before we get started I want to advise you again that you have the right to remain silent, but should you elect to talk to us, anything you say can, and possibly will be used against you in a court of law. You don't have to answer any questions without a lawyer present. If you have somebody you'd like to use, we can wait until he or she arrives before we begin. If you don't have, or can't afford a lawyer, the court will appoint one for you at no expense. Do you understand what I've just said?"

"I understand what you said, somebody's already told us all of that, but we don't need a lawyer since we haven't done anything. What I don't understand is why we're here," Olivia Dautery said, speaking on behalf of herself and Bill Toma, who sat quietly with his eyes downcast.

"Are you saying that you don't want a lawyer?" Chief Bowman asked.

"I'm saying that I don't...that is, we don't need a lawyer because we haven't done anything. We've been at home all day long and haven't left Cypress Hill, all day or all night, that is, until you hauled us in here. Now, ask your questions and then take us home. It's way past our bedtime."

"Very well," Chief Bowman began, "but should you decide at any point that you want a lawyer, we can get you one."

"Quit talking about lawyers and ask your damn questions," Dautery protested loudly, "you're wasting our time."

"It's well known that there is a long-standing rivalry, if not downright enmity between you two and Miss Murdock, that is, between yourself and Mr. Toma, and Miss Murdock. Would you care to elaborate on that?"

"It's simple enough," Dautery said. "She's brazenly slain several members of our animal family, shot them in cold blood. Then she dragged their lifeless bodies through the hedgerow and onto her propertyto justify her callous actions, stating that they'd been trespassing. Anybody could see that she killed them first on our property and then dragged them across the yard and into her flower garden. The woman's horrible."

"How many of your animals has she killed in this manner?" Chief Bowman asked.

"Does it matter? The woman's mean and crazy. Have you ever just seen someone who's mean just for mean's sake? Well that's her."

"So you don't like her?"

"No?" Dautery asked sarcastically. "Of course I don't like her, who would? But that doesn't mean that I killed her. God'll take care of her, sooner or later. People like that always get what they've got coming to them in the long run. I wouldn't waste good ammunition," Dautery said. "You've asked me, and I've told you. Can we go now?"

"Who said anything about a gun, Miss Dautery? And isn't it true, that you threatened to `blow her head off?' I believe that those were your own words, were they not?" Bowman asked.

"Sure, I might've said something like that. I told her that if she killed another one of my animals that I was going to come after her. She knew that. I believe that a person has a legal right to protect her own property. I've done nothing wrong. I don't know where she is. I've already told you that I heard either gunshots or a car backfiring. You know that already. Pay attention!"

"You don't seem particularly upset that she might be dead."

"I hope that she's alright, but I'm not going to say that I like her. I don't like her, but I don't know where she is. It would be hypocritical of me to engage in some charade concerning my deep sense of personal loss at the possibility that she might be missing or might be dead, don't you think?"

"Has she been at your house recently?"

"No. Why would she come over to see us? She's not welcome at Cypress Hill and she knows it. She'd no more come see us than we'd go see her," Dautery said.

"So, she hasn't been over to see you at your house in…how long would you say? Six months? A year? What?" Chief Bowman asked.

"I think she came by five years or so ago to complain about something, while we were sitting on the front porch," Dautery said.

"No, it's been longer than that," Bill Toma ventured, looking up for the first time.

"Well, how long, Mr. Toma?" Chief Bowman asked.

"More than five years," he said. "That's what I remember."

"Why did she come over then, whenever it might have been? What was the reason for her visit?" Chief Bowman asked.

Toma and Dautery looked at each other, trying to remember why Miss Murdock had come by. "I remember now," Toma said, smiling and looking simple-minded.

"That's right Bill," Dautery said, taking up the thought. "She accused us of having caused her car to get a flat tire. She said that she had run over a board from our front porch and said that had caused her to have a flat tire. Yes, that's what it was."

"She's right," Toma agreed. "She appeared quite vexed, but Olivia told her…"

"I told her that if that was what had happened, then we were sorry for any inconvenience and expense that might have caused her," Dautery said. "We were very nice about the alleged incident. But that wasn't enough for her. Her tire had already been fixed, so obviously she wasn't particularly concerned about the tire. The tire was merely a pretext for her to come snooping around, and also provided her the opportunity to berate us verbally for an occurrence which had nothing to do with us, that is, if she ever even had a flat tire."

"How do you mean that?" Chief Bowman asked. "Didn't a board from your porch cause her car to have a flat tire?"

"That's what she alleged. That was her version. I never saw any supporting evidence. It appeared to me to be nothing more than an idle claim," Dautery said. "I hardly see how we could've been considered responsible for her lack of driving skills. I advised her that in the future, the condition of her tires might better be served if she simply watched where the hell she was driving."

"That's good advice," Tom laughed quietly to his brother and the detective in the other room.

"Don't forget about the goat?" Toma said quietly, addressing Olivia Dautery.

"That's right," Dautery bristled. "She brazenly accused us of permitting one of our goats to `dance upon the hood of her car.' I believe that was the expression she used.

"Obviously she doesn't know much about animals," Toma ventured.

"What do you mean?" Chief Bowman asked.

"He means precisely that goats, and other animals, neither ask, nor require permission from anyone for participation in any activities which they might deem to be desirable, that is, from their perspective, of course," Dautery said, interrupting her partner.

"Well, did one of your goats bang up her car?" Chief Bowman asked.

"Again, that would be a matter of conjecture," Dautery stated flatly, "but if you brought us here to talk about goats, we can do that at a reasonable hour on some other day. You appear to be wasting our time."

Chief Bowman had been somewhat taken off guard by these two, specifically Olivia Dautery. She had an excellent vocabulary and a quick and biting way with words. She clearly showed no regard for the missing woman, and there is or was definitely a hostility between the two women. Toma, on the other hand looked `damaged' for lack of a better word. He was more or less just `present.' The woman was clearly the `brains' of the pair, ifsuch a term could be used in this situation. They were obviously both well-bred and well-educated, but to look at them as they sat there was somewhat disorienting, even to the chief of police. In the first place, their shabby, unkempt appearance belied their patrician bloodlines which were as significant as anyone's in Halcyon, with the exception of Mark Delgado's and Miss Murdock's. They were literally dressed in rags, and not designer clothes which had disintegrated with age, but literally rags. Additionally, the pair were filthy, and they stank. There was no immediately identifiable particular or predominant smell or odor, just a pervasive stench which was ever present, hovering around them like an invisible fog. Dautery's despicable appearance in no way diminished the arrogance of her bearing. She was obviously comfortable speaking her mind and felt no sense of the potential gravity of her present circumstances. Her filthy attire didn't in any way lessen her sense of her own importance or self-worth. It was this which seemed most peculiar to Chief Bowman.

"Which one of you killed her?" Bowman asked directly, changing his entire approach to throw the pair off guard. This question appeared to agitate Bill Toma who suddenly became visibly nervous, and immediately began rocking back and forth mechanically on the seat of the chair, his hands tucked beneath his thighs.

"It's hot in here," Toma observed meekly. "Can we go home now?"

Olivia Dautery's reaction to the question was quite the opposite. "I'm offended by the nature of your accusation and I'm not...I'm simply not going to answer any question which is both absurdly stupid and personally offensive. I'll recap this for you since you don't appear to have heard anything I've said so far. So pay attention this time. I don't like Jeannie Murdock, she's always been a horse's ass, and that's why she became a spinster. Who could she have ever found who would have loved her as much as she loves herself? Neither one of us, that is, either Mr.Toma or myself, had or has anything to do with anything that happened to or might have happened to her tonight or at any other time. Are we clear so far? Good. She's the one who threatened me. She's the one with the itchy trigger finger and the big pistol. She's the one with a well-deserved reputation as a bloodthirsty killer, not me, and not us. Now if I were you...how do you know that the blood which you claim to have found in her house is even hers? Have you performed any sort of DNA test? She probably shot some hapless drifter in cold blood, and even now, as you waste our time here, is burying his lifeless body in a shallow grave out in the woods somewhere."

"Excuse me for a moment," Chief Bowman said, and stepped out of the room.

"I'm ready to go home, can we go home now?" Toma asked her.

"We'll be leaving soon enough. They can't prove anything. They don'thave anything on us and they can't hold us without charging us. Also, I've seen enough of those moronic TV crime dramas to know they're watching and recording us right now behind that big fake mirror. In other words, don't say anything." Dautery said, holding up her middle finger at the two-way mirror.

"Maybe we should get a lawyer like they said," Toma speculated. "But one thing's for sure, I don't want anything the government is selling."

"Of course you don't, and I don't either. There's likely nothing wrong with that bitch at all, and this is something she cooked up. She probably gave a large donation to the Fraternal Order of Police, or some other group of white trash union thugs. This is Murdock's doing. She's still after Cypress Hill, she and Mark Delgado, that so-called cousin of hers. They're like that dead singer Jerry Lee Lewis from across the river in Ferriday who married his 12 year old cousin about two hundred years ago," she laughed. "He was at least straightforward about it, and man enough to tell the world to kiss his hind quarters. And what kind of man lives with his mother until he's nearly sixty years old? Delgado is either a pervert, a weirdo, or someone else who has something to hide. I don't trust either one of those two, and I doubt that the Murdock woman is missing at all. This is something she and Delgado have fabricated to try and steal our house again through yet more legal wrangling."

"Well, you know best, Olivia," Toma agreed.

"I know the New York style bait and switch when I see it."

Chief Bowman reentered the room carrying a large brown man's overcoat and looking at Toma, asked him if it belonged to him.

"Now what would he want with a man's winter overcoat this time of year in Halcyon, Mississippi?" Dautery replied.

"I want Mr. Toma to answer the question," Chief Bowman replied. "Again, Mr. Toma, is this your coat?"

"No," Toma answered, "it isn't mine."

"You mean you've never seen this coat before?"

"I've told you already, that coat doesn't belong to me."

"He's told you twice that it's not his coat. Quit badgering him," Dautery said. "And why are you so preoccupied with some overcoat?"

"This coat, which I believe belongs to one of you, was found at the crime scene, and I suspect that it provides a material link to you both. I suspect that its presence at the scene of the crime establishes that you two were at the house of Miss Murdock sometime earlier tonight. In your haste to leave the house after the crime, I imagine you forgot it. I will ask you again. Mr. Toma, is this your coat?" Chief Bowman inquired.

"No sir, it isn't," Toma replied for the third time.

“I know that this coat was at your house earlier today,” Chief Bowman stated accusingly.

“You `imagine,’ you `suspect,’ you `believe,’ and now, suddenly, thirty seconds later, `you know.’ The fact is you know nothing of the kind,” Dautery said angrily. “That coat could have come from any wino anywhere, some poor unfortunate soul, down on his luck who you snatched from the street in your haste to convict some innocent of a parking violation. If you’re attempting to imply that one of us went to the trouble to lug that heavy coat over to Miss Murdock’s house in order to implicate ourselves in the commission of a crime, then I seriously question your grasp of even the most basic police work. That is an illogical premise, ergo, it follows that any conclusion based upon it would, of necessity, therefore be incorrect.”

“Well then, why don’t you tell me about the coat,” Chief Bowman ordered.

“I have nothing further to say about the coat, Miss Murdock, or anything else. When you find her, that is, if she’s actually missing, this questioning will be proven to have been unnecessary. We have nothing further to say tonight, either one of us. Either charge us, or release us. That’s the law.”

“You seem hostile and uncooperative, for someone who claims to have nothing to hide,” Chief Bowman replied. “I can keep you both for 48 hours without charging you with anything, and that’s what I’m going to do. You will be placed in separate facilities within this complex, shown to the showers, and given fresh clothes for the time you’re to be here.”

“Of course I might seem hostile. I am hostile. Wouldn’t that be normal? I’m being held against my will on suspicion of a crime which may or may not even have occurred. And if by uncooperative you mean that I’m unwilling to implicate either of us by making false statements which fit your preconceived and prejudicial notions, then yes, by all means, please do consider both of us uncooperative...and hostile."

"Someone will be here momentarily to show you to your quarters. I trust you will find your accommodations here to be satisfactory," Chief Bowman said, as he stood to leave. "We'll resume in the morning."

5.

Cypress Hill

"It's late Tom," D.A. Bill Roberts said, "you should probably go back to the hotel now. I don't think anything else is going to happen tonight and I've got to get some sleep. I'll see you at the house tomorrow morning, say at around 10:00. Mark, run him back to the Moro, will you? Thanks."

"No, that's OK, I've got the rental. Thanks for letting me hang around, it was interesting watching the way things work. This was a lot more exciting than anything else I would have done tonight, but I'm tired. Jet lag, I guess. I'll see you in the morning. Goodnight everybody, thanks again."

"Yeah, you be careful. We'll see you tomorrow. We have a search warrant now, so I'm going back into Cypress Hill," Chief Bowman began. "When we were there earlier, it was without a warrant, and I want to handle this one strictly by the book. I'm really not sure what we're looking for there since I doubt that Miss Murdock's body is going to be found in the house. But it's a big place. Who wants to go with me?

"OK, Carl, you can ride with me. Let's go,"Bowman said, volunteering Carl Draper. "Has anybody heard anything from

George Wilson and his dogs?"

"Not yet," one of the deputies said, looking around the room for confirmation, "but he called and said that he was on his way. Heshould be here any minute."

"Well, call me when he gets here, or if there're any other developments. I'm surprised he isn't here yet. I don't think Miss Murdock is on the property at Eldorado, or somebody would have found her by now. Bob, call the coroner, no, on second thought hold up on that. There's no point in waking him up unnecessarily. We'll probably need him soon enough."

Chief Bowman and Sgt. Carl Draper jumped into the cruiser and drove the short distance back to Cypress Hill where the chief was pleased to find a patrol car parked at each the end of the street halting both pedestrian and automobile traffic. There was already a crowd of several dozen people standing around, as well as a mobile camera truck and several reporters from the NBC affiliate station in Jackson, Mississippi. Further down the street another police cruiser was parked in front of Cypress Hill, securing the location against any curiosity seekers, its blue lights spinning quietly. Chief Bowman parked beside it.

"It's been quiet around here for the last couple of hours," the patrol officer said. "Are y'all going back in there tonight?"

"Yeah, we're going in now."

"Good luck. I wouldn't go inside that place if you paid me, especially at night."

"You're not afraid of...ghosts...are you?" Draper mocked, holding his arms over his head and waving his fingers back and forth.

"I might or might not believe in ghosts, but I do believe in fleas, ticks, roaches, mosquitoes, fire ants, mice, rats, copperheads, rattlesnakes, spiders, deadly bacteria and the numerous as yet unclassified viral strains you are certain to find inside that dump, but that's alright, Carl, I'm sure you'll have a good time."

"Quit clowning, you two," Chief Bowman said, "this isn't going to be pleasant. Get your flashlight, Carl, and let's get this over with."

Chief Bowman led the way across the treacherous front porch, lighting it carefully as he proceeded, being cautious not to step through a rotten board, or on an exposed nail, or trip over any of the junk randomly stacked and scattered there.

"What is all of this crap?" Sgt. Draper asked in disbelief. "I've never seen anything like this. Why would anybody have wagon wheels on the front porch? And lying on their sides for God's sake. That's just asking for a broken leg."

"Or tires? Or boards with exposed nails pointing upward? Or heaps of gasoline and kerosene infused rags?" The chief asked as he slowly stepped over piles of debris.

"God damn it!" Sgt. Draper cursed, startled as a roosting chicken jumped out from under a broken chair he accidentally hit with his foot.

"Watch your step," Bowman advised, "This is a very dangerous place. There has to be a front porch light switch inside this doorway somewhere. If I can locate it we'll both be better off. In fact, just stay there for a second until I find it. It must be here somewhere. Yeah, here it is. That's better," he said as the front porch lights came on. "Yeah, and here's the hall light switch. Damn, what a mess," Bowman exclaimed as the light from the chandelier illuminated the large hallway.

Draper looked toward the ceiling, amazed by the elegance of the chandelier. It was a massive four-tiered gilded bronze gasolier, of the type found in many of the larger antebellum homes of Halcyon, which had at some point, in more prosperous times, been converted from gas to electricity. It was probably worth more than $20,000, he speculated, as is, not that he would have known with certainty. It was suspended from an elegant and ornate plaster medallion, or rosette, of immense proportions. Its light enabled him to also see the detailed plaster cornice work around the edges of the ceiling perimeter, some of which was missing and had fallen and broken a crystal vase, and covered a small gold stenciled mahogany pier table with powder and chunks of broken plaster. At the far end of the long entrance hall was a large spiral staircase which wound gracefully to the second floor. It was as nice as any he'd ever seen. His eyes were drawn to the wallpaper, probably French Zuber, not that he was an expert on antebellum French wallpaper. Zuber was the only kind he'd ever heard of, and he wouldn't have heard of it at all if he hadn't worked as a boy scout during the annual spring pilgrimage. Large sheets had peeled from one of the walls and were just hanging there, halfway between the floor and the ceiling, suspended in time, he reflected, between the dead past and the very uncertain future of this house. He suppressed the urge to pull all of them down, at least the ones he could reach. The inherent magnificence of the large hallway was diminished by the filth on the floor. "What is that stench?" Draper asked loudly, trying hard not to gag, an involuntary response to his surroundings.

"You mean bouquet," Chief Bowman laughed. "I detect the subtle layered blend of fragrances comprised of the competing, but altogether compelling essences of chicken shit, dog shit, goat shit, cow shit...did I omit anything?"

"You neglected to mention rodent piss," Draper laughed. "What are we looking for precisely, Chief?"

"I'm not really sure. Generally, I'd say tell me if you see anything unusual, or something out of the ordinary, but under the circumstances, I'd be more likely to ask you to report anything which could be considered `normal.' I've never seen anything like this. Firearms, I guess. There are probably plenty in the house."

"These people are filthy. How can anybody live like this? Nobody would believe this."

"I guess that this is what happens when the money runs out. And it appears that it has," Chief Bowman observed, as the beam of his Maglite came to rest upon a life-size bust of Confederate General Robert E. Lee. It could've been either marble or bronze, it was covered with so many layers of dirt that it was impossible to tell.

"Poverty is one thing. I can understand poverty, I grew up poor. This is more than that. This is filth. This is the nastiest place I've ever seen, or smelled," Draper said, as his flashlight's beam came to rest on a large Jersey cow, standing placidly in one of the rooms off the central hallway. "And the heat just makes it worse. There's no telling what we're likely to step in or on, or trip over."

"Just watch and be careful. I don't want either one of us falling through the floor," Bowman said, "and that's a real possibility."

They kept close together, managing to find light switches as they progressed, but they weren't the standard wall-mounted up and down light switches of modern times, or even the dual button switches of the 1920s, but round dials which made a metallic grinding sound as they were turned clockwise to activate them. Bowman observed that the wiring was external, meaning it was not hidden behind the walls, out of sight, as in modern houses, but was contained in narrow rectangular tubes affixed parallel to the foot-high baseboards. Every five feet or so there would be a junction box positioned along the baseboard, which contained regular electrical outlets. The large chandeliers in the first-floor parlors had conduits running from the baseboards up the walls and across the ceilings which supplied them with electricity. It was a common practice in the early 1900s when antebellum houses were first retrofitted with electricity. In fact, the wiring in most of these houses was a combination of the original fabric covered knob and tube wiring in which two parallel wires ran side by side inside the walls or above the ceiling, and modern romex wiring. It was primitive and dangerous, and was the first type of residential wiring used. The intense Halcyon heat had in most cases literally transformed the braided fabric insulation into powder, leaving the bare metal wires totally exposed, just waiting for the intrusion of some gnawing little rodent to finish the job and burn the house down. Chief Bowman was not happy about turning on any of the inside lights anywhere in the house and halfway expected a puff of smoke each time he used a switch. There were no other options in this house as the flashlights which they carried were totally inadequate to provide sufficient light, either for their own safety, or the discovery of anything which might serve as evidence.

The exploration of the first floor produced nothing but revealed even more filth and squalor than the deplorable outside condition of the house suggested. The large elegant Persian rugs in both the ladies' and gentlemen's parlors were so discolored from dirt and stained by animal feces and urine that they were unrecognizable. There were matching gilt mirrors atop each of the heavy black marble mantles, but each were missing plaster in places, and the silver backing had degenerated leaving the mirrored surfaces darkly translucent, spotted, streaked, and ghostly. A gilded French bronze clock, now covered with dust, rested silently on one of the mantles, its hands having stopped in happier times. The heavy ornate cast iron grate of a fireplace at one end of the gentlemen's parlor had been pulled away from the brick and was propped up haphazardly against the surrounding marble. A magnificent nine-foot-long 1860s Austrian Bosendorfer rosewood concert grand piano was imposing even now, with its broken bow styling and ornately carved legs, but it was covered with dirt and many of its keys were warped, stuck together, and missing ivory. A look inside its case revealed broken and rusted strings and evidence of its obvious and long-time use as a chicken roost. It was a total loss. Tables were overturned, resting on their sides, with broken legs reaching outward. Upholstered chairs showed exposed rusted springs and missing stuffing which had been removed by goats. Feathers of some sort were visible nearly everywhere, either from the chickens and ducks which roamed the premises freely, or perhaps from a ripped mattress somewhere upstairs. Large tropical roaches scurried rapidly across the floors and other surfaces, obviously unbothered by either the presence of light, or the human intrusion into what had now clearly become their domain. Shattered glass shards littered the floor along with broken picture frames and ripped canvas portraits stacked on the floor against the walls. Warped, swollen, water-logged books, empty metal tins, and rusted coffee cans served as containers for broken pens, pencils, and multiple pairs of scissors.

The kitchens of these great houses had originally been built away from the main house in a separate building to diminish the chance of an accidental fire destroying the main structure. A kitchen had been added at the rear of this house at some point, probably in the 1890s, judging from the enamel sink and hand operated water pump overhanging it. This was the nastiest room in the house yet, with garbage, paper sacks, and the remains of uneaten food, piled on both exquisite china plates and fast food containers. Mice openly darted across the floor in plain sight. The sink was filled with rusted iron skillets and food and mold encrusted metal pans and plates, stacked a full foot or higher above the counter level. Delicate but darkly tarnished sterling silver knives, forks, and spoons littered the marble kitchen counter tops and floor.

Further exploration revealed the presence of a bathroom which had been added as an afterthought under the servants' stairway off the side of the main first floor hallway. Since the original houses did not have indoor plumbing, under the back stairs was a site frequently selected for a retrofit. Such was the case here. The toilet lid was thankfully closed but the unsanitary conditions there rivaled those of the kitchen, the filthiest place in the house by far.

"What an elegant stairway," Chief Bowman observed as he carefully placed his foot upon the first step of a winding and graceful spiral stairway which, following the curved contour of the wall, led to the second floor. "You should probably wait until I get to the top before you try it, just in case it doesn't hold. It looks solid enough, even though it's free-standing."

The mess upstairs was even worse, if possible, with the large central hallway, normally used as the den or family room in times past, piled with junk. Rotting pieces of fabric and other clothing were strewn about the floor and provided bedding for goats and roosting places for ducks and chickens. A large and exquisitely carved rosewood armoire overflowed with shredded formal gowns of discolored silk and velvet. A faded and moth eaten Confederate uniform, probably that of Brigadier General Dautery, was visible in the cabinet where a protective door had once been. A formerly beautiful Regency sofa, positioned against one of the walls, had been destroyed by the attentions of meandering goats and the intrusion of water and fallen plaster from a leak in the ceiling overhead. The heat and stench were even more pronounced and overpowering on the second floor.

Bill Toma's bedroom.

Each of the four upstairs bedrooms contained a large rosewood or mahogany four-post tester bed. The fabric from the crowning testers was ripped and hung in tattered shreds like the rotting curtains of an abandoned hearse. What appeared to be Olivia Dautery's bedroom, due solely to the presence of women's clothing, was somewhat `cleaner' than the other upstairs bedrooms, if that word could be used at all in this context. Her beautiful mahogany bed had a six foot tall headboard, and four, ten foot tall elegantly fluted posts, but there was no mattress at all, just an empty space where it had once been. Over to the right of the bed, against the wall, were five chairs, each of a different size and style, along with a small low table resembling a piano bench. These precariously supported a filthy, stained, and mildewed mattress, its sides drooping at different levels and angles. There were no sheets, only a couple of knotted rugs which served either as covers or additional padding for this makeshift bed. Dirty articles of clothing hung from the backs of the chairs, and clothes were also scattered indiscriminately across the floor. There were strips of what appeared to be cooked meat each of which had been carefully placed upon a rusted mattress frame. The overwhelming smell of kerosene which permeated the room was traced to two recently used rusty steel smudge pots which had been placed in front of the fireplace.

Bill Toma's room, or what Chief Bowman assumed to be his sleeping quarters, was literally beyond belief, and far more cluttered than Dautery's. Moth-eaten blankets and shredded curtains were piled four feet high atop the mattress of his large rosewood four-poster bed, providing no level surface anywhere on the bed, let alone a place where someone could lie down, or even sit. Clothes, papers, chairs, sheets, rotting books and other refuse littered the floor. Toma's sleeping accommodations appeared to consist of a pile of filthy rags on the floor. There was scarcely an exposed spot anyplace where someone could step, so littered was the room. The entire scene, throughout the house, as bizarre as it would have been under any circumstances, was magnified further by the strange blending of elegance and filth, and the underlying insanity which permitted these conditions to exist simultaneously in the same place.

"There's nothing here," Bowman exclaimed. "Let's get out of this place before one of us is exposed to some as yet unidentified bacteria or virus. I've really never seen anything like this. I'm going to take positive steps to have this place condemned. This is a definite public health risk as well as a general nuisance. It would take an experienced big city crime scene unit working here more than a month before anyone could even imagine calling this place `secured.'"

"The sooner we can get out of here the better, Chief. I'm on duty until 6:00 a.m. If you don't mind, I'd like to take a shower as soon as we get back to the station. This has already been an experience I'll never forget. I feel like things are crawling on me," Draper said.

"They probably are," Bowman replied. "There are some outbuildings and a garage which we've got to check first, so let's get that over with and get the hell out of here."

"Who's going to feed these animals?" Draper wondered aloud, "I mean if Dautery and Toma are going to be in jail."

"I don't know, and I can't worry about it right now," Bowman said, as he shined his flashlight upon the edges of the floor. "Watch your step."

"Wait, what's this?" Draper asked.

"What?"

"I know the muzzle of a 1911 Colt when I see one," Draper replied, as he bent over and with gloved hand withdrew a pistol from beneath the corner of a rotten, moth infested Persian rug pushed up against the wall by the front door.

"That's a .45 all right," Bowman agreed, aiming his Maglite down toward the edge of the carpet. "There's something else though," he said, moving the corner of the rug back further with the edge of his shoe, exposing the black grip of what appeared to be a nickel-plated revolver. "It looks like a 1890s or later Smith & Wesson .32. It's probably what we're looking for, and here, take this .45 too. Put them both in the trunk in evidence bags. We've still got to check the garage. We're through here for tonight after that, but I'm sending forensics over here tomorrow. Let's go."

The ramshackle two-story brick outbuilding appeared to be from the same period as the residence and probably had been a carriage house originally. Its exterior had been altered more than once judging from its lack of any specific architectural continuity. It was every bit as filthy inside as Cypress Hill, but apart from broken furniture, empty paint cans, and piled up rags, was basically empty. There was a rusted, dirt-covered 1950s Packard sedan with four flat tires in one part of the building, but no trace anywhere of Miss Murdock.

This night was turning out so-so for Chief Bowman. The discovery of a body was generally, though not always, the first phase of any murder investigation, and yet no body had been found. To make matters worse, it was really hot outside, and humid, and the darkness of the night had reduced visibility to near zero. "Let's get out of here," Chief Bowman said. "At least we have what I believe to be the murder weapon, that is, if there has been a murder. There has definitely been a shooting though, and this .32 will probably prove to be the gun that lodged the bullet in the wall. This is likely Miss Murdock's .45 that Tom Roberts told us about."

"Chief, you should probably go home and let the duty officer call you if there are any further developments," Draper said. "You've had a long day."

"You're right, I can barely keep my eyes open and it's almost 3:30. I'm going to drop you off at the station and see if I can get a few winks. Tell Farrel to call me if, that is, as soon as they find her. I've got to get some sleep."

6.

Solomon for the Defense

In Los Angeles, California, in the upscale residential area of Mt. Olympus, celebrity attorney Mark Solomonsat down in a comfortable chair, clad only in a tee shirt and boxer shorts, and flipped on the TV, channel surfing, looking for business in much the same way lawyers of the past had chased ambulances. At this point, he no longer needed the money, although he still made plenty. Solomon wasn't offended by the term `ambulance chaser,' nor was he offended by his success, or its comfortable trappings. He worked hard for the money he made, and he performed a public service, providing the best legal representation to those who could afford his fee. Had he compromised his personal ethics along the way? No, he was admittedly amoral, much like a shark or a rattlesnake. He did what he did. There was no karmic reaction in his own mind, as far as he was concerned, and since he didn't believe in such things anyway, it follows that they don't exist. Besides, is a shark to be blamed for doing what it does? Of course not. A shark's purpose is to kill, eat, and reproduce. That's as basic as it gets. Solomon's sole function is to protect his clients and to make money. In a perfect world, some imaginary utopian society, he might personally be concerned with their actual guilt or innocence, but not in this one. He withdrew a large cigar, an Hoyo De Monterey Excalibur # 1, from a highly polished rosewood box, punctured its end with an ice pick, rolled it around gently between his thumb and forefinger, and then lit it slowly, holding the flame of his butane lighter just beneath the cigar's end, rolling it again as he fired up the edges. These are better than anything now coming out of Cuba these days, he reflected fondly, the soil there has been ruined through decades of improper agricultural practices.

Solomon's musings were suddenly distracted by a full-screen image of a magnificent plantation house on the large wall-mounted television screen. The beautiful but generic and robotic blonde anchorwoman proceeded to tell a tale of a rich, missing Halcyon, Mississippi socialite with international connections, who'd just disappeared, leaving nothing but several pools of blood. Two rustic-looking southerners, a man and a woman, had been taken by the police and were being held on suspicion of murder, even though a body had yet to be found. "An abundance of evidence, particularly large amounts of blood found in various places both inside and outside the missing woman's house, leave little hope that she will be found alive. The suspects, rather the detainees, and I repeat that they are only `persons of interest' at this point, are neighbors of the missing woman. They live in a gigantic decaying antebellum mansion called Cypress Hill, which is referred to locally as `The Animal house.'"

"Why is it called that Susan?" the handsomely plastic co-anchor asked.

"It seems, Stan, that the house has been overrun, and with the owners' permission, by various types of livestock, including goats, cattle, hogs, chickens, and other animals."

"You mean the animals live in the house?"

"Yes, that's right Stan, it appears that these animals have total access, 24/7, in or out of the house."

"Well, that is a strange story indeed Susan."

"What's stranger still, is that the `persons of interest' in the Halcyon woman's disappearance are former southern aristocrats with roots to both Jefferson Davis and Robert E. Lee. The missing woman has an equally aristocratic background, with a large Newport, Rhode Island mansion, and a former Russian ambassador in her background. We'll keep you updated about this extremely interesting story as soon as more details become available."

"Let's hope that they find her alive and well," Stan smiled. "Back to the recent congressional battles. Wait, it appears that the two former aristocrats are being…have now been charged with murder."

"That means they must have found the missing woman's body," the female news anchor observed. "Is there any word on that?"

"No," Stan replied. "All we know is that the two suspects have now been formally charged. There are no further details available at this time, but we'll keep you posted on this bizarre and interesting story from Halcyon, Mississippi, so please stay tuned."

Solomon reached over and picked up the phone from the table, dialing Walter Eubanks, his second in command at Solomon, Solomon, and Solomon. "I want you to call Williams Aviation and have the jet ready to leave at 8:00 a.m. in the morning, yes this morning. Get the usual crew together, we're going to Halcyon, Mississippi. If we need backup later, they can fly commercial. I want our full press corps on board for this project."

"This must be big, or you wouldn't be pulling out all stops this early. What is it?" Eubanks asked.

"It's likely to be a very high-profile murder case. Find the best hotel in Halcyon and book us for three days to start with. Be sure to get whatever corporate discounts are available before you commit to a length of stay, or a specific number of rooms. Whatever price they offer, no matter how low it might seem by California standards, tell them that if they can do better, we'll book the rooms for a longer duration, and that we'll take more rooms if we can get a better rate. That place is probably hot as hell, and I doubt that there's anybody there this time of the year anyway, unless it's someone actively seeking malaria, the West Nile Virus, or some other equally pernicious insect related malaise. In other words, they should be thankful for our business this time of year. Make sure they show us their appreciation."

"What about Mr. Caine's possession for resale trial?"

"Hal can take care of that. He can ask for a postponement if he likes. Caine is out on his own recognizance anyway. It's not like he's wasting away in some Mexican jail. Have Hal tell him that we need to do some additional discovery, and also tell him to make sure accounts receivable bills Caine for the extra time and trouble of having to reschedule. He can afford it. Morris and his crew can handle anything else in our absence."

"What's this about, boss?"

"I don't want to explain it but once, so I'll cover everything on the plane tomorrow. The situation is still developing, but this is something I know I'm going to want to fool with."

"How long are we staying?"

"I really don't know."

"Well, how should I tell everybody to pack?"

"I don't know that either, since I've never been to Halcyon, but I'm certain it's going to be hot, just like it was that time we handled that case in Jackson, Mississippi a couple of years ago. Tell them to use their own discretion. They should probably bring enough clothes for at least a week, initially. I want to be in the air and on the way by 8:00 a.m. sharp, so notify the pilots."

"OK Mark, I'll see you then." Eubanks hung up the phone and looked at the clock. 4:05 am. "The bastard never sleeps!"

7.

Mon Reve

The phone rang loudly on Black County District Attorney Roberts' bedside table. He reached sleepily to answer it, anything to stop that horrible ringing. 5:45 a.m., he noted. It was Sgt. Farrel. "Sir, we've found her. She's dead."

"When? Where?"

"Just now. Davis found her. She'd been carried to some pile of weeds and brush and dumped there, by whoever the killer or killers were."

"Where?" Roberts asked. "On her property, or at Cypress Hill?"

"Near the edge of her property, but at Cypress Hill. I can't say for sure since the property lines aren't marked, but the scene has been secured, pending your arrival. I just got off the phone with Chief Bowman. He said to call you and that he'd meet you there."

"I'll be right over," Roberts said, as he jumped out of the bed.

"What is it, honey?" his wife asked.

"They've found her."

"Is she all right?"

"No, she's dead. Murdered. I've got to get over there."

"I'm sorry to hear that, but remember, the funeral is at 2:00 this afternoon."

"I know. I'll be there, but I think it would probably be best if I meet you at the funeral home around 1:30. I doubt that I'll have time to come by the house, but I have a suit at the station. I'll change there."

It was already getting hot as the district attorney stepped into the bright Halcyon morning sunlight, and it probably would break 100 degrees again by noon. Despite his lack of sleep over the past several days, Roberts was now running on a combination of adrenaline, Red Bull, and soon, strong black coffee with plenty of sugar. This would have to keep him moving and focused for the rest of the day. Perhaps he could get some sleep tonight, though just now, that seemed doubtful.

The body of Miss Murdock had been found and photographed at the place where she'd been dumped in a wooded area on the Cypress Hill property, near Eldorado. It was evident that she'd been shot. The Black County Coroner Dr. James Traughber was still at the scene when the district attorney arrived, and had already determined that Miss Murdock had been dead when dropped there, probably in an effort to hide the crime. He'd established the time of death to have been sometime between 7:30 and 9:30 p.m. of the preceding evening. Cause of death: multiple gunshot wounds with more than one delivered at close range. An autopsy would be more conclusive. In the meantime, the district attorney speculated that whoever was responsible for the crime was probably not a skilled marksman, and not particularly intelligent either. The latter point was indicated by the poorly executed intention to cover the crime by hiding the body, as if the massive amount of blood found at the scene would somehow escape notice. A trail of broken weeds and stalks which couldn't be seen in last night's darkness, clearly led through the brush and onto the property of Cypress Hill, further supporting the district attorney's intuitive feeling that Toma and Dautery were directly responsible. "Did you get that trail of broken brush?" he asked the police chief.

"Yeah," Bowman said, "as black as it was last night, I'm not surprised that we couldn't see it. It goes straight back to Cypress Hill. Anyone else other than Toma and Dautery would have taken the road and not cut through the brush to Cypress Hill. The scene has been photographed. Let's go back to the station. I'll meet you there."

As the district attorney wheeled his black Dodge Charger onto First Street he could already see the presence of the media as well as a crowd of probably fifty or sixty people who had gathered outside the police station, despite the early morning heat. "Son of a bitch," he whispered. He knew that this would happen. In a never ending world-wide 24-hour news cycle, the outlets were starved for anything, especially anything sensational and unusual. If this had happened anywhere other than in Halcyon, it would scarcely have warranted any mention at all, but because there hadn't been any significant hurricanes yet this season, or any especially egregious domestic mass murders recently, this would provide camera fodder for media outlets needing anything to stay on the air. There were five or six camera trucks in sight, and probably half a dozen more which he couldn't yet see, parked around the corner.

The good news was that none of these out of town reporters, or their camera crews knew who he was. Hopefully he could just park behind the station at Dr. Thompson's office, and sneak in the side door of the station unnoticed. Presumably the officer of the day had enough sense to keep everybody contained outside in one area.

The Roberts funeral that afternoon at Mon Reve, drew a capacity crowd as expected. The decedent had been well-liked and had done much for both the community and for individuals, many of whom he'd represented in legal matters at no charge. As the preacher spoke, Tom's mind wandered. This tie is choking me. That Beau Brummel, if he's really the one who invented the tie, well, he's dead already, otherwise he should be shot. Roberts didn't even hear the guest speaker, who extolled Tom's father, as the service progressed, endowing him posthumously with virtues which, while he'd possessed in life, had been for the most part experienced by persons other than himself. From a family standpoint, Tom had been the `last hog at the trough' as their yardman would have put it. But the whole thing was surreal anyway. In the first place, Tom thought, all funeral always smell like death. A combination of embalming fluid, cleaning solutions, and massive floral overkill, whether from actual flowers, themselves dead, or the cans of floral air freshener merely drew attention to the reality of the situation. But what reality was that? His father was `gone to glory', `had passed', `had passed away' The truth is that the man is dead, but what the hell does that really mean? How can someone be somewhere for a very long time and then not be somewhere? It doesn't make any sense. Thank God that the old man had shown enough foresight to be cremated. What could possibly be more barbaric than having an `open casket' where a bunch of people come stare at you? And those funeral directors, what a ghastly bunch. They're probably real-life vampires. They're as white as marble tombstones, and generally as cold. Even here in the deep-south, they're pale and deathly looking. Do they ever go outside, into the sunlight?

In the South, he reflected, as his mind wandered, a funeral is a social event. People dress up and arrive in their best clothes and cars. They come to pay their respects, but also to see and be seen, yet another one of the many strange and curious aspects of human behavior.

"And he was a great family man," the preacher continued, "he placed his family above all else, above his legal work, before what little free timehe had, even ahead of his…" and the preacher paused for maximum effect, "golf."A warm muffled laughter followed, just the effect sought by this windbag of a preacher. Tom tuned him out again, looking at his watch. Hopefully this wouldn't be a tag team match, where this pompous orator introduced another speaker, who would also ramble incoherently for another thirty minutes or so before passing the baton to the next speaker who would transport the gathered flock across the oratory, or is it oratorical finish line? Just then he saw Leah, across the room to the right, several rows away.

She happened to look in his direction just then, and their eyes met. She smiled, and so did Tom, but with the reservation befitting this somber occasion. He noticed that she didn't appear to be sitting with anyone, that is, she seemed to be by herself. Not that it mattered. He'd loved and lost. That's the way it was, that's the way it is. `Better to have loved and lost, than never to have loved at all.' The words came to him unsolicited, a famous quote from, Shakespeare? Probably, not that the words, or their author particularly mattered. `It's been ten years,' he reminded himself. These words had become a mantra which he repeated silently anytime he thought of her. `It's been ten years.' It was annoyingly distracting to be troubled by her memory. As they say, she'd lived `rent free' in his head for the last decade. He didn't even know who she was. Hell, he hadn't even known who she was back when he thought he did.

Well, it turned out to be a tag team match after all, with a second, and then a third speaker. Tom tuned them both out and really thought about his father's death for the first time. The sudden realization that he'd never be able to see him again, or hear his voice was sobering. More than that, it was saddening. Although Tom's father had been tough, he'd never been mean, and much of Tom's current success could be directly traced back to the lessons his father had taught him, lessons that in many cases were learned rather reluctantly, but subsequently confirmed through Tom's own experiences. While each had been delivered frequently as a full lecture, they could all be condensed into a series of several dozen simple but meaningful sound bites. "Do the best you can do, not the least you can do," now determined how Tom approached every situation. "Do the right thing," was another one. "Nobody owes you anything, and nobody's going to give you anything," had been drummed into his head for as long as he could remember. In reality, Tom had been given much, by many people, as his father probably knew that he would, if he worked hard enough, but the real lesson, the underlying one had been to teach Tom to become self-reliant. "Self-esteem, and the respect of your peers are earned through accomplishment. You're not entitled to anything you haven't earned." Another one, was "Choose your commitments carefully, but once you've agreed to something, you must do it, since you should keep your word." All of these maxims and platitudes had been instilled in him so frequently because his father realized that they provide the foundation upon which a person exists.

As he sat there now, Tom clearly remembered his father's parting words before Tom left for California. "It's almost like you're running away, but you can't run away from yourself. Sometimes what you think you're running from, you're really running to, and that's maybe what's happening with you. I think every man has to make his own way, and there's always the unseen hand of fate, or destiny. I wanted us to all be just one big happy family, but it's not up to me, so you do what you need to do, with my blessings. Your mother is distraught, and we'll all miss you, but you're like I was at your age, hungry to break free and find out who you are and what you're supposed to do. I believe that you'll find where, and more importantly, who you're supposed to be, if you're honest and do the best you can do. The main thing is, don't lose your soul. Keep it and protect it above all else."

It was the closest thing to a traditional `father and son' talk he'd ever had, and it had been the first and the last. His father had never mentioned anythingabout it ever again, and never asked any deep questions about Tom's life in California. He seemed content that Tom had secured a job with the postal service, had good benefits and a retirement package. Was he proud of Tom? He'd never know. Tom would've liked to have been able to tell his fatherabout what he really did for a living, and to thank him. That above all else, to thank him for those annoying lectures, and what seemed at the time to be merely repetitious platitudes. They'd served him well as a compass, and had truly guided him safely through uncharted territory.

Tom was returned to the present by the closing remarks and final prayer of the third speaker. Private burial of the decedent's ashes in the family plot were announced for a later, undetermined date. Tom joined other family members in bidding farewell to those who'd taken time out of their Saturday afternoon to come pay their respects, one of whom was Leah. He didn't know how it happened, but one thing led to another and afterward, he found himself driving unexpectedly up Hwy. 61 North toward Port Gibson, with her in the passenger seat of his rented Lincoln. Just south of Port Gibson he veered off to the left toward the ruins of Windsor, a gigantic antebellum mansion which had burned in a spectacular 1875 fire. Tom turned off the main highway and followed a meandering dirt and gravel road which wound through a tunnel of huge live oaks, their magnificent branches draped with long strands of Spanish moss which waved in the afternoon breeze of an approaching storm.

The majestic ruins of Windsor were visible in the distance, its massive three-story tall round fluted brick columns still forming a perimeter surrounding the area where the mansion had once stood. The cement fluting which originally covered the surface of the columns had fallen off some of them in places, exposing their still solid brick construction beneath. Even now, nearly a century and a half after the house burned, the ruins were still magnificent. The gigantic columns seemed to have literally sprouted from the verdant earth, as much an outgrowth of the southern soil as cotton, sugar, or tobacco. Pale green ferns with serrated edges reached skyward from crevices in some of the ornate but rusted cast iron Corinthian capitals which topped the tallmoss and vine-covered columns.

The hour and a half ride north from Halcyon had passed quickly and the conversation had been pleasant, but confined entirely to surface level topics. The bitter subject of their breakup remained unaddressed by an unspoken mutual agreement, but remained ever present, overshadowing anything else they might talk about. Tom parked in front of the first row of columns, lowered the windows, and turned off the car. Leah looked out of the window at the ruined columns which were so tall that they appeared to almost converge in the distance, high overhead.

"I…" he said, speaking at the same time as his companion. "Ladies first."

"No…you," she said.

"I was just going to say how nice you look," Tom said. "The truth is that I wanted…well, I'd hoped that if I ever saw you again, you'd be old and ugly with a couple of howling kids tugging at your dress."

"Why would you wish that on anybody?" Leah asked, genuinely surprised by the observation.

"I thought that it would be easier for me, than remembering you as you were…are. That's all. I didn't wish anything bad for you. I just…"

"I understand," she said, "you look just the same as you did, too, as I remember you." The fact of the matter is that he looked better to her now than he ever had. Apparently, California life had been good for him. He'd always been self-confident, sure of himself, but now, she sensed, there was something different about him, which seemed to substantiate what she'd formerly regarded merely as his own high opinion of himself, some accomplishment, perhaps, or possibly, just a definite sense of purpose heretofore lacking. He was the same as he'd been ten years ago, but somehow different. And she was finally free or that big mistake, that disastrous so-called marriage. She'd listened to everybody and everything but her own intuition. "Tom comes from a good family," her mother had repeatedly cautioned her, "and his brother is on the way up, but Tom just seems to lack direction. He isn't marriage material." It had been the biggest mistake of her life, almost ten years wasted on somebody she'd liked but never loved, mainly because he'd seemed focused and could promise a `good life.' But the good life hadn't been that good after all. And now here she was again, back where she'd started, but not quite. Now she was here looking at someone she'd loved, and who'd once loved her, but who'd now moved on, seemingly none the worse for the experience. `You don't miss the water until the well runs dry,' she thought, wistfully.

This was dangerous territory for Tom. Sure, she was beautiful, just now, and ripe, more so than she'd ever been ten years ago in her twenties, and now presumably available. And here she was again, sitting next to him, just the way it had been when they'd first driven up here at night in that old Cadillac convertible of his father's with the top down, the night heat so thick that it felt like the ocean. That had been so incredible, the standard against all subsequent sexual experiences had been judged. But it wasn't the same, not now. He was no longer the fool that he'd been back then. He remembered the words of a country song `Don't Touch Me There.' Since her betrayal he'd kept his heart in the proverbial `lock box.' No love, no loss, much pleasure. Infinitely preferable to being chained down. Freedom to come and go, and the freedom to stay, if he so desired, for as long or short a time as he wished.

And so, here she was again, sitting in the car with him just like it had been long ago, and she truly looked better than ever. He noticed the vein in her neck as she spoke, and could not help but remembering how sensitive her neck had been and how ardently she'd responded to his kisses there. And her eyes and body language seemed to convey her willingness to resume where they'd left off, beginning right this moment, if he so desired. But he never made the same mistake twice. It was a rule he lived by. If someone in business betrayed him or broke his trust, he never forgot it. In his business it wasn't an infrequent occurrence, and while he wasn't into revenge, as such, if anybody, an actor he'd formerly liked and helped, for example, had screwed him, but was someone he still had to do business with, a lucrative role might quietly go to another actor in his stable instead, someone not already known to be disloyal. Loyalty is everything. Money comes and goes, but loyalty or lack of it is at the essence of who somebody is. It's one of the foundation bricks upon which a person is built. Ironically, he hadn't thought that much about it before Leah's unexpected betrayal. Perhaps that's what had made him now so obsessive about the subject of loyalty. She might've learned her lesson, since `mankind learns through suffering,' as the ancients said, but the real point is, if she'd been right for him to begin with, it would have never been an issue in the first place. And better to have found out then rather than later, who she really was. Still, the temptation was there, and he wanted her now, more than ever, emotionally and physically. They both sat inside the car with their backs propped against opposite doors, their fingers casually interlaced and touching lightly over the seat backs. It was all he could do to resist her now because he knew in his heart that he still loved her, but for once in his life, he'd let reason triumph over impulse. It was like they said at Alcoholics Anonymous, `one drink is too many, and a thousand aren't enough.' It was the same thing just now with her. One kiss would be too many, and everything wouldn't be enough. Sure, he could give in, he certainly wanted to. But how would he feel a week from now, back in his own world? He didn't want to be consumed with missing her, and his work didn't allow for emotional distractions. Tom started the car as the first drops of rain hit the windshield, and they drove through the storm in silence for the most part, all the way back to the funeral home, but the emotional tension was palpable. By the time they reached the funeral home, where she'd left her car, the rain had diminished to a drizzle. He pulled up next to her light blue Toyota and stopped, leaving the engine running in his car as he struggled to find the right words to say. She stopped him by placing her finger over his lips and saying, "Shhhhh, it's all right, just kiss me."

8.

Lucien Dale

"They've lawyered up," Sgt. Draper whispered to Chief Bowman as the chief cut an angry path through the throng of reporters waiting for him outside the criminal justice center. It was no surprise to Chief Bowman, the current district attorney, or anyone else at the station that Toma snd Dautery had retained an attorney. It wasn't some big-time lawyer from New Orleans, Memphis, or Baton Rouge, after all, as they'd feared, but worse, much worse.It was Mark Solomon, from Los Angeles, a former criminal defense lawyer who'd successfully handled several high-profile murder and divorce cases, received an appointment as a federal judge, and publicly resigned the prestigious post two years later because he `wasn't making enough money.' Not only that, he'd brought along an entourage of junior attorneys, clerks, students and assistants, as well as a couple of representatives from his L.A. publicity and management firm with him to Halcyon. The lawyer actually had a manager, and a press agent, like a singer, or an actor. He'd turn this trial into a circus and his crew would create and control media spin. They'd basically taken over the 1927 Moro, Halcyon's historic downtown hotel, and were in the process of adding additional phone and cable lines even now, setting up a `Command Center' as he brazenly called it.

Solomon had arrived at the facility where Dautery and Toma were being held unannounced, his entire legal team in tow, loudly demanded and been given one of the meeting rooms at the criminal justice center as opposed to a smaller interview room designed specifically for attorney client interviews. Everyone with any social significance had been at the funeral of the district attorney's father on the edge of town when the lawyer had arrived, so there'd been nobody with the authority to stop him. He'd bulldozed into the place with his crew in tow, verbally overpowering the small staff holding the fort until the funeral was over, demanding to see his clients immediately.

Solomon had burst into the conference room like a bantam rooster, pushing the door open, surveying his surroundings for a moment, before turning to one of his assistants and saying, "Have you checked this room for hidden microphones?"

"Yes sir, I have."

"Well do it again, now. I'm not taking any chances in this place. Every room here could be, and probably is bugged. Shhh!" he whispered loudly, holding his index finger in front of his mouth and looking at the defendants. Solomon's group of about fifteen people sat silently as well for the few minutes it took for one of them to walk around the room waving some sort of detector which would indicate the presence of a hidden microphone. Toma and Dautery sat there in silence, alternately watching the procedure, looking back and forth at each other, and at the crowd of out-of-towners in the room with them.

Solomon was tall and thin, they observed, slightly more than six feet tall, with dark, intense eyes, and a commanding and powerful personal presence which seemed to overwhelm the room. His booming baritone voice intensified that impression. He was also immaculately dressed in a flamboyant pale blue sharkskin suit which, given its perfect tailoring, fit him like a glove. His hands, nails, and dark but slightly graying hair were perfectly manicured, and he resembled, more than anything else, a male model in some high-end fashion magazine. He was the living embodiment of the phrase `tall, dark, and handsome.'

After the room had been cleared and Solomon given the thumbs up, he stood and waved his hand around the room with one broad sweeping motion, flipping his wrist and hand upwardly in some sort of grandiose theatrical gesture, bowed slightly, and stated loudly to the perplexed defendants, "I am Mark Solomon, and this is my posse, your `dream team,' as we say in Los Angeles. The first thing we're going to do is get you some decent clothing,"he said to Dautery and Toma. "The wearing of this rustic `prison garb' has obviously placed the both of you in a diminished psychological state, making it more difficult for you to speak or act in your own defense. The presumption of innocence is inherent in the judicial system and your current attire suggests the opposite, to you, the employees of this facility, and to members of the press." Solomon knew that he would not be able to secure the defendants street clothes, but he intended to make an issue of it with the prosecution anyway, putting it in a defensive position from the outset. "The second thing," he continued, "is that you need to be released at once on your own recognizance. Again, you have the constitutional right to the presumption of innocence."

Before either of them had the opportunity to even respond, Solomon interrupted himself, "Gayle, would you be so kind as to inquire of our hosts what type of refreshments they might desire, and then send one of your assistants out into the lounge, waiting room, or even outside of the building if necessary, to secure whatever they might wish, barring alcoholic beverages, of course."

Solomon stood at the end of the conference table looking at the headline of the special latest edition of the *Halcyon Democrat*, as his assistant took the defendants' drink orders. `Pair Charged in Murder of Wealthy Socialite,'it read in large bold type. "This is good," he said addressing his seated team, "it sways the potential jurors in favor of the defendants to start with."

"What do you mean, sir?" one of his student clerks asked.

"What is the subliminal message suggested by this headline? There is little sympathy...." Solomon stopped mid-sentence and rose from his chair. "Class," he shouted, for the moment ignoring the defendants, "this is the local paper here, the (looking down), yes, the *Halcyon Democrat.* Look at these headlines," he said again, holding the paper up, "`Pair Charged in Murder of Wealthy Socialite.' Can anyone tell me what this headline suggests as pertains to our present situation here?"

One of the junior attorneys stood and said, "Given the current class warfare instigated by the government-media complex, it would seem to suggest sir, that the decedent is somehow less of a human being, less of an elderly woman, and more of a social pariah, that is, given her wealth and patrician background."

"That's exactly right, Marvin. You may be seated. This is what I mean when I say that high profile cases are won in advance through the manipulation and control of the media. The press are invariably the thirteenth juror. There is no such thing as a sequestered jury, at least not from a local jury pool. They've already reached their own conclusions before they're ever selected for actual jury duty or enter the courtroom for trial. Any competent and successful defense attorney knows this. An honest and sincere juror may believe himself or herself to be impartial, and capable of responding only to the evidence as presented, but we all have preexisting biases based upon our own personal life experiences which influence our actions, opinions, anddecisions at the most basic level, that is, subconsciously, or subliminally. How might this headline have been better worded from the standpoint of the prosecutor?"

Susan Dawson, a third-year law student, and Solomon intern, stood up and answered the question. "Sir, it would have been much more prejudicial to the defense if the headline had read something along the lines of `Pair Charged in Home Invasion Murder of Elderly Woman.'"

"That's right," Solomon said, "but why? Again why? You have to understand the `why' if you want to manipulate and control public opinion."

"The `why,' sir, is that people are much more inclined to feel sympathy for an elderly woman, living alone who has been murdered within her own home, a sacred place, than they would some wealthy socialite, who is much more likely to be considered to be a member of the currently unpopular class known as the `idle rich.'"

"You're right, Susan. Did you hear what she said?" Solomon asked. "The political class here in the U.S. has maintained control of the population since the early 1960s largely through pitting groups against each other. The gays and the straights, the blacks and the whites, the blacks and the Mexicans, the Jews against the Muslims, the haves versus the have-nots, the list is endless. `Divide and conquer,' is much more than merely an idle expression. Today, in this current economic climate, the battle is largely waged around the struggle between the so-called rich and the so-called poor. Neither class is generally speaking, either really rich or really poor in reality, but perception is what counts in terms of public opinion. We're going to use this to benefit our clients here, and her point is right. One's home is considered one's sanctuary, a place of refuge, a sacred place, as she rightly put it. A lonely old lady, a spinster, if you will, murdered and abducted from the sanctity of her own home is a much more sympathetic character than an aloof, wealthy socialite. Keep that in mind. Now, in any relationship we maintain with the press, either locally or nationally, Nikki Daniels will be the point man on this case. Nikki, that is, we, will be portraying the defendants as the real victims in this situation. It is they who were taken from their own home in the middle of the night, abducted themselves, if you will, by bumbling, incompetent police, by legally sanctioned night riders reminiscent of the Ku Klux Klan. While Miss Murdock was certainly killed by someone, it wasn't these two. First, we're going to get the story from the defendants, their story, and based upon that, we will formulate a specific defensive strategy. We're going to seek to establish that the crime scene was greatly compromised, and that the accused were questioned without an attorney present."

The defendants had been sitting there as if they were in a movie of some sort, invisible witnesses to speculations concerning somebody else. Suddenly, it was about them after all, as Solomon turned his full attention upon them.

"Mr. Toma, if you will, please tell me everything that happened on the day of Miss Murdock's disappearance. I want to know everything you did, every conversation you had with anyone, anywhere, about anything. So, start from the beginning. What time did you wake up?"

"I generally go to my room at around 8:30 or 9:00 every night and read until I fall asleep. That time varies, but usually I'm asleep well before midnight, so that's what I did Wednesday night. I woke up Thursday morning at around eight o'clock. Olivia, Miss Dautery, had cooked some breakfast. After that I went to the tool shed and got a sledge hammer and slaughtered a hog out in the back yard."

"What time was that?" Solomon asked. "Approximately?"

"I don't know what time that was. It was in the morning."

"It was at around 9:30," Miss Dautery interrupted, "What difference does it make? It's been established that Miss Murdock had a visitor at around 10:00 in the morning, the district attorney's brother, to be specific. She wasn't reported missing until around 9:00 p.m. when her cousin, boyfriend, or whatever, came calling. Her maid had been at the house until at least 5:00 p.m., just as she was five days a week, that is, Monday through Friday, so what either of us did in the morning has no bearing on anything. Let's move on to something which might have some actual relevance to, that is, to our present circumstances."

Her aggressive and defensive attitude caught Solomon off guard, but not for long. "You wouldn't by chance be from New York?" he asked her, attempting to introduce a bit of levity into the room's suddenly chilled atmosphere.

"No, I'm not from New York," she answered, "but I lived in the city for awhile, Manhattan. I used to write for *Atlantic Monthly, The New York Times*, *Harper's*, and other publications. You might have heard of them. Where did you say you're from?"

"I'm from California, via Long Island, and N.Y.U. You seem to have a certain New York attitude about you, for lack of a better term. While it's a trait I consider to be admirable personally, Miss Dautery, it's important that you answer any questions myself or any of this team might ask, no matter how trivial they might seem to you. You two have been charged with the robbery and murder of your neighbor, Miss Jeannie Murdock, and while I may be convinced in my heart of hearts that you are innocent of these charges, there are many potential jurors who are not so certain to be as sure of your innocence as we are. It's important that you recognize that we, that is, all of us have come this great distance from California, at our own expense, on our own time, specifically to represent to you, to stand as a bulwark against a district attorney who is actively seeking to enhance his personal reputation by making an example of the both of you. You need to understand that the authorities are out to either kill you outright or put you both in prison for life. They will seek to turn you against each other and force a confession from one of you which implicates the other. My experience indicates that they won't especially care which one of you turns state's evidence, whoever they deem to be the easiest to manipulate. For these and other reasons, it'is extremely important that you answer every question any of us might ask, no matter how insignificant it might seem to you. We need an air tight alibi for both of you, and the best way to get that is to establish a clear, correct and detailed timeline both in the days leading up to the murder of Miss Murdock, and especially on the day on which she disappeared. It's important that this be done while the memory is fresh, because an actual trial might not take place for many months, possibly even a year or longer. A lot can be forgotten in a year or more, so if you please, regard us as friends..., family, if you will, and respond to us accordingly."

"Very well," Olivia Dautery said calmly. "You've come a long way to help us, and since you already know that we don't have any money with which to pay you, and you've come anyway, at your own expense, you shall find us both extremely cooperative henceforward. My apologies to all of you if I've said anything which might have possibly seemed hostile. The truth is that we've been treated disrespectfully by the police, our animals need to be fed, and we haven't slept much, so we're both a bit on edge, and we're ready to go home. We haven't done anything to anybody, but since they don't have any other `suspects' they've settled upon us as the path of least resistance. In the interim, who'll feed our animals?"

"We'll check with the authorities and see what can be done. For the moment, I'm going to leave you in the capable hands of my staff. They will question you extensively and will establish a comprehensive timeline. Please be patient with them as they are here to assist me in helping exonerate both of you. In the meantime, I'll be working to secure your release on your own recognizance."

"Now, let's start with Thursday morning," Solomon heard as he left the room.

At the Moro Hotel a command center had been established in the penthouse with cable and satellite feeds from all of the news outlets as well as the major networks. Five television monitors had been set up with computers on two large conference tables which had been pushed together. Debra Harriswould record and catalogue any reports out of or about Halcyon and feed them to Nikki Daniels, Solomon's legal assistant, herself a lawyer. "What do we have so far Debra?" Daniels asked, calling the command center on her cell phone from the lounge of the police station.

"The story is airing hourly on FOX and BBC in addition to national network affiliates. Things are becoming more detailed now, but there's still a lack of specific relevant information and the police are denying access to either house, although the road bordering both properties is open again. There are quite a few curiosity seekers as well as camera crews from Jackson, Baton Rouge, New Orleans, and Vicksburg."

"Here's what I want to do," Nikki Daniels said. "I'm going to get access to that decaying house as soon as possible, and I'm taking a camera crew in with me. We're going to portray these two as innocent victims of an ongoing war waged by the decedent and her cousin, who was also supposedly her longtime lover. I want you to send somebody over to the local paper, the *Halcyon Democrat,* and find out everything you can about all of the people involved. Who are they? How are they perceived in town?"

"I can answer that last question now," Debra replied, "It's a preliminary evaluation, and I'll delve deeper into it, but from what I can tell, Miss Murdock was respected by the bon ton here, not because of her gracious way of dealing with the locals, but because of her background and her immense wealth. I was told that she was `old money.' It seems as if that's a big deal in Halcyon, maybe in the south in general. Apparently, she had little to do with anyone here, socially, at least. It seems that she wasn't particularly well-liked by anyone but the upper class, and there is definitely a class caste system here. Liked might be the wrong word. I think that everyone at the upper end wanted her to at least know who they were. She'd been socially active at one point, back when her father had been alive, but basically didn't care what anybody thought about her one way or the other. And she was rich. She drove a new Aston Martin of some sort, that is, before she stopped driving, and was known to pull up onto the curb in front of a store and honk the horn loudly and impatiently, literally, until somebody actually came out to see what she wanted."

"What store?" Daniels asked.

"Any store. She didn't want to be bothered by having to actually go inside. Eventually her car broke down. I think that the brakes went out and nobody around here could fix them. At that point she began riding a bicycle which she wrapped in newspaper or butcher paper of some sort, supposedly to protect it from fading by the sun. She wrapped her car in paper also, after she stopped driving it. She was very interesting according to general consensus, and eccentric, but not particularly well-liked, apparently by anyone other than her cousin, Mark Delgado, and the district attorney's mother."

"That's good for us, that is, for the defendants. News outlets are probably going to be after the same information as we are, so I want your crew to beat them to the punch. I'm going to schedule a news conference this afternoon. In the meantime, I want you to get the feel of this place. Where does the sympathy of the town lie? What are the details concerning the long-standing feud between the decedent and the defendants? I also want to know everything about both of those houses, Eldorado, and Cypress Hill. I want to control the public perception of these two defendants. Is there some place where the locals hang out around here?" Daniels asked.

"Yes, there is a restaurant called the `The Kitchen.' It's on the property of Lady of the Lake, one of the largest and most magnificent of the mansions here. I believe that the restaurant is owned by one of several garden clubs. It's been around since the 1940s, and is where most of the locals eat lunch, that is, the locals at the upper end of the social register. It's also patronized heavily by tourists, especially during both pilgrimages, but there aren't many tourists here this time of year as it's generally considered too hot."

"With good reason. Here's what I want to do. I think you and I'll go over there for lunch and see what we can find out. There's probably somebody who's been working there forever, a cook, maid, or hostess. He or she should be able to provide us with some of the backline story on everybody involved. Mark and I will pick you up at 11:30. By the way, when is Miss Murdock's funeral?"

"The funeral is scheduled for August 6, at 2:00 p.m. at Trinity Episcopal Church."

"Good work Debra. Be downstairs in front of the hotel on the First Street side. Most of the streets around here are one way."

Lady of the Lake was unlike anything Nikki Daniels had ever seen. It was unlike anything any of them had ever seen. The same could be said of Halcyon. Period. Gigantic moss-draped live oak trees lined both sides of the narrow streets, buckling the sidewalks with their serpentine roots, their branches forming a shaded canopy overhead. Lady of the Lake was perched upon a hill pretty much in the center of town, with no lake anywhere nearby. The huge glossy black iron gates were hinged upon ornate square iron posts and opened to a gently sloping curved driveway which led to the front steps. There, a series of incredibly large hewn stone steps led up to a portico of immense proportions. Words like large, massive, gigantic, magnificent, were all inadequate to describe what the visitor beheld.

The house was above all else majestic and imposing. There were many houses in Beverly Hills far larger than this one, as well as in some of the newer upscale residential areas of Los Angeles, most of which, in the latter case, were filled with McMansions, large, expensive, highly detailed monstrosities, which despite their custom building and high cost seemed temporary at best. Lady of the Lake, on the contrary, seemed to say. `I am theproduct of real wealth, not that worthless currency, credit, and high debt with which you operate. I was here long before you arrived and will be standing long after you're forgotten. I am forever.' That's the message conveyed by most of the great houses of Halcyon, like Sheraton Hall, Waverly, Tomfoolery, Ivory, Twelve Oaks, Concordia, Longview, Forsythe, and many others. But that haughty architectural bravado is an illusion after all, and many of the great houses of Halcyon and indeed the entire Mississippi Valley were anything but enduring. Miss Murdock's cousin Mark Delgado's ancestral home, Live Oaks, had burned to the ground, Windy Hill had rotted and been razed, the magnificent Homewood had burned in 1940, the 1840 Harper House mansion had been demolished in 1902, and within the last decade, even the historic Tomfoolery had succumbed to flames and now remained nothing but a burned, gutted shell, stripped of its beautiful architectural details, and its stately walls covered with third-world graffiti.

The The Kitchen restaurant was located directly behind the main house, Lady of the Lake, but on the property next to a small, private swimming pool. The fragrance of tea olive and blooming azaleas permeated the air with a sweetly decaying bouquet which involuntarily brought one's senses fully into the present, and yet at the same time reminded one of another place, an emotional place rather than a physical one, a vague tugging upon one's heart strings which was undeniable. It hit Nikki Daniels that way. "I don't think I ever want to leave this place," she said, barely able to catch her breath due to a sudden overwhelming and unanticipated emotional rush.

"You mean Halcyon?" Solomon asked quizzically.

"I'm not talking about Halcyon, although obviously that's part of it," she answered wistfully. "No, I mean I never want to leave how I feel, I mean right now. I think, somehow this must be who I really am, or maybe was once, long ago. I am this, the gently waving Spanish moss, caressed by the warm breeze, the sweet floral fragrance everywhere, the flowering crepe myrtles the size of trees. I really don't know how to describe it, but it's almost like being in love."

"That's crazy talk," Solomon answered. "This isn't who you are at all, you're from Santa Monica. You'd wither and die like that flower on the ground over there. You wouldn't make it five minutes on your own in this place. It's in the middle of nowhere and there's nothing to do here. You'd be bored to death. I guess it's a good place to die though, if that's what you have in mind. There's a big hospital here, I think. This place would drive me insane. This murder is probably the only noteworthy event that's happened here since the Civil War, which, by the way, still seems to be a major though mostly unspoken preoccupation of the locals, for some reason."

The dining room part of the The Kitchen restaurant was basically a big, square one-story room with a high ceiling numerous tables, and minimal decorations. There were some vintageHalcyon Pilgrimage posters adorning the walls in places, and curtained windows permitted a limited view of the outside. Each of the square tables was covered with a thick white cotton tablecloth and accented with fresh flowers in a small clear glass vase. Otherwise, there was nothing remarkable about it, that is, except the food. Solomon, and his three companions were among the first to arrive, but within half an hour the place had filled to capacity. Daniels noted the small colorful freshly cut flowers in the vase and wondered to herself what they might be, and if they were local. Just about any upscale restaurant in L.A. had fresh flowers on the table, though nobody noticed them. There were flowers all over Halcyon, in yards, along the streets, and in residential and commercial areas. The roads, yards, and sidewalks were littered with them. You couldn't help but notice them, the entire city seemed like one big flower. She appreciated the fact that someone had taken the trouble to put flowers on each table in the restaurant. The person or persons who'd been told to do this probably didn't even pay attention to the job. Somebody was supposed to put flowers out. Somebody else's job consisted of placing tablecloths and arranging forks, spoons, and knives just so. It's so easy to be preoccupied with a job that one scarcely notices the work being done. Nikki Daniels noticed the flowers though, and was appreciative.

Solomon felt like a fish out of water. This wasn't like L.A. at all. The Kitchen lacked both the subdued hi-tech ambience, and the anonymity of a California eatery, at least of the type he frequented, and yet, as far as he could tell, there were no shaved headed tattooed louts lurking about like there were in L.A. There, it was difficult to tell who had money and who didn't. Appearance was generally no longer a clear indicator, especially in the entertainment circles in which he traveled. In Halcyon, at least, everybody pretty much looked like who they were. Somebody who looked like a bum probably was, but come to think of it, he hadn't seen anyone who fit that description here, at least not yet. The people he'd seen so far were well groomed andnice looking. In fact, everyone in the restaurant was well-dressed except for a couple of mid-western tourists, recognizable by their unkempt general appearance and the presence of those hideous vinyl so-called fanny packs worn like an additional belly, generally located beneath a larger real one, as was the case in this instance.

As if sensing their thoughts, a man in a blue seersucker suit at a nearby table leaned over and whispered to Solomon, "Probably, Wisconsin, Indiana, or Minnesota. Tthey stand out like a sore thumb here, but they're all welcome nonetheless. It's a pleasure to meet you Mr. Solomon," the well-dressed stranger said, extending his hand. "I'm Lucien Dale, a local lawyer. I imagine you're here because of the so-called Animal House Murder."

"It's a pleasure to meet you, sir." Solomon replied, standing and extending his hand, thrilled to be recognized in any place as remote as Halcyon, Mississippi. "Won't you please join us, we'd love to speak with you."

The local attorney hesitated initially, due to a natural upper class southern reticence, but quickly changed his mind. After all, this was `the' Mark Solomon, one of the most successful celebrity trial lawyers in America. It was truly an honor to be asked to join Solomon's table, even if Solomon's intention was simply to pump him for information.

"What's good here?" Solomon asked as Dale seated himself. "This is Nikki Daniels, my head of everything, and Debra Harris, her right-hand man, I mean woman."

"It's a pleasure to meet all of you." Dale replied cordially, "and everything's good here. Well, I wouldn't personally recommend the sushi, unless you like raw catfish."

"This restaurant really has catfish sushi?" Solomon asked in stunned disbelief.

Debra Harris, being from the south, understood the joke and quickly covered her mouth with her napkin to keep from laughing out loud. The Mississippi Lawyer had just caught Solomon off guard, a very difficult feat.

"I'm just kidding about that, although catfish is the largest cash crop in the state now. We are the number one producer of farm raised catfish in the nation, but everything at this place is really good. It's the most popular lunch spot in town."

"That's encouraging," Solomon replied. "Are you a Halcyon native?"

"Yes, I am. Most of us are."

"What can you tell me about the two suspects?" Solomon asked.

"Are you representing them? You must be."

"Yes, I am."

"Well, they're very interesting people, as you will find out soon enough. In Halcyon eccentricity is a virtue, though not one equally esteemed by everybody. The annual pilgrimages are about all Halcyon has going for it, that is, if you discount the wonderful climate, the pleasant and gracious populace, the beautiful architecture, and picturesque scenery. There is, of course, that so-called riverboat casino at the landing in the part of town known as the river front, but then there are similar casinos all the way up and down the river, so you really can't count that. Anyway, during the pilgrimagesHalcyon puts on its best face and lives up to its well-deserved reputation for hospitality. Visitors come literally from all over the world to see what the antebellum south was like. Toma and Dautery began advertising, inviting pilgrimage visitors to come to the `Animal House,' while they were in town. Their decaying mansion, Cypress Hill, is alternately called the Animal House or the Goat House, depending on who you happen to be talking to. This intentionally blatant and illegal posting enraged certain members of the current so-called upper crust, particularly the sponsors of the event, as they felt it cast a dark shadow over the entire proceedings, and in essence was a deliberate mockery of the pilgrimage."

"Why?" asked Nikki Daniels. "I doubt that any visitors to Cypress Hill would seriously diminish the garden club's revenue."

"The revenue loss was nonexistent," Dale explained "since Toma and Dautery's house was not on any of the official tours, for which visitors paid one set fee to see several houses. But many people are fascinated by decay, and without getting into some long-winded examination of the subject, let me just say that true decay, whether it be personal or architectural, is the next evolutionary step beyond perfection. When something is at its highest point, down is the next stop. In other words, only something superior to begin with is ever capable of being decadent. From an architectural standpoint, a particle board shack can never be decadent, because it was nothing to begin with. Cypress Hill, on the other hand, was magnificent from the outset, a seemingly minor distinction, but in fact a significant one, especially in terms of Southern culture.

"As regards the two defendants, they're the very embodiment of the term southern decadence. They represent an image that Halcyonians at the upper end of the current social scale, and indeed Southerners in general, wish to put behind them...us, specifically the decline of our former aristocracy. While their presence was well known to everybody in town, it was only when they began touting their own decadence, reveling in it, shamelessly rolling around in it like hogs in mud, that they ran afoul of the powers that be. Formerly they'd been merely a quaint local curiosity, but this brazen effrontery toward the current ruling class from two of its own high-ranking members...defectors, for lack of a better word, made them folk heroes, outlaws, of sorts to those who do not come from such distinguished backgrounds. Despite the presence of many grand houses here, the fact is, that the percentage of people who actually own and inhabit them is very small compared to the population in general. Longview, for example, is owned by the D.A.R. Lady of the Lake, and Tomachichi, are owned by garden clubs, and I use the term in a generic manner. In that sense, these houses really do belong to all of us.

"So, while the silk stocking gang, and those who are involved in the pilgrimage are horrified by Cypress Hill, et al, the public in general has embraced them, that is, the defendants, to rather a large degree."

"They live in that big mansion," Solomon observed. "It must have been elegant at some point. What happened?"

"Well, Toma inherited a fairly large fortune I suppose. Large enough at any rate. He was once esteemed by the decedent and her consort, rather I should say cousin, since that is a matter of actual fact rather than mere speculation, and they traveled in the same circles. In any event, both Toma, and Dauterywere from southern aristocracy, not the social climbing junior league type, but long-standing wealth spanning generations. Cypress Hill became vacant, I remember, and he moved in. It had been in his family somehow, although I don't remember the particulars. Bill Toma had been expected to become a concert pianist of international renown, that is, prior to the accident in which his hand was crushed by a falling window. He recovered, and continued playing, but it wasn't the same. He wasn't the same. Olivia Dautery had fallen on hard times as well, so, as I recollect, Toma offered her the shelter of Cypress Hill, and together they entertained the bon-ton, but ultimately, they ceased having people over and no longer went out. I guess Toma realized that his musical career was never going to materialize. At that point, whenever that was, he seemed to have given up altogether. He sort of withdrew into himself. He stopped dressing normally and began wearing old feedbags with holes cut in them for his arms, legs, and head. He stopped shaving and grew a long beard, giving him the appearance of some feral mountain man from Appalachia. He'd frequently wander around town and sometimes the police would take him home, you know, give him a ride back to Cypress Hill. He became sort of a local curiosity."

"You mean like a `village idiot?'"Solomon suggested.

"Not at all, actually. He'd graduated from Vanderbilt, played classical piano, and was extremely well-read and well-bred. The library at Cypress Hill rivaled that of any of the great houses in

Halcyon, that is, before it was devoured by meandering goats and destroyed by water damage from a leaking roof."

"It must have been the result of a long-standing depression," Nikki Daniels speculated. "Things like that sometimes happen more frequently than one might think, but seldom to that degree. Usually the decline is slow, the result of repeated setbacks. In this case, the injury to his hand was probably the defining event which initiated everything."

"You're probably right about that," Solomon agreed, "but what happened to the money?"

"Nobody really knows. It was rumored that Bill buried it somewhere on the property, and he might have. The rumor was so prevalent that upon several occasions the police actually arrested amateur treasure seekers for trespassing, and Olivia Dautery was reprimanded for shooting at a couple of teenagers who'd been digging in her yard. No charges were filed, in regard to her shooting at trespassers, but that kept people away for awhile. However, it was not unusual for Dautery and Toma to find freshly dug holes in the yard some mornings. No money was ever found, or if it was, it wasn't reported, not that it would have been anyway. Their money probably just ran out at some point.

"Eventually, Toma and Dautery were totally abandoned by the aristocracy as Toma's behavior became stranger. He began referring to himself as Oswald Lobrecue, a pseudonym he probably adopted from some obscure literary work. Former friends would pass him on the street and offer greetings. He would reply, his face absolutely expressionless, `I'm not who you imagine me to be. I am Oswald Lobrecue.' The former beauty Olivia Dautery, began dressing like a peasant as well, wearing inexpensive dresses while her out-of-style couture gowns became the food of moths. And then, at some juncture, they began bringing animals home. At first it was cats, then ducks, and goats, and eventually even hogs and cattle. They roamed the house unhindered. You can imagine the results."

"Be that as it may, I understand that they're generally well-liked," Solomon observed.

"Yes, for the most part, though that wasn't always the case. After the bon-ton turned on them they became the butt of pranks, crank calls in the middle of the night, you know that type of thing. As I said, Toma was basically emotionally absent. Olivia, on the other hand, was quite handy with a shotgun and earned the reputation of being someone you don't want to mess with. Parents warned their adolescent sons and daughters to give the place wide berth. No, they weren't especially liked, that is, until they began to open their house while the pilgrimage was underway. Having been shunned by their former high-toned friends, they'd come to be considered as feral and dangerous by the local black citizenry, and decadent freaks by the middle-class whites. Once they began opening their decrepit mansion to the public during pilgrimage, however, they became sort of local folk heroes of the underclass, that is, their flagrant mockery of the pilgrimage changed the public perception of them. Visitors toured the house, even locals, though not unaccompanied. Bill played piano on some beat up old upright, for his paying guests, gave lectures on the antebellum south, and Olivia read selections from her poetry. The visitors stepped around or over the livestock. It was rather ingenious, that is, if they were actually financially destitute. They might arguably have been unbalanced, but they were by no means either ignorant or stupid. They're now considered to be interesting curiosities by most Halcyon folks, rather than dangerous and potentially violent, a consideration which could prove beneficial to your defense. In fact, I could state without reservation that they are known to everyone in Black County, black or white, and generally, favorably regarded by all except the social-climbing status seekers.

"The same can't be said for the decedent and her cousin, Mark

Delgado, who are regarded as arrogant, but then you must understand the politics of the deep-south. The white ruling class have now been outnumbered by the Negro descendants of the sugar and cotton plantation workers. They, the blacks, are now the mayors, city councilmen, aldermen, constables and frequently the sheriffs, of nearly every city and town in both Mississippi and Louisiana. They win by sheer numbers, and are not particularly concerned with so-called historic preservation, especially as it pertains to the symbols of their former oppression, specifically elaborate plantation houses and mercantile buildings constructed under duress by their enslaved ancestors. The preservation or loss of white antebellum architecture is of absolutely no consequence to the black political class whatsoever. Note that I said political class, not ruling class. That's a big distinction. In the south the ruling class is composed of the moneyed class. It is and has always been that way. Money rules, and those who have the money make the rules. In Halcyon, and New Orleans, especially, but to a lesser degree in other smaller cities, or rather towns, historical preservation is a thin line. The black politicians hardly welcome the preservation of the monuments to their bondage, and yet at the same time, it is by and large this historic architecture which ironically sustains their individual political ambitions. If it weren't for these houses and the pilgrimages, that is, the fall and spring open houses, Halcyon would be every bit as dead as Port Gibson to the north, just above Natchez."

"But what about the riverboat casinos? Haven't they altered the balance between the political and ruling classes? And which group is allied with that bunch at the casinos?" Solomon asked.

"The presence of so-called riverboat casinos is not that significant in terms of the overall balance of power in Halcyon. In the first place, there are many such casinos beginning just south of Shelby County, across the state line from Memphis, way to the north. There are casinos all the way down the river, in Mississippi, from Tunica County, through Coahoma County, that is, Clarksdale, and all the way down the river, to Black County, that is Halcyon, and of course, there are casinos in New Orleans. Halcyon is, sort of the last in line, in terms of casinos. Inpractical terms, the casino is of minimal significance in the scheme of things here, although that's changing now. Note the presence of the new hotel in the middle of town. It wouldn't have been allowed thirty years ago, andperhaps shouldn't have been built now. Casinos in general are now as common as flies, and frequently as short-lived.

"But back to what I was saying. The balance is comfortably maintained by neither side rubbing the other side's nose in it. But despite historical antecedents, the fact is that we all get along fairly well, better than in the north. And contrary to the popular myth promulgated by the northern media as fact, most southerners want to see successful blacks. So-called southern culture would not exist without them, nor they without us. Here as in the rest of America, the disparity between the races is primarily a middle-class phenomenon. At the lower end of the social and financial scale, as well as at the upper end, there are few racial problems, and there is free and open association between blacks and whites, and all are comfortable with it."

"But what about those three civil rights workers from up north who were murdered in the early 1960s?" Solomon asked. "Doesn't that legacy continue, even to this day?"

"That happened, and it was inexcusable, but that event was not perpetrated by the residents of Mississippi in general, but rather by some insane racist zealots. It was an unfortunate and turbulent time in our nation's history, and Mississippi, I'm sad to say, wasn't always as welcoming as it is now. In fact, even as late as 1940, there was a program here sponsored by local merchants called `Penny Day.' Every Saturday, merchants placed pennies in a coin box outside the door of their businesses, and I quote, for `old darky beggars,' as the author of one book about our fair city phrased it. `Penny Day is a thoughtful, good natured gesture to the needy Negro from his white folks,' she wrote."

"That's horrible," Nikki said.

"Of course it is, but that's the way it was back then. I don't remember the practice in my lifetime, but I remember my parents and grandparents talking about it. But racial strife wasn't just in Mississippi, Alabama, or even the south, in general, for that matter. You remember all of the civil discord, the looting and burning in California, Detroit, Chicago, and elsewhere. It was far worse than what happened in Mississippi. The fact is that even now, more black folks are probably murdered in any given month in Chicago by each other, than were killed nationwide during the entire civil rights movement, but nobody talks about that, do they? Hell, there were thirty something murders in Baltimore last month, nearly all of them, black on black.

"But let me continue. In the case of Mark Delgado, and Miss Murdock, I believe that it can be said accurately that they were equally contemptuous of everybody, black or white. In fact, I was told that the decedent's, that is, Miss Murdock's maid, Hattie, had been discovered to have wrought some Voodoo charm against her, which, speaking frankly, is, in some circles, seriously considered the real reason for her murder."

"Voodoo?" Solomon asked, scarcely able to believe that he had really heard the word used seriously in a normal conversation. "You mean someone could actually believe that the decedent was killed by some sort of `black magic?'"

"Obviously, the actual murder weapon was a small caliber pistol, a .32, if I'm not mistaken, but there are those who would, well, actually do believe, that the killer or killers, whoever they may have been, were not acting under their own power, but were being directed, that is, manipulated by darker forces," Dale observed.

"You mean they were driven to commit murder as the result of some Voodoo charm or amulet?" Nikki Daniels asked, intrigued by the absurdity of the concept. "You mean against their will?"

"Yes, but bear with me. I'm not a physician, but my brother Samuel, in Jackson, is a psychiatrist, with an M.D. from Johns Hopkins, speaking of Baltimore. He deals both constantly and extensively with schizophrenia, or `Skippy Freeman,' as it's often referred to in these parts. What's the difference between someone who is directed to commit a crime by `voices' and someone who has had his will temporarily usurped by some other means of control? I'm not saying that I personally believe any of that, I'm merely saying that there are those who do, and plenty of them.

"Additionally, if you replace or reword some of the basic tenets of so-called Voodoo, replacing them with medical, that is, with the appropriate clinical and scientific terms and definitions used routinely in psychiatric circles, there are few actual differences."

"Are you saying that you consider the decedent's maid to be a suspect?" Solomon asked.

"No, not at all. She, that is, the maid, had probably been mistreated and talked down to for years by Miss Murdock. Hattie is not a murderer, not as the word is commonly used, though that may clearly have been her purpose, in a passive sort of way. On second thought, I would say that it was clearly her intention to kill Miss Murdock, probably by causing her to waste away over time through some lingering illness, like cancer for instance. I'm told that she'd taken a photograph of Miss Murdock, and carefully blackened the eyes and mouth, obscuring them with some sort of magic marker, and then sewn the eyes and mouth shut with coarse black thread. She then placed the `item' under a well-traveled rug within Miss Murdock's house. I suspect a careful search of the house will produce more similarly sinister `charms,' if it hasn't already."

“Technically, then, the maid should at least be charged with attempted murder,” Solomon said.

“Technically, yes,” Dale agreed, “in that she believed the action taken would produce that desired result, and since the object of her malice did, in fact actually die, then she should indeed be charged with actual murder in the first degree.”

“But then, that would be absurd,” Solomon answered, “since the murder weapon was a .32 caliber revolver.”

“Of course it would,” Dale concurred. “To get a conviction it would be necessary to establish a causal relationship between the actual talisman, the killer or killers, and the death of Miss Murdock, which of course would be impossible, and yet this was certainly a deliberate attempt to commit murder. I merely mention this as a very real consideration in terms of potential jurors.”

“This is making me dizzy,” Debra Harris observed, “what do you mean?”

“I mean specifically that a jury pool comprised of older black women would be more likely to lean toward an acquittal based upon their belief that they, that is, the defendants, if not actually innocent of the charges altogether, were forced to act against their inherent natures through the agency of unseen forces or `powers,’ for lack of better definition. In other words, they would be deemed to have been compelled to murder through no fault of their own. The enmity existing between the defendants and the decedent would have generated a certain psychic tension, and provided the darker powers a channel of expression, or the means of fulfilling the intentions of the maid, Hattie.”

Just then a waitress appeared to take their lunch orders. When she left the conversation resumed. “Well Mr. Dale, then, who do you think killed the woman?” Solomon asked.

“I have no comment upon that subject, but I will say that in my opinion, the district attorney, Bill Roberts, will have a hard time seating a jury sympathetic to the prosecution, that is, unless some as yet undiscovered evidence is forthcoming."

"Why do you say that?" Nikki Daniels asked.

"Toma and Dautery are generally well-liked, as I mentioned, not that they're necessarily well-known personally by the people who like them. Let's just say that they're regarded as sympathetic characters who've been railroaded by a bumbling, incompetent police department. It's the underdog syndrome. People tend to have sympathy for those whom they feel to be victims of injustice. But that's not to say that they won't ultimately be tried and convicted anyway."

"Would you be interested in serving as co-counsel?" Solomon asked. "It would be pro-bono work, of course, as is the case with us, but it would be interesting, and I could certainly use your help. I sincerely believe the two are innocent, and it would be highly beneficial to their defense if you would join us, inasmuch as you have an understanding of the way things work around here that we could never grasp."

"Well, it would be an honor to work with you," Dale replied, "and I do know everybody in town. I served as the Black County district attorney myself for nearly eight years, prior to Bill Roberts taking over. I thank you for the invitation, and yes, count me in. Here's my card. I'm at your service, but tell me if you don't mind, what your present strategy is."

"First and foremost, we want to control the press," Solomon said, "both nationally and locally, and I believe we can do that, and of course we want to portray the defendants as unfairly victimized, private citizens down on their luck, who were tormented by the decedent. We need to transform the dead woman from an innocent person murdered in her own house, into someone who was rude and unpleasant to nearly everyone she dealt with."

"I agree so far," Dale said, "that was how she was generally perceived, but you must be careful in your wording as regards the victim. If you succeed in making her sound too bad, there is always the possibility that such a portrayal can backfire in that it increases the legitimacy of motive for the prosecution. In other words, you don't want to make her sound so bad that the defendants had no alternative but to kill her. She merely needs to be an unpleasant, that is, unsympathetic character, to the jury. She needs to be bad enough that someone else with a true and legitimate motive, sought to, and succeeded in killing her. In other words, while she taunted and tormented the defendants, they restrained themselves from avenging her because they were, by nature, nice people who meant no harm to anyone, and who minded their own business, but I defer to your experience and expertise on the subject of homicide."

"It's indeed a very thin line," Solomon agreed. "Somebody obviously had a genuine motive for killing the woman. There's always a motive. Find the motive and it will invariably point you to the murderer. This case will come down to that sooner or later, but it's not my concern, it's the prosecution's problem. In my own personal experience as a defense attorney though, I've noticed that murder is usually about money, or sex, or some offshoot of either. It's generally about money in the final analysis, especially since sex is not now the precious commodity it once was, at least in terms of availability. Still, rage, jealously, passion, or resentment, are very real considerations. On the other hand, this could simply be a case of robbery that went wrong, but I seriously doubt it, for several reasons. In the first place, I gather the decedent was the type of person who would have told any intruder to go to hell. Apparently, she wasn't afraid of anyone or anything. She obviously didn't like the two defendants, but she was ready for them, more prepared than actually afraid. However, since the door was unlocked, I must conclude that her killer was known to her, and probably someone she knew well, as there was no sign of forced entry. I doubt that she would have opened the door to either of the defendants, or to anyone else, certainly not someone unknown to her."

"That's as may be," Dale agreed, "but within a certain segment of the community, it has already been determined that the underlying cause of Murdock's death was Voodoo, no matter who actually pulled the trigger, or what the actual motive may have been, therefore a jury consisting of older black women, as I said, would seem to be in the best possible interests of the defense. And before you suggest that it's `racist' to point out the obvious, it's no more racist than noting that some white person happens to be a Catholic, or a Presbyterian."

"Granted, but does anybody really believe that stuff?" Nikki Daniels asked.

"It's not as absurd as it seems, as I've already explained. In fact, it's completely logical, that is, if the thread of logic is pursued far enough."

"What do you mean?" Daniels asked.

"We inhabit a spiritual world, and Voodoo is a spiritual religion, and in that sense, is every bit as valid as any other religion. I don't know what your personal religious beliefs may be, but should you examine them logically, that is, from the standpoint of an outsider, an impartial observer, if you wish, you'd probably conclude that they're illogical, just as much as so-called Voodoo might seem to us," Dale observed.

"I'll grant that point," Solomon interrupted, "but still..."

"Let's approach it another way," Dale suggested. "Say you wake up one Day and don't feel so well. Perhaps you have an unfamiliar and occasional pain or numbness in your left arm. Maybe you strained it at the gym lifting weights, or playing tennis. You apply what you regard as critical thinking and reach that conclusion. It's nothing specific, and like I said, more intermittent, so you do your best to forget about it. Still the discomfort persists. You have a vague but increasing uneasiness as a result. Someone at your office notices that you seem preoccupied and might even suggest that you're working too hard, perhaps not getting enough sleep, or they might actually tell you that `you don't look so well,' that perhaps, you should take a couple of days off. Your mind works beneath the conscious level reminding you of several people known personally to you who have died from heart attacks at approximately your age, or even younger. Your fear increases both consciously and unconsciously, so you go see a doctor, who runs a battery of tests, and determines that you must have merely strained your lower arm after all. The numbness remains, but now it no longer matters to you, since someone you respect, a physician, an authority figure, has said that you're fine and not to worry."

"Certainly, that's what I would do. That's what anyone with any sense would do," Solomon agreed.

"At that point, your subconscious mind stops working against you, having been instructed by your rational conscious mind that there is no cause for alarm. All right now, say someone suspects that he or she may have been `cursed' or `crossed,' for lack of a better word. Perhaps that person has suffered a series of strange and uncharacteristic setbacks or misfortunes as of late, say their dog died, or their car had a flat tire, two days in a row, or maybe they feel a certain general but unspecified malaise, or a sense of impending dread. The actual event or condition doesn't really matter. In this instance, he or she suspects that the cause of whatever the misfortune, or other out of the ordinary events might be, has its roots in the spiritual realm. He or she seeks the same assurance and comfort that you do, and consults a doctor, in this instance, a general practitioner from the world of spiritual medicine, a Voodoo priest, a `root doctor,' if you prefer, and is offered the same comfort that your heart specialist gave you. This visit shuts off the underlying subconscious fear which might have physically produced the dreaded effects eventually from beneath the surface, from the unconscious realm."

"Yes, but my doctor is actually a professionally educated medical scientist. The Voodoo doctor is not working with science, but with superstition," Solomon argued.

"Of course, technically, you are right, but the results are the same."

"Not at all," Solomon countered.

"Well let me ask you this," Dale continued, "How many times have you heard of cases where someone had been given a clean bill of health by his doctor a week, or a month, before dying from a heart attack or some other undiagnosed illness? I know of two cases personally, and I imagine you've heard of at least one similar instance yourself."

"Granted," Solomon agreed, "but what's your point?"

"My point is that in some circles the Voodoo priest, or root doctor, as he's more frequently called, is considered to be every bit as `scientific' as you consider your heart specialist to be, and in the real world, his results are often every bit as effective as those of the heart specialist."

"You sound as if you believe in Voodoo yourself, Mr. Dale?" Nikki Daniels smiled.

"I believe in everything and nothing, Miss Daniels. I merely repeat that a jury composed of older black women would be beneficial to the defense given the reasons I've already suggested. Additionally, both the decedent and Mark Delgado were not especially liked within the black community. As I understand it, black maids have been replaced by Mexicans in the rest of the country. In the deep-south, however, we still have black maids. I was raised by one, and so was nearly everyone I know. They're a part of who I am. Be that as it may, they talk among each other, and to those of us whom they trust. As a matter of consequence, we hear things. Mark Delgado's maid, Chantelle, was given a Christmas bonus, if you will, of four dollars from the multi-millionaire Mark Delgado, an act of unprecedented largesse from his point of view, but an insult from the standpoint of everyone else."

"I agree," Solomon answered quickly, "that's insulting and offensive. It's actually degrading."

"Anyway, while the black population here have no particular feelings about Toma and Dautery one way or the other, other than that they are probably crazy and their house, Cypress Hill, is certainly `haunted,' they have an active dislike for the decedent and Delgado. Hatred and contempt might be better descriptions of their feelings. That, in combination with the underlying belief that Voodoo was the real cause for Miss Murdock's death, which is generally regarded as justifiable homicide in that sector, means that a black jury is less likely to convict Toma and Dautery for any reason.

"And one more thing. In this case there is a legitimate motive from the standpoint of the prosecution. The mansion Cypress Hill was owned by Toma, as he'd inherited it. It was subsequently sold for back taxes on the courthouse steps at public auction several years ago, unbeknownst to either Toma or Dautery, until after the fact. And guess who the buyer was?"

"Miss Murdock?" Solomon asked.

"Yes and no," Dale shot back. "It was bought by Mark Delgado."

"So he owned the house at the time of the murder?" Daniels asked. "But what would he want with it?"

"No, not at the time of the murder. He probably intended to tear it down, which would of course have literally thrown Toma and Dautery onto the street, made them homeless. As soon as the sale was concluded, Delgado attempted to take possession of the house and evict Toma and Dautery. When Dautery found out what had happened, she went before the judge, and persuaded him that Toma was not competent to handle his own affairs, or he wouldn't have forgotten to pay the property tax. The judge temporarily suspended the sale until he could determine the facts of the situation. After several months of unsuccessful legal wrangling by Delgado and Murdock, Judge Dawson set aside the sale and ruled that Toma could retain ownership of the property if he paid the taxes and penalties owed at the time of the sale. The taxes were paid in full that day. The judge appointed Dautery to be Toma's guardian, and subsequently, allowed her to adopt him, as strange as that sounds."

"She adopted him?" Daniels asked incredulously, "You mean as her son?"

"That's right, but by this time there was open enmity between the former friends and neighbors apart from and preceding the judge's ruling. The existing hostility was merely further exacerbated by the judge's decision. Mark Delgado, no doubt goaded and encouraged by Miss Murdock, had sought to get rid of the problem neighbors once and for all, but had failed due to a judge's ruling. Delgado now openly vowed to get rid of them by any means necessary, but having given it his best shot and lost, found Toma and Dautery even less concerned with their animals roaming over there and tearing up Murdock's garden and shrubs. You might even say that Dautery baited them, provoked them intentionally, if you will, actually allowing her animals to go over there. Having personally known all of the parties involved, I'd say that this is what happened, and you should note that Dautery is extremely confrontational, every bit as much as the decedent was."

"Yes, I've experienced that side of her already," Solomon agreed. "She was combative upon our first meeting, but only until she grasped that we were here to help her. She and her `son,'" he laughed, "had been charged with murder and felt as if they were being unjustly railroaded into some sort of kangaroo court type of situation. I certainly understand her initial hostility. I hadn't, at first, determined whether I considered her either guilty or innocent, but her genuine outrage helped convince me that they're both innocent. It should be clear to anyone that Toma is `damaged.' He's obviously incapable of even taking care of his own basic needs."

"Not so fast, Mr. Solomon. Toma is the one who butchers and eviscerates the goats and other animals the two of them eat. He kills the animals coldly and methodically. Additionally, he's in good physical health, that is, he's physically capable of killing a large animal with a knife, in cold blood, and probably with a cudgel or sledge hammer as well, beating its brains in. It isn't that much of a stretch that he could kill anyone who threatened Miss Dautery, who is basically his caretaker. He seems totally incapable of functioning without her."

"I suppose you're right," Solomon reluctantly agreed, "but the decedent was killed by a bullet, not a knife."

"Yes, but one of the two guns which were found at Cypress Hillhas been determined to be the murder weapon, a .32 caliber Smith & Wesson, and the other one is a model 1911 Colt .45, of the type known to have been owned by the decedent, Miss Murdock. And there are other guns over there at Cypress Hill. You can count on that," Dale responded. "Everybody in the state of Mississippi has at least one gun in their house, and you can bet several more will turn up at Cypress Hill, but in this case, that is, most likely later rather than sooner, given the filth in that place, but there are other guns over there to be sure, and Chief Bowman and his men are no doubt looking for them now, although the location of additional firearms will be redundant as the murder weapon has already been found. I mention this only because the prosecution might attempt to imply that the possession of multiple firearms somehow suggests an innate predeliction toward potential violence."

"I don't like the turn this conversation is taking," Solomon observed. "Both of those pistols had been wiped clean of finger prints, and neither of them are registered to anyone, so while the .32 is definitely the murder weapon, it doesn't have the fingerprints of either defendant, and neither does the .45. Both pistols were obviously planted there, at Cypress Hill, after the fact, by whoever actually committed the murder in an attempt to falsely implicate the defendants."

"Again, yes and no. That's the talk around town, but both pistols have been sent to the lab in Jackson, I suspect that fingerprints willbe discovered. It's not as easy to wipe a gun down as people are led to imagine on TV, as I'm sure you, of all people, know. But apart from that, I'm merely saying that there is an underlying something here in Halcyon," the lawyer said, "which...that is, there's always more here than meets the eye. Seemingly nice people are capable of extreme brutality, as you know, probably better than I do, but there is an evil presence afoot here despite the warm temperatures, beautiful flowers and gently waving Spanish moss. Visitors don't see it, temporarily blinded, as they are, by the magnificence of this place. They don't even sense it, and yet for us, it underlies everything here. From the massacre of the French settlers by the Indians at Ft. Wood, to its brutal revenge, to the frequent robberies, rapes, and murders in the old days down by`The Riverfront,' as it's known locally, Halcyon has a bloody history, and it's an unspoken, that is, unmentioned thread which binds all of us who call Halcyon home. This really is a haunted place, one with many ghosts, and if the defendants are innocent, that means the killer or killers, are still out there...out here, rather."

Nikki Daniels shuddered as Dale spoke, and Solomon listened intently, seemingly spellbound by the lawyer's words which seemed for the moment like some sort of hypnotic soliloquy. "You're scaring me," she said.

"What? Oh, I'm sorry," the lawyer said, seeming to suddenly emerge from his near trance. "Don't mind me. I think overall, the defense has the advantage at present. Just tell me what I can do to help. Oh yes, there's one more thing that certainly qualifies as a real motive, at least for Dautery, though I doubt Roberts will bring it up, though he might. It would be rather unsportsman like of him to do so."

"What's that" Solomon asked?

"Well, Dautery wasn't always an old maid. She was once young and beautiful, and was to be married to someone from New York. You know she lived there for several years and was quite successful. I can't remember the man's name now, but he was from a prominent New York publishing family. Dautery brought him to Halcyon and introduced him to everyone who was anybody here. He was feted by the bon ton and seemed to love the town and intended to move here as soon as he and Dautery were married. He'd even placed a down payment on one of the large houses here. Anyway, everything was beautiful until he was introduced to Jeannie Murdock, by her good friend Olivia Dautery. It was a classic example of the old storyline from the song `Tennessee Waltz.' Dautery's fiancé fell in love with Jeannie Murdock immediately, and she fell in love with him. He basically dumped Olivia Dautery a couple of weeks before they were to be married here, and left for Newport, Rhode Island with Jeannie Murdock. The wedding invitations had already been sent. Dautery had her bridesmaids, and her wedding dress had arrived from Paris."

"That's horrible," Daniels observed.

"It was especially bad since Dautery and the man had already taken a marriage license, and everyone in Halcyon knew about it. Well, Jeannie Murdock toyed with Dautery's fiancé for a few weeks but tired of him soon enough and sent him packing, back to New York. Murdock returned to Halcyon, acting as if nothing had happened. It was all just a game to her, but the man had been the love of Dautery's life. Dautery returned to New York, greatly embarrassed, immediately quit her job, and moved back to Halcyon for good. She never got over it, and as you know, she never married. It was just a lark to Murdock, but her friends here, that is, their mutual friends, more or less turned against Jeannie Murdock after that. Murdock didn't care though, since she thought herself so far above all of them anyway, it didn't matter to her one way or the other. She wasn't really a nice person."

"Well, that's as good a motive as I've ever heard for murder," Solomon said.

"That's not the end of the story. It gets worse. Dautery's former fiancé, sincerely repentant, attempted reconciliation with Olivia Dautery, but she refused to ever see him or speak with him again. Several months later, truly heartbroken over his actions, he killed himself over the matter, a bullet through the heart. But like I said, I don't think the district attorney will bring any of this up in court," Dale observed. "After all, it was a long while ago, and it has no bearing on the present case. It would be in very poor taste to even mention it."

Solomon knew that it had plenty of bearing on the case, and District Attorney Roberts will surely introduce the matter in some way, whenever he deems appropriate. It might be something he holds back until necessary, or he could simply start with it. In any case, Solomon suddenly thought less of his new co-counsel's legal abilities as a result of his observations. But then, maybe trials aren't as vicious here as they are in L.A. In any case, Solomon would be prepared now that he'd been forewarned.

9.

Preliminaries

Solomon intended to physically take over the criminal justice center, both to gather information and to annoy the prosecution. He'd just met District Attorney Bill Roberts for the first time, and was in the process of demanding a suite of offices on the premises when he suddenly spied a familiar figure coming through the front door. It was Tom Roberts from Los Angeles, personal agent for some of his top legal clients. "Excuse me for a moment," he said, breaking away from the district attorney, "I see a friend of mine. I'll be right back. Tom, what in the hell are you doing here? Is this going to be a movie already?" he shouted loudly as he walked briskly across the room and embraced Tom Roberts warmly. "Damn, it's good to see a familiar face. What in the hell are you doing here in Halcyon?"

Tom's brother, the district attorney looked on in disbelief. How could his own brother, Tom, a mere mailman, be on such good terms with one of the most famous entertainment attorneys in America? It didn't make any sense.

"Mark," Tom whispered, "The district attorney is my brother. Don't say anything, please. He thinks I'm a mailman, and I really want to keep it that way."

"A mailman?" Solomon laughed loudly, glancing quickly over his shoulder at the obviously perplexed district attorney.

"I'll explain later. I'm in Halcyon for my father's funeral, which was yesterday. I thought you knew I'm from Halcyon. He's going to ask some questions about our friendship. Just tell him that you represented the postal workers union and you used me as a witness or something."

"Sure, I get you," Solomon said, backing away and winking. "I'm sorry to hear about your father, please accept my sympathy, and of course I do remember that you're from Halcyon. You just never mention the place, and I decided to take this case on the spur of the moment and didn't make the connection. Look, I've got to get back to work, but I'm staying at the hotel here, the Moro. You call over there and talk to Nikki Daniels. You remember her don't you? Well, no matter. She has my schedule. We're going to dinner somewhere, you and me, tomorrow night. I insist. How long are you going to be in town?"

"I was originally going back today, but I've already cancelled my flight. I think I'm going to hang around a few days, maybe a week. I don't know yet. This might be a movie. I'm thinking of having a script writer sent over. I'd heard you were in town."

"Well, let's do dinner tomorrow night then, as late as possible. Call Nikki and she'll schedule the time. It's in the book. I'm putting it in the book now," Solomon said, pointing to the side of his head and smiling.

"I'll look forward to it," Tom said. "Go easy on my brother, now."

"If he's anything like you, I'd better be on guard myself," Solomon laughed.

Tom looked across the hallway at his brother, not knowing what to say, so he just smiled sheepishly and shrugged his shoulders. At that moment his cell phone rang. Saved by the bell. He looked at the phone and noted the prefix on the incoming call, 601. A local call. "Hello." It was Leah. "Lunch? What time is it? Sure. I was going to visit Bill, but I can see he's tied up. Sure, First Street Pasta. Twenty minutes. See you there."

It was nice to think about their visit after the funeral yesterday and the drive to the ruins of Windsor. It had been both fun and nostalgic, and he still had strong feelings for her, but she was like cocaine. Just because she was in the room, so to speak, didn't mean he had to partake. Well, he reflected, cocaine was a bad analogy since he hated cocaine. He'd tried it on several occasions and all it did was make his teeth numb. Well, it made his teeth numb and made him restless and angry. Coffee did the same thing and was less expensive, and legal. Cocaine had once been fashionable back in the 1980s, but only losers used it now.

"I'll call you later," he shouted at his brother, who seemed to be getting the worst of it from Mark Solomon. Bill waved absentmindedly, occupied as he was under the circumstances by the demands of the defense attorney.

"I need unfettered access to the defendants in order to provide an adequate defense, so I'm asking that you release them on their own recognizance. They pose absolutely no flight risk of any kind, are obviously destitute, and lack both the means and the ability to flee. They don't even own a car. They have no prior criminal record of any kind, not even a parking ticket. They pose no danger to either themselves or anyone else. I can think of no reason at all to hold them. The U.S. Constitution guarantees the presumption of innocence. In short, holding them under the present circumstances denies them this basic right inherent in American citizenship. They should be released immediately, at once, and in the interest of justice...well, justice is their right, and we demand it."

"You seem to have forgotten that a woman with whom they are known to have had a longstanding, and hostile relationship has been murdered," the district attorney replied.

"As far as I'm able to determine, there is no actual evidence against them," Solomon said angrily. "The guns now in your possession were obviously intentionally planted by a third party, in some misguided and amateurish attempt to incriminate them."

"That's for a judge and the Grand Jury to determine," Roberts replied. "In the meantime, they've been charged and will remain at this facility."

"I want offices here so that I can have unlimited access to my clients," Solomon demanded, ignoring the district attorney's response.

"You expect us to provide you with offices at state expense?" the D.A. asked, scarcely able to believe that such a suggestion had been made.

"The state would pay for the defense of the two defendants and provide their defense attorney a temporary office anyway. We're saving the state the cost of an attorney. I don't understand your objection. As the district attorney, I'm certain that you don't want to enter the courtroom in this case, with the taint of a defense which was denied the basic tools necessary to provide adequate counsel." Solomon knew that the request, or rather demand was absurd, but it again placed the prosecution in a defensive position, forcing the D.A. to waste time and energy, and keeping him off balance, no matter how slightly.

"That's out of the question. It's not even a remote possibility," the district attorney answered defensively.

"In that case I return to my original request. I want the defendants released on their own recognizance," Solomon demanded.

"The police chief had presented Judge Channing with the evidence he had against them and the judge issued an arrest warrant for the pair. They had their initial appearance before the judge well within the 48-hour period mandated by law. Their names, mailing address, and place of residence were established. They were again read their rights and asked if they had counsel, and told that a lawyer would be appointed for them in the event they couldn't afford one, or did not have one. They said they had counsel en route, meaning yourself. They were given copies of the charges against them. You have those charges. Now, I've got work to do. Good day."

"Then I'm calling on the judge," Solomon stated loudly. "I'm going to talk to the judge!"

ELSEWHERE

"The D.A. has an extremely weak case, in my opinion," Walter Eubanks, Solomon's office manager speculated as they drove back to the hotel.

"The prosecution is supposed to be at a disadvantage, given the constitutional guarantee of the legal presumption of innocence," Solomon stated. "That having been said, I don't think that the district attorney has much of a case either, but never underestimate a jury, any jury, especially in a small southern town. It can literally go either way, and the actual facts may have little bearing on the verdict."

"Does that mean you're considering seeking a change of venue?"

"Not at all," Solomon replied. "We're holding all of the cards, at least at this point. The defendants are already folk, or anti-establishment heroes. The local and national press coverage is all on their side, portraying them as underdogs who've fallen on hard times. I wouldn't consider a change of venue. I want to seat a jury of their peers, specifically the poor and outcast."

"Do you expect additional charges to be filed against the pair?"

"No, I don't. Of course the prosecution can file more charges right up until the first witness has been duly sworn in at the actual trial, I mean even after the jury has been selected and seated and the trial started. But of course, you know that already. To answer your question though, they've already played their hand," Solomon surmised.

"They obviously want a speedy trial," Eubanks observed.

"Another right of citizenship, of course," Solomon answered, "although I hardly consider the federally mandated 270 days to be `speedy' under any circumstances."

"A request for any kind of continuance on their behalf from our end, that is, from the defense, would, of course, nullify that time requirement."

"Yes, it would effectively waive the defendants' rights to a so-called speedy trial, but a continuance or delay of any kind is the last thing any of us want, including the prosecution. I imagine Roberts wants to go to trial as quickly as possible before his case evaporates entirely."

"How do you view the potential jury pool here?" Eubanks asked.

"Well, it's hard to say. Here as elsewhere, everyone registered to vote is a potential juror. Normally, the more intelligent people are able to avoid jury duty, and I'm sure that's the way it is here, in Halcyon. A potential problem, though I'm not sure yet whether it's our problem or the district attorney's, is that given the sensational nature of this trial, I doubt that anyone is going to be attempting to avoid jury duty, but you never know."

"Well, anyone over sixty-five is exempted from jury duty, as well as anyone who's served on any jury within the last two years," Eubanks stated, "though, of course, it's necessary to appear when called, in order to claimeither exemption. I know that much," the office manager said. "I just wondered if it's the same here."

"The initial number of potential jurors called from the voter rolls will be eighty at first, and narrowed down to twelve active jurors with two alternates, just the same as elsewhere," Solomon stated, "and of course, it's necessary to be able to read and write to be a juror, but then it's doubtful that anyone, that is, any legal citizen would fall into that category now, though illiteracy was a legitimate concern in the past, especially in the south."

"Explain the jury selection process again, though I should know it by now," Solomon's office manager said. "It could be different in Mississippi."

"Both the prosecution and the defense can reject any potential juror for any reason. This is referred to as `unlimited challenges for cause.' Of course, it can't be an arbitrary rejection. In other words, any challenge for any potential juror must be explained to the judge."

"On what basis could a juror be successfully challenged?"

"In a murder trial, as is the case here, any potential juror who'd had a friend, relative, or spouse, who'd been murdered, for example, could be reasonably assumed to have a bias against any defendant charged in a similar crime. In other words, any bias or prejudice is legitimate ground for rejecting any juror," Solomon said. "There is also what's known as a preemptory challenge. That means that either side can reject nine jurors without cause or explanation. After that, any challenge must be presented to the judge. And as you know, generally speaking, the less intelligent the juror, the better."

"Why do you say that Mark?"

"Perhaps I should rephrase that. In my experience as a defense attorney, I've found that it's harder to persuade people who think too much. They have to weigh too many outside considerations, and are less likely to reach a conclusion of either guilt or innocence based strictly upon the evidence presented. The less intelligent, or perhaps I should say, those with less varied life experiences and less education, often seem more able to grasp the essence of the situation without embellishing it with a lot of `what ifs.'"

"What tangible evidence exists against the defendants?" Eubanks asked.

"As far as I'm concerned, nothing. The prosecution has the murder weapon, as well as what is presumed to be the decedent's .45 caliber pistol, but there's no doubt in my mind that the guns were planted in the defendants' residence, probably while they were being held at the police station. Their fingerprints are supposedly not on either weapon, although the actual results are not yet in from the crime lab in Jackson. The defendants were tested for gunshot residue and nothing was found."

"They could have been wearing gloves."

"Yes, it's possible, but unlikely. Besides, latex gloves do not protect against gunshot residue, not that they seem the type to go out and buy a box of latex gloves. And other gloves, work gloves, for example seem too clumsy, too cumbersome. I really don't think these two people had anything to do with this murder. There is a body, however, and a woman, a known enemy of theirs, was murdered. The district attorney really believes that they're the murderers, and apparently the judge must believe that there is a high evidentiary probability of their involvement as well, or he wouldn't have issued a warrant for their arrest to begin with. I think they're innocent. That's why we're here. I can't trust their fate to some public defender, but the fact is, we're the outsiders, and these will be local jurors, some of whom will resent us specifically because we are outsiders. And like I said, no jury is ever predictable even under the best circumstances. Any jury can go either way with or without regard to the facts.

"Despite what I would consider to be the lack of present evidence, doesn't mean that additional, and possibly significant evidence won't be forthcoming prior to trial. At this point it will be up to a grand jury, but as I said, we're holding all of the cards at the moment, and Nikki tells me that the media spin, so far at least, is in favor of the defendants. But the truth is that we actually know very little about them. What I want to do is get everybody together at the hotel in say, half an hour. Call Nikki and set that up. We need to go over everything and see where we stand at present. Call Lucien Dale, that local lawyer I met at lunch. See if he's free to join us. Nikki has his number."

A few minutes later Solomon entered the command center with his office manager, Walter Eubanks, trailing after him like the smoke of an expensive cigar. "I want to know everything there is to know about Toma and Dautery," he said, addressing his class. "Who are they? I want to know the same thing about the decedent and her cousin, Delgado? Yes, Delgado. Where did they go to school? How do they know each other? There is an established and long-standing history of open hostility between the defendants and the decedent, although it's common knowledge that they were once close friends. When did hostilities begin between the defendants and the decedent? What precipitated them? Was there one specific event? Did one of them run over the other's dog? Was there any dispute over boundary or property lines? Everything has a starting point, and there was one here. I want to know what it was. I trust all of you are working on this now. Excuse me, I've got to take this call. Nikki? My car's here? Yes, at the hotel? You're in the lobby? No, tell the driver to turn around and take it back to California and have someone park it in my space in the office garage. Yes, I'm sure. I know, but I've changed my mind. I don't want to be Hollywooding it around here. This isn't L.A. or New York. A big show of power and prestige could be counterproductive here and could actually work against us. We're outsiders, and I don't want that working against us. No, the rentals are fine, send it back to L.A. I don't want anyone in town even seeing its California plates. No, you don't have to do it now. Yeah, it can sit there for a few Days. No, I don't care. Wait. Never mind. On second thought, keep it here, I might need it at some point, just make sure that it's backed up against the garage wall at the hotel. I don't want anyone seeing the California license plates. Thanks Nikki. Yeah, at the hotel, upstairs at the command center, come on up. Bye. Excuse me…now, where were we?"

10.

The Way We Weren't

Milano was a local favorite in Halcyon which served a basic but tasty offering of dishes with an Italian flare. The main dining room in the front of the building was a small `L' shaped area, but there was a larger, walled outdoor patio in the back. WhenTom Roberts arrived, Leah was already seated and waiting for him. He suddenly remembered that she always liked to eat outdoors if possible, but was pleased she'd chosen to sit inside today, given the heat of Halcyon in summer. She smiled when she saw him enter. He was dressed casually, just like she remembered him, in bright madras shorts with a light blue oxford cloth shirt, its tail hanging down covering a brown alligator belt, no doubt, and the pistol he always carried in his front pants pocket. "Let me see your belt," she demanded. He raised his shirt tail just enough to reveal part of a brown alligator belt. "Some things never change," she said.

"The more things change, the more they stay the same," he replied.

"Always the joker," she laughed. And it was true, she reflected. Tom had a sense of humor which had always kept her in stitches, not that he told jokes per se, but that he was just a bit off center. She fondly remembered a time that somebody had parked in a handicapped spot who didn't belong there, one of his absolute pet peeves. Tom had seen the woman get out of her car and head through the door of a local department store at a fast pace, meaning she obviously wasn't disabled. Without a word Tom suddenly stopped his car, removed a tin capped cardboard jar of Royal Crown Hair Dressing, a really fragrant concoction of perfumed petroleum jelly with the consistency of Vaseline. He ran up to the vacated car, dipped his finger into the can and applied a liberal amount to the underside of the car's driver's side door handle, returned to his car and waited. He didn't have long to wait. The woman sauntered out casually in about five minutes, unlocked and began to open her car door. Boy, did she get a surprise. She began cursing, stomping, and looking around. Tom backed up, lowered his window and said, "Don't park in a handicapped space. You're lucky I didn't call the police." Strange that she should remember that incident now.

Tom sat down and a waitress immediately approached. "What's good?" he asked.

"Everything," the waitress answered with a smile.

"That's encouraging, what do you want to drink Leah?"

"Iced tea for me," she replied.

"Yeah, me too," Tom said. "No, on second thought, bring me a San Pellegrino, in the bottle, no glass." He suddenly remembered the nuclear reactor located upriver from Halcyon and thought better of drinking anything containing local water.

"Let me guess," Leah smiled, looking at him with one raised eyebrow, "it's the nuclear plant."

"Well, I'm not saying that there is any direct correlation between various cancers and a possibly radioactive water supply, and there's probably a nuclear reactor positioned immediately upstream, just above wherever San Pellegrino is bottled, but if there is, I don't know about it. I know about the one here. I'm sure it's safe, but for me, better safe than sorry."

"Like I said, some things never change."

"I should think you'd find comfort in anything constant these days," he said, smiling. "By the way, do you still have my cat?"

"Yes I do," she answered, remembering the time Tom had stopped his car abruptly right in the middle of Highway 61, and quickly jumped out and rescued a kitten from the middle of the highway, at great personal risk to himself. He'd been almost hit by a large transport truck in the process.

"She's twelve years old now, but, for the most part, still doing all right."

"What happened? I mean, why did you get divorced?" Tom suddenly asked without warning, jumping right into the middle of the subject they'd both avoided. "My brother told me that you were divorced. For some reason, he thought that I'd heard about it in California, though how I could've done so is a mystery."

"Do you really want to know?" she asked.

"Yes, I'd like to know, since you dumped me, for him," Tom said. He had nothing to lose by asking. He could be on a plane back home anytime he felt like it, none the worse for this, or any other experience. He restrained himself from saying, `A God damned dentist?' though he certainly felt like it. It wasn't that he didn't like dentists, per se, it's just that the person she'd chosen over him happened to have been a dentist, therefore he disliked his former rival as a `dentist.' If he'd been a lawyer, he would have felt the same about lawyers. He knew better than to insult her ex-husband on any grounds even though Tom perceived him to be a doofus, because that would be the same thing as insulting her intelligence and lack of taste, although her actions in the matter had clearly established both. That had been the worst thing, after the heartbreak and loss of course, the fact that she'd chosen some goofy-looking bastard with plastic looking gospel hair. It's one thing to be dumped for some extremely handsome person of great wealth and accomplishment. It was another thing altogether to be shunned in favor of some goof, as had been the case here. But it's always the same old story. Men will frequently see a beautiful woman with some goofy-looking weirdo and marvel that she could have possibly chosen somebody that goofy-looking. It's never the other way around, that is, some shabby-looking old hag with a really handsome man.

"Well, as you know, my mother didn't think that you were `marriage material.' That was the term she used, and since my father had run off with another woman, some `Jezebel,' as you may also remember...anyway, I think that she viewed you as some sort of Lothario. She thought that you and I would get married and that you'd run off with somebody else, sooner or later. She just wanted to spare me what she'd gone through."

Tom had asked, and he wanted to know, so he restrained himself from saying what he thought of Leah's mother, or of Leah's lack of a self-determining intelligence, and of her duplicity. He could never forgive her betrayal, not now, not ten years later, not ever. This was an untenable position for him, because as he looked at her just now, he felt like he had when they'd been together. He still loved her.

"Mom met Rob when her own dentist retired. He'd taken over Dr. Hagar's practice. She noticed that he wasn't married and told him about me. I won't bore you with the details, but he seemed to like me, and we hit it off, more or less. It was incessant from my mother. She talked about your father's girlfriend, compared you to him, and said that you…we…I would end up the same way."

"Well, it seems that I was the only person in town who didn't know about Dad's girlfriend," Tom said.

"Anyway, like they say, you attract what you fear. In this case, I guess I attracted what Mom feared. I arrived at his office one day after hours. We were supposed to go to dinner at Waverly, with the Wilsons. You remember George Wilson. Anyway, the front door was unlocked so I just walked in. I assumed he, Rob, was in one of the patient rooms cleaning up. There wasn't anybody else there, or so I thought. You know me, I'm not the type to walk into a place and start shouting, `Hey, where are you?' so I just thought I'd wait around in his office. I knew that he'd show up soon, since we were supposed to go out with the Wilsons. Anyway, Rob was sitting in the chair behind his desk when I ambled in. It looked like there was a small dog jumping around on his lap, some terrier of some sort, or something like that. It didn't register at first, because I knew he didn't have a dog at the office anymore. They'd had a really sweet Westie that stayed at the office and sat on patients' laps and calmed them down. Everybody really loved that dog, Debbie, that was the dog's name, but the dog had gotten old and had been given to one of the patients about two years earlier. So, like I said, I was a little disoriented at first. Then I noticed that it wasn't a dog after all, just a bitch. It was his hygienist, LeDonna. She was giving him a blow job right in his desk chair. That was that. You should've seen that wormy little bastard when he looked up and saw me standing there. The look on his face was really classic."

"What did you do?" Tom asked, for the moment genuinely intrigued.

"I said calmly `We're supposed to be meeting the Wilsons at Waverly, but it appears you have some late work at the office. I'll see you over there.' I turned around and walked out the way I came in. She never looked up, just kept at it, right in front of me, I mean even after she heard my voice and knew that I was there. I think she wanted me to catch them."

"Well, did you go to Waverly for dinner?"

"No. I called my brother and told him what had happened, and that I didn't want Rob coming back to the house. He made a phone call to a friend of his who runs a security company and a couple of really beefy uniformed security guards showed up before Rob got there. I knew that he'd go to Waverly first, and that would buy me time to change the locks, which of course I did."

"You always were sort of a handyman," Tom recollected.

"I changed the alarm code, the password, and the locks, and that was that. Your brother was kind enough to represent me in the divorce, although there was no court battle since Rob didn't want to lose any patients over the matter. He wasn't as concerned about losing his wife. I got pretty much everything, given the circumstances. Rob lost most of his patients anyway as a result, and he and that bimbo hygienist of his, LeDonna, moved to Jackson. I think he's working now at one of those corporate family practice clinics that have about ten dentists all working next to each other at the same time. Good riddance! He was really, and I mean this, really one of the most boring people I've ever met. And he was totally inept, and I mean inept in every way. And his teeth, my God, they were like something from an Edgar Allan Poe tale. They were so artificially white that they almost glowed in the dark. I have no idea what I ever saw in that fool."

"Well, what happened that night when he came home? Surely, he came home."

"Well, he came home, all right, and wanted to come in, but that didn't happen. The security guys told him that he'd best be on his way."

"`But this is my house, I live here,'" he shouted angrily. "He was really pissed."

"'That's something you can take up with your lawyer tomorrow, if you like' I heard one of the security men say, `but you need to leave here now. You're not going in that house, and you're trespassing.' He argued with them quietly for a few minutes, but both of those security guys were gym rats with biceps as big as country hams. That skinny little weasel wasn't about to try anything. He just left in a huff, peeling out of the driveway in that yuppie little BMW of his. He actually got a ticket for speeding when he pulled onto Highway 61."

"Well, you'd been married for nearly ten years, I'd have thought that you would've given him a second chance, or something," Tom observed.

"I would have stayed with him, at least as long as Mom was alive, that is, if I hadn't caught him with that bimbo, although it was really just a matter of time. The truth is that I didn't even like him. In fact, I don't think he liked me either, so in a way, I can't really blame him. Under the circumstances it was the best possible outcome for me."

"Now see, that's something I don't understand. I wouldn't stay with somebody I didn't like for any reason, and I'd do whatever it took to get out of a bad situation, and wouldn't care what it cost. I've never cared what anybody thinks about anything having to do with my personal life. Freedom is everything, freedom to stay or freedom to go, at least to me. I'm never going to get married. I don't want some lawyer, or some government worker, telling me I have to stay with somebody I'd rather not be with. No thanks."

"You wanted to marry me," Leah said, "once upon a time."

Her statement caught him completely off guard. It was true enough, but he really didn't know how to respond. "Your mother shouldn't have been so down on me," he said, stalling for time to formulate an appropriate reply. "The fact of the matter is that no man has enough experience or self-knowledge at age twenty-five to know what he wants to do for the rest of his life. And seriously, marriage should be the last thing on anybody's mind at that age, man or woman. But yeah, I wanted to marry you, and yes, you broke my heart, if that's what you wanted to hear," he said coldly, looking straight into her eyes.

"I'm sorry. I guess I need to know that there was someone who loved me just because he loved me. I'm sorry, I shouldn't have said that." she said, turning away, unable to look into his eyes, and unwilling for him to see what was in hers. "I know I hurt you. I'm so sorry."

"I love you still," he said, suddenly, without thinking. "I just don't know what that means."

"Me too," she said, looking into his eyes again.

11.

Dinner at Waverly

"Yeah," Solomon said gruffly, answering his cell phone. "That's great, hold on...Tom, Nikki," he said addressing his dinner companions, "that mysterious overcoat at the crime scene belongs to some itinerant logger who'd been renting a shack on Toma and Dautery's property. He hadn't paid them rent so they took his coat as collateral, just like they said to begin with. They told Debra Harris that there was some receipt and I.O.U. they'd gotten from him, and that it was in a drawer. One of our interns actually found it in all of that mess over at that house of theirs. Dautery actually had a receipt."

"Fabulous," Nikki Daniels laughed, thrilled at the way things were breaking for the defendants. "It doesn't prove that Toma and Dautery didn't place the overcoat at the scene," she said, whispering to Tom, "and why would they? But it does heighten the perception that they were telling the truth to begin with."

"Hush, the both of you," Solomon said. "There's something else. It what? Good work Walter. You take the whole crew out to dinner tomorrow, I mean everybody. Yeah, I'll tell you what. Bring them over here to Waverly. Damn, that's good news too."

"What?" Daniels asked.

"The blood on Toma's shirt turned out to be hog's blood, just like he said originally. I really don't see that there will be a trial. There's no evidence. I can't help but think that the D.A. will drop the charges quickly. It appears that we're here for nothing after all," Solomon said, "but who knows? Maybe if we hadn't blown into town like a tornado, these two innocent people might have been tried, and even convicted."

"Well, I wouldn't celebrate just yet," Tom said. "I can't speak for my brother, but he really believes Toma and Dautery are the killers, and although he may be wrong, I don't imagine that he'll drop the charges. My guess is that he'll go to trial. There are other factors in play, and additional evidence that will be forthcoming. I don't know what that is yet, he just said something else was pending. I know you're a tough bastard in a courtroom, but when my brother gets hold of something, he's like a bulldog. He doesn't let go. I agree that there doesn't look like there is much of a case against them on the surface, but Halcyon is a deep place with many layers. It's kind of like Indian food, you know, how the flavors are so subtle. Well, Halcyon is like that in a way. There are many almost imperceptible layers between the surface and what lies beneath the surface. They're so subtle that you don't notice them at first, but they're all interrelated, and by the time you get to the bottom, everything has changed. This place isn't as out front as L.A. Things aren't always what they appear to be here."

"Well, we'll just have to see about that. I agree that the south, Halcyon...isn't like L.A. and there are no doubt many layers here, but to pursue your analogy, a sharp knife will cut through a cake no matter how many layers it has. My knife is double-edged. Reason and logic are one side of that blade, and knowledge, skill, and experience are the other. Either edge of that knife will cut through anything. Toma and Dautery are getting off no matter what. If the charges against the defendants are dropped, so much the better. If not, we'll win in open court. I love a good fight, and I didn't come all the way out here to lose. The burden of proof is on the prosecution, while reasonable doubt is all I have to establish, and I could do that if we went to trial this afternoon, without any additional preparation. With no gunpowder residue, and no real motive, there's nothing at all to build a case on," Solomon stated confidently. "They have nothing."

"All right Mark," Tom said, "Look at it this way. There are plenty of people who hate their neighbors. I've got to give my brother that much, so that's a situation a juror might..."

"Let's drop all of this...really, it'll take care of itself one way or the other," Solomon said. "I'm just happy to see you outside of the same old places, not that there's anything wrong with the same old places. So this is where you grew up? It's certainly one of the most beautiful locations I've ever seen. Now that I've seen this place in person, I'm surprised you haven't had a movie shot here yet. It's a perfect location, but it's hotter here than at home, although the heat doesn't bother me as much as I thought it would. Pretty as it is though, I'd go crazy here, I need action. Hell, you're the same way. You can't sit still ten minutes, you're always fidgeting. Just look at your foot, I see it tapping right now," he smiled.

"I'm not nervous or fidgety, in fact I'm quite relaxed, but there's always a heavy up-tempo bass line running through my circuits, and that's why I'm always shaking my foot, if my legs are crossed, but you're right, I can't sit still very long. I have to be doing something. I do love this place, and it was a wonderful place to grow up, but I've got to be doing something all the time, accomplishing something, it's how I'm wired. No, you're right. I can't sit still."

Nikki Daniels laughed to herself at the boyish charm of their dinner companion. She knew all about Tom, that he was one of the top agents in Hollywood and had a reputation of taking what he wanted, and yet despite his toughness in business, he managed to be well-liked even by those he bested. He genuinely enjoyed people and it showed, and that was a big part of his success. Just because he might have gotten an actor more than he was actually worth for a particular picture didn't mean that everyone couldn't be happy. When Tom came to meet a producer, director, or someone in charge of casting, he'd already read and studied the script, so he knew what he was talking about in terms or prospective roles for his clients within the scope of the project under discussion. Instead of saying `Jim Smith' would be able to play the role of a doctor, he would go into great detail, saying that Jim Smith's grandfather had been a doctor, and that little Jimmy had hung around the office with his grandfather as a child during the summers. When he sought to persuade a director, he'd already studied the director as well, knew his work, and knew what line to follow. It was almost a Zen thing for Tom. He literally could get in to see anybody in Hollywood with a phone call. Nikki had seen him coming to visit her boss, Solomon, on occasion. She'd actually met him once, about six months ago, and was a bit crestfallen that he didn't seem to remember her, but he was attentive enough now, looking at her frequently, and including her in the conversation, making certain that she felt comfortable in their surroundings. What she liked about him was his absolutely unpretentious manner. He was rich but didn't flaunt it. He also had a reputation for being good in bed, which didn't hurt either, though he was known to be discreet, that is, he didn't talk about the girls he dated, but they did, and favorably.

Despite the fact that Tom was outgoing socially, he was private personally. The rumor was that he'd been dumped at the altar by somebody from his hometown ten years ago, that she'd broken his heart, and that was why he never stayed with anybody too long. Supposedly, he'd never recovered and had vowed `never to love again.' He probably hadn't said that, but it had been said about him. He was rumored to be very hard to get to know apart from business, that is, personally, but looking at him just now, across the table, that appeared unlikely. He seemed warm and outgoing, very engaging, with deep blue eyes that when looking into hers briefly, seemed to instinctively read more about her than she would have him know, and yet, maybe his warmth was just part of his business arsenal. No, he wouldn't be `on' with Solomon as they were close friends socially, this is probably how he really is. Her speculations were brought to a sudden end by Solomon's voice.

"What's happening with the script for `Death Doesn't Sleep'? Did Nick approve the changes?"

"Unofficially yes, officially, no. He's holding out," Tom said. "He doesn't want the shooting schedule they want to put him on. It's too much work for what he's being paid."

"Seven million isn't chicken feed and the studio has expenses. Nick shouldn't rock the boat. He's starting to get a reputation of being difficult to work with," Solomon observed, "You know how that worked out for him at Paramount."

"You're right of course, but you know how it is. I have a thin line to walk. Every agent in town is after him all the time, seeking to secure him as a client, and he's come off three big films in a row. His ego is redlining. It's all I can do to keep him focused on the road ahead," Tom stated.

"They're all the same, well not `all' the same, but mostly," Solomon laughed. "It must be something in the water, something they drink. They have no concept of the meaning of the word `gratitude.' They actually believe that they're really `that good.' And then one day, the work runs out and they wonder what happened. They fire their agent, manager, accountant, and lawyer. They get divorced...again. Then they come begging. It's still the same old story."

"Well, the agent is always the first to go, as you know," Tom laughed. "It's `what have you done for me lately?'"

"Yes, that's true," Solomon agreed, "but I'm the one who has to clean up all the crap they cause themselves and their associates. Drug problems, binding legal contracts ignored or broken, frequent and nasty divorces, adultery, overdue commissions, tax problems, irreversible career errors. We're both in the same boat. The only difference is that you advise them before they do the wrong thing, and I have to clean up the mess after the fact."

"A manager and an agent are in a strange position," Tom cited. "We see the dangers to their careers and reputations if they decide upon a specific course of action which, to anyone on the outside, would seem obviously detrimental and self-destructive. At some level they know that something which they're contemplating is wrong both morally and tactically, but they seem unable to help themselves, and do it anyway. They start believing the hype that they read about themselves in the trades, the very stuff they're paying their press agents to write. From what I can tell, it's always been that way. Work dries up for these people, often without any real reason, and usually without advance notice."

"Well," Solomon observed, "you never know, but I do know that work often dries up and disappears without any specific or tangible reason. The actors with really long-term success treat it like a business and minimize their risks. They are the product, and they market, promote, maintain and protect that product. Public scandals about their private lives are kept to a minimum. They show up on time, don't make stupid demands, and concentrate on their work. They seldom divorce, openly do drugs, or appear obnoxious in public, consequently they have longevity. On top of that, they live well, and sometimes even excessively, but not stupidly."

"Speaking of excess, what happened to that Ferrari you had?"

"It was a death trap. Well it was for me at least. It was really just too fast, and it didn't like heavy traffic. I got rid of it, before it killed somebody. You know how kids are. Sooner or later one of ours would have taken it for a spin without my knowledge or permission. No, it was an accident just waiting to happen. I bought a Bentley V-12, and I'm happy with it, but I have no idea who actually made the damn thing. These car companies change owners as frequently as actors change wives and husbands. Maserati, Jaguar, Lamborghini, Ferrari, hell, who knows anymore? But, it hasn't been a problem, whoever made it."

"My Phantom hasn't been any trouble either, but then I hardly drive it, so I can't really say, and besides, that old Lincoln convertible is kind of my trademark."

"I love that car," Nikki Daniels said, "I've seen it all over town. Anytime I see it parked somewhere I think, `well, that Tom Roberts must be somewhere around.'"

"Well I didn't know you liked cars so much, and I'm flattered that you sometimes think of me. I'll have to take you for a ride sometime," Tom said.

"Ride?" she asked, flirting a little. "No, no, no, I want to drive."

"Are you serious?" Tom asked, looking deeply into her eyes.

"Yes, I am. My grandfather had a black one with red leather seats when I was a child in Lake Forest, Illinois. I'd spend my summers there. I don't know what model it was, but it looked like yours and the rear doors opened backwards."

"Seriously? Well, I'll be glad to let you drive."

"I'll take you up on that," she smiled, "when we get back home, however…, and this may not be a good time for you, under the circumstances, but I'd love for you to take me on a twenty or thirty minute tour of the town and show me some of the houses, and tell me a little bit about them, and about Halcyon, since you're a native. I've never seen anything like this place."

"Sure, I'll be glad to do that, whenever you want. You've got my cell number in Mark's phone book, so just call me whenever it works for you. It would be fun seeing how much I actually remember."

"What about 9:30 or 10:00 tomorrow morning?" she asked.

"Nikki," Solomon interrupted, "Tom's probably got things he needs to be doing…"

"No Mark, it would be my pleasure, really. I'd love to show her around, that is, if it OK with you. I plan to run for 45 minutes in the morning, so that gives me plenty of time. Nikki, why don't you meet me in the lobby, then at 9:30?"

"It's a deal," Daniels said, extending her hand to Tom and smiling.

The meal was superb, and it was indeed pleasant for Tom to be spending time with Solomon. They played tennis or racquet ball together several times a month, and spoke business on nearly a daily basis, but it was nice to have a friend from his other life actually have some sense of where he came from, of his roots. And Nikki Daniels, where had he been keeping her hidden? Tom found her very interesting and attractive, but in Hollywood you never know who is with whom. Solomon was a married family man, but in the circles in which they both trafficked, marriage, as such, didn't necessarily mean exclusivity. Nikki Daniels could be Solomon's mistress. If not, Tom would definitely like to know her better.

Tom excused himself, located the waiter and paid the bill. He returned, and standing by the table said, "It's been a delightful evening, but I'm really tired, and it's getting late. I'm going back to the hotel and get some sleep. Miss Murdock's funeral is tomorrow, and I'll be attending. I used to cut her yard when I was a kid. Anyway, I've already paid the bill, and I'll check in with you tomorrow. Good night."

Daniels and Solomon thanked him but lingered an additional fifteen minutes or so over another glass of wine. "You didn't mention the anonymous note you received today," she said, as sheremoved a folded piece of paper from her purse.

"It would've embarrassed Tom, this being his home town," Solomon replied.

"You don't seem particularly upset by it. I'd think you'd be more concerned. I'd be."

"'Go home while you still can!' Is that supposed to frighten me?"

"It frightens me."

"Well, it doesn't scare me, it makes me curious. It merely serves to further convince me that our clients are innocent. It means that somebody doesn't want us on the case. The underlying question is why?"

"You aren't going to show it to the D.A. are you?" Daniels asked with irritation.

"No, why should I?"

"Don't be so damn macho, Mark. I don't think it's something that should be taken lightly."

"You know me. I can handle myself, and if I ever started down the road of fear there's no telling where I'd end up. I've been threatened before, many times, and you'll note that I'm still standing. My experience has been that people who talk, don't do anything but talk. People who act don't threaten, they act."

"Well you can ignore it if you want Mark, but I think you should show it to somebody. If not the police, or the D.A., at least let me show it to Lucian Dale and get his thoughts on its credibility as a threat."

"No, I said I don't want it shown or even mentioned to anybody. Let it go."

12.

Let's Put Our Love in Motion

Jeannie Murdock's funeral is tomorrow, Tom reflected, as he drove back to the Moro Hotel. Her body had been transported to the morgue in Jackson, autopsied, and returned to Halcyon this morning. Since she didn't have any friends to speak of, there was no visitation. Two funerals in one week, Tom reflected, that's a big deal for a small town, and Halcyon really was a small town. It was a warm, almost tropical night with a strong breeze off the Mississippi River. He parked and stood on the highest part of the bluff overlooking the river, just like he used to do. There was something peaceful and rejuvenating for him just standing there overlooking the river, despite the sheer drop of several hundred feet on the other side of this wire mesh fence. As he stood there, he remembered that old Cadillac convertible of his parked where he always parked it when he would come to the bluff. The barges could be seen far away, moving slowly and silently up and down the river, seen, but not heard, except for an occasional low muffled foghorn blast. To the south, the bridge across the river to Louisiana was clearly visible, its lights flickering in the velvety darkness. He saw them now, and remembered Halcyon as it had been then, a decade ago, and earlier. There was now some new multi-story hotel right in the middle of downtown overlooking the river and blocking the view from the rear windows of the Moro. Under other circumstances he would've cursed the developers and the city council for allowing the construction of such an architectural abomination in the middle of an historic district, but standing there just now, on the bluff, it didn't seem to matter for some reason. Nothing stays the same, he reflected. The only constant in life is change. That's just the way it is. Hollywood seemed far away now, further than the half a continent which it actually was. The nostalgia he felt as he stood there reminded him that beneath the surface glitter and his success, he was still alone. For a few minutes he felt truly alone, and let the feeling overtake him, yielding to it, willing to see where it might lead. "Do your worst," he said, defiantly accepting the reality of the human condition as it applied to him. "I'm not this," he resolutely said to himself. "I'm not Halcyon, I'm not the loser I was when I left here ten years ago. It was her loss, not mine. If things hadn't turned out the way they had, I'd probably still be here, nonproductive, and rotting away. Solomon was right. I can't sit still, I have to be doing something. I've got to keep moving." Then he took one last look at the river and turned away. Back to his car and back to the hotel.

The lobby of the Moro was similar to that of the Peabody in Memphis, or the Read House in Chattanooga, or Nashville's Hermitage Hotel, but much smaller. There was a grand piano, elegant architectural detailing, and an open view to the surrounding second floor mezzanine. Tom preferred older, grand hotels rather than soulless hi-tech multi-story chrome and glass towers, and sought them out. Any of the hotel towers in New York, Atlanta, Dallas, L.A., or anywhere else in the world for that matter, could just as easily have been office buildings, for all the intrinsic warmth they possessed. These old hotels had been built as hotels, and each had its own personality. The manager at the Moro, for example, had been there almost thirty years, and still remembered Tom. The manager wasn't some corporate guy from somewhere else, dispatched from the head office by the board of directors for a 12-month stint in exile.

Tom entered the hotel through the back door from the parking lot, passing the side of the check in desk on his left. "You have a visitor, Mr. Roberts," the desk clerk said as he passed, "she's seated on the mezzanine."

"Who is it?" he asked.

"She didn't say, sir."

"Thanks," Tom said, as he walked over to the grand stairway to the second level. He wondered who it could be, as he strode up the stairs and turned the corner. It was Leah. "What are you doing here?" he asked as soon as he saw her, both surprised and pleased. "It's after eleven, how long have you been waiting here?" he asked, before she'd had a chance to answer the first question.

"I hope you don't mind," she said, "I just needed to see you. That's all. I needed to talk to you."

"Sure," he said, "This is a pleasant surprise, but is everything OK? Are you alright?"

"Yeah, I just…."

"Do you want to sit here or go upstairs?" he asked innocently, "I've really got to pee. You can wait here for a minute or come upstairs to the room with me, if you want."

"I'll come with you."

"Let's take the stairs," he said, wanting the exercise.

"Let me guess," she laughed, "you're on the lowest floor you could get in case of fire?"

"Damn straight. You remember reading about that fire at the old MGM Grand in Las Vegas, I always stay on the lowest floor possible wherever I go." This type of peculiar eccentricity on his part would have annoyed her ten years ago, but now, after all that had passed between them, she didn't mind. They reached his room and he withdrew the key card from his pocket and inserted it into the slot. A green light flashed, and he turned the handle and pulled the door open. Most hotel room doors opened inward, but the Moro's doors opened outward, as they should. "Come on in and make yourself comfortable. I'll be right out. Do you need the bathroom?"

"No," she said, taking a seat on the bed.

Tom was thankful that he had to pee, as it bought him some time, however brief, in which to reorient himself. What does she want? What should I say? He didn't know what to make of the situation. He was glad to see her, but really didn't know what to say. The last thing he wanted to do was to give her the old L.A. `What can I do for you?' which basically means, `You're wasting my time and I don't want to fool with you, but my own self-interest requires that I appear courteous in case I might need something from you later, no matter how unlikely that prospect seems to me just now.' No, he was glad to see her but very much afraid, terrified in fact. It was one thing to look across the table at her in a public place as he had at lunch yesterday. That was safe for him, neutral and non-threatening. Her presence, here, alone in his bedroom, on the other side of the door was very dangerous to his sense of security because he still loved her. He could face that. What was hard to face was the fact that his bond with her had been different than anything with any other woman he'd ever known. Their passionate sexual relationship, for him at least, had always been an outgrowth of his love for her, an emotional need for closeness, an almost spiritual communion which translated into physical expression. It had never been just lust in the traditional sense, nor their unions planned. Their lovemaking had always just happened naturally. He'd been in love with her since the first time he saw her. It had been a spiritual thing for him, almost religious, and her betrayal had devastated him. He didn't know what to say to her just now. What could he say? He needed to protect himself. That was the most important thing.

He exited the bathroom and found her sitting on the bed, and took a seat in a nearby chair, just to be safe. "What's up? Are you OK?"

"Yeah, I just...why are you sitting over there?"

"You know why," Tom answered, "I'm afraid of you."

Leah smiled at the thought that he still found her desirable, and somewhat dangerous after ten years. "I've waited all of this time to see you," she said, "don't be so stand offish."

It was a tough call for him, but he relented and took a seat on the bed next to her. "I can always be on a plane out of here in the morning," he silently told himself, as she suddenly pulled him to her.

13.

Halcyon

"Hey, you look nice," Tom said, looking up at Nikki from his *Wall Street Journal* in the Moro lobby. And she did, dressed as she was in a sleeveless turquoise cotton shirt and bright linen shorts.

"Well, thanks. Did you have a nice run?"

"Yeah, I did about five miles in 45 minutes. That's pretty slow, but it's already hot. You ready?"

"I sure am. I've been reading up on Halcyon, but there's a lot to learn."

"Where do you want to start?"

"You're my tour guide, so I'll leave that up to you. Mark has given me the day off, for a change, well the morning at least, that is, until Miss Murdock's funeral this afternoon."

"Well then, let's go. This will be an opportunity for me to see how much I remember, as well as what I've forgotten. To tell the truth, I really don't think about this place when I'm in California. There's no need to. It's an ever present part of who I am, but it's more about my past than my present," Tom said as they stepped through the rear door of the hotel, to the parking lot and into the rented Lincoln.

"First of all, you should know that Halcyon is supposedly the third oldest actual city in North America, after St. Augustine, Florida, and Natchez to the north. But of course, that's crap. Jamestown, Virginia, and other areas of the northeast were settled before Halcyon. From 1714 to 1763, Halcyon belonged to the French, as did Natchez, as I recollect. From 1764 to 1780, it belonged to England. Then it returned to Spanish hands until 1798, when the first American flag was hoisted from a spot up there on the hill, by an American surveyor, Major Thomas Thornton. There's some confusion, at least for me, as far as the dates are concerned, because supposedly the Spanish were still occupying Ft. Black in 1798, and Thornton raised the flag from the hill in defiance, within sight of the fort. But the house was supposedly built in 1797 by James Rhea. There was a tavern nearby called Maryanne's Tavern, and the two structures were frequently confused, so that this house is really `the House on Thornton's Hill,' but it's still often referred to as Maryanne's Tavern by locals. This is probably more information than you actually need to know. I don't remember, and could be wrong."

"No, tell me. It's interesting."

"Anyway, it was built in 1797, of brick, and wood which was taken from barges. It clearly has a West Indies appearance, similar to some of the surviving down river sugar plantations of the same era. Homeplace, for example in Hahnville on River Road west of New Orleans, looks a lot like this house, so does Whitney Plantation. Exterior stairways to the second gallery were common in the south in the early 1800s, and this is a classic example. When people think of Mississippi River plantations, they usually imagine a giant two-story mansion surrounded by 28 white brick columns and galleries on all four sides, sort of like Oak Alley, or even Waverly here in Halcyon, but those houses, and there were at one time many of them, came forty to fifty years later. The first Louisiana plantation houses looked much like this. Like most old houses, this one has been used for a variety of different purposes in its long history. It was once a high school, a dormitory for cotton workers, and no telling what else. It was saved and restored by the Halcyon Garden Club, I think, sometime during the 1930s. As you can see, it's built on a high brick foundation, which is surrounded by an additional, outer brick wall. There were also primitive drawbridges at one time, which were raised at night to keep marauders and outlaws at bay. Given its prominent location, it's one of the most recognizable landmarks in Halcyon.

"Now this white brick house, Tomachichi was built in 1794, and high above street level as well, but for a different reason. The Spanish had mistakenly determined that the source of yellow fever was to be found below ground, and therefore prohibited the excavation of land within the city. For this reason, Tomachichi was built atop the crest of a hill, which had been where the first American soldiers had camped at the beginning of 1798. Again, conflicting dates. Since the house was supposedly started while Halcyon was under Spanish rule, the Greek revival elements were no doubt added later. As you can see, from this angle, it's a two-story house, but having a recessed front porch and entry supported by two, one-story columns, has the appearance of being smaller than it actually is, but look at the side of the house. It's really massive. It's strange to think that this house is more than two hundred years old. There are larger houses in Halcyon, but this is certainly one of my favorites.

"This one is Tomahawk, and it was built around 1836, restored at some point by the Foreign Legion, and more recently, by some doctor in the 1980s. It may still be for sale. The last time I checked, the asking price was $1,250,000, which is in my estimation a real bargain. If I intended to live here again, I'd certainly buy it myself, except that it doesn't have off street parking, which is a problem for me, given my love of cars. Tomahawk reminds me quite a bit of

Canebreak, which I'll take you by in a little while."

"Why's that?"

"Well, although the entrance to this giant red brick house is actually above street level by nearly a full story, and Canebreak's entrance is at basically ground level, the two houses are similar in appearance. This one, like Canebreak has a two-story portico supported by four, large, two-story columns, that is, two Ionic columns on either side of the front door. But you can see that the four columns and front gallery do not stretch across the entire front of the house. It's the same with Canebreak, which like this house, Tomahawk, has a full second story gallery in the rear with supporting columns which extend the entire length of the back of the house, but only four in the front. The rear gallery afforded privacy for the family and was a sort of social area. The front columns of Tomahawk are larger than those at Canebreak, but then, Canebreak is an earlier house."

"You sure know a lot about architecture."

"Not really, but if you live here, you're bound to absorb a certain amount of information through osmosis, if nothing else. And I forgot to mention, Tomahawk was given to the city at some point and housed the Halcyon Institute, the city's first public school.

"Now this is Lady of the Lake, and behind it is the The Kitchen, where you ate lunch the other day. It's considered by many visitors as well as locals to be the grandest house in Halcyon. Its location on top of a hill in the center of town probably has something to do with that perception, but everything about it was built to last. Did you take the tour?"

"No, but I'd like to see at least one of these great houses on the inside. Your family owns Forsythe? I read about it in one of the books on Halcyon. It looks magnificent," she said.

"It sounds like you're asking for a tour."

"Yes, I guess I am, that is, if it isn't inconvenient, and, since I doubt that any of us will be here during the pilgrimage...."

"Sure, that's fine," Tom offered, "but let's save that for last. We're going next to ride by Etienne Hall. It was built in 1857, and is currently undergoing restoration. It was probably the last of the big mansions built before the war. It's also one of my favorites. It has four large columns across the front which support a pediment roof, as you can see. It's finished in stucco over brick. You'll note that the stucco was cut in such a way as to provide the illusion that the house is constructed of large blocks of stone. This practice was not uncommon back then. A friend of mine owns a mansion in Holly Springs, Mississippi, named Grey Gables. It's an earlier house than Etienne Hall, but also made of brick which has been covered with scored stucco to give the appearance that it's made of cut stone. Etienne Hall is generally considered to be the best example of pure Greek revival architecture in Halcyon, but the truth is, that claim could be equally made for several other houses here. One other thing about this house is that it was reportedly damaged in 1862 by bombardment from the Carstairs, a Union gunboat. I forgot to mention that Halcyon was a part of the Confederate States from 1861 to 1863.

"Now this magnificent place is Roundtree, and also known as Crazyman, and it was designed by architect Samuel Sloan and built in 1858."

"It's beautiful," Daniels agreed. "It doesn't look like any house I've ever seen."

"It's almost unique in plantation culture, and is considered a mixture of Italianate and Moorish. There are none of the giant two-story columns generally associated with plantation houses. As you can see, it is round in shape, constructed of red brick, and three stories high, with the third story recessed from the two lower levels. It looks more like a wedding cake than anything else. Perhaps the most distinguishing feature is the incredible amount of woodwork surrounding each layer, that is, each section. I believe that the brick had been painted white at some point, but has now been stripped back to its natural color by. It is vaguely reminiscent of the domed Longwood in Natchez to the north. Sloane designed both houses and this one was actually finished before the war, while Longwood was not. In the case of Longwood, the war came, and the family lost its fortune, and except for the ground floor, which may actually be the basement. It's the only part of the house that was actually completed there. The workmen's tools still remain where they left them.

"Next, I'd like to run by Canebreak, one of the greatest of all of the houses in Halcyon. I was told that it burned several years ago, but that it was still standing, although now in ruins, despite the fact that some historic organization here had sought to save it by putting on a temporary roof. It's unique for several reasons. In the first place it was both magnificent, and elegantly furnished. It's also old, built in 1820. Unlike some of the houses in town, this one is situated on a large tract of land, and was in private hands when it burned."

"Is that it?" she asked, looking through a distant field of moss draped live oaks, at a large house with four columns across the front.

"That's it," Roberts said, turning onto a winding driveway and ignoring signs which read `No Trespassing' and 'Keep Out.'

"This is unbelievable," she said.

The driveway was approximately a quarter mile and wound around to the left before gently curving in the opposite direction. Suddenly the house was visible in the distance at the left, magnificent, imposing, and ghostly. Tom parked in front of it, like he owned it. "Come on," he said, stepping out of the car and walking around to open her door. "Let's go."

"Are you sure?" Daniels asked. "This place doesn't look especially safe," she observed. "Besides, there might be some maniac living here."

"It's safe enough," Roberts laughed quietly, "and you can see that there's a new roof on the house."

Nikki Daniels wasn't comforted by his observations. The grass hadn't been cut in several years, and weeds had engulfed the house at the lower level. It was just like Lucien Dale had said the first day she met him at the The Kitchen restaurant, decay is much more interesting than perfection. The house was much more fascinating in ruins than it had appeared in photographs of Halcyon interiors, but somehow, frightening. Still, it seemed to beckon her within.

"Is it going to be restored?"

"I don't really know. It's doubtful at this point. If it was, it should've already happened by now. The way I understand it is that the owner won't sell it and won't fix it."

"What a waste. Whoever owns it should be locked up. This is criminal."

Roberts swung the large paneled front door inward, revealing a long unobstructed hallway from the front of the house straight through to the rear, and another door, transom, and side panel windows identical to the front entrance. The scene they beheld was one of scorched walls, blistered doors, and missing plaster cornices, and yet, despite the havoc caused by the fire, the house was not a total loss, and could be restored by any competent construction company.

"Look at those beautiful doorways," Daniels said, "they're in very good condition considering the heat that they were exposed to, but where are the stairs?"

"They're no doubt behind those two large doors down the hall on the left, that is, if they weren't consumed by the fire. Judging from the remarkably well-preserved lathing on the ceiling above us, most of the major damage occurred upstairs. Take a left into the first room and let's have a look around." The wallpaper had been scorched, and for the most part destroyed, and yet some of it had survived, enough at least, that samples could be taken so that it could be duplicated. The window casements were in fairly good condition except for missing glass panes. Tom carefully opened one of the two doors to the hidden stairway and found it generally intact despite having been exposed to extreme heat. It ascended gracefully to the second floor, and surprisingly still retained its banister.

"I'm going up first, very slowly, just in case this thing isn't as solid as it looks."

Knowing that Roberts wouldn't be dissuaded from climbing the stairs, she warned him, "Please, be careful."

Testing each step carefully with one foot and increasing pressure, Roberts determined that the stairs were indeed safe, and called from the landing midway to the second floor for her to follow him. Upstairs was indeed where most of the damage had occurred, and there were no lathing boards forming a ceiling surface. Instead it was possible to see the underside of the roof which had been recently replaced with temporary shingles. "Obviously the entire roof was completely burned away during the fire. The walls look solid enough for the most part, except for some missing bricks surrounding the absent window casements. The heat here was obviously intense."

"There's somebody here," Daniels said nervously, stopping and listening.

"Let's go back downstairs," Roberts replied, ignoring her concerns but detecting a faint but unsettling trace of cigarette smoke. "there's nothing to see here but bare walls." But Roberts sensed there was indeed somebody who'd been here recently, or was perhaps still here, even now. It was probably some transient or drifter who'd moved in, but still many of the so-called `homeless' were insane and violent. He stuck his hand into his front pocket and silently flipped the safety switch upward on his ever present PPK, just in case. Nikki followed him down the stairway, through the double doors and into the front hall.

They were unpleasantly surprised to suddenly see two rough looking men, probably in their mid-thirties, one of whom was sitting atop a pile of lumber, and smoking a cigarette. The other one was standing in front of the lumber and to their left. "I told you, they'd be back down here in just a minute, buddy, that all we'd have to do was wait."

"You sure did, but I was hoping they might give us a sex show. It looks like they seen a ghost or something up there. Did all see a ghost?"

"My friend asked you a question," the one standing said, seeking to intimidate them.

"Wait for me in the car," Roberts directed calmly, handing Nikki the keys.

"Now hold on there baby, not so fast, we thought maybe you might like to have a little fun. Your pussy boyfriend here, we'll even let him watch. We ain't that bad looking are we?" the seated man asked, while grinding his cigarette into the floor.

As Nikki started toward the door the other man reached for her. At that point Roberts quickly swung his left leg sideways, catching the right side of the man's face hard with his shoe, instantly knocking him to the floor. The seated man stood up quickly, intending to make some sort of move against Roberts, but found himself face to face with the business end of Roberts' raised pistol. Roberts backed silently out of the door behind Nikki Daniels who unlocked and started the car.

"Hey Jimmy, that's them lawyers I seen on the TV."

"I don't give a shit who you are," the injured man said, rising from the floor and rubbing his jaw briskly, "you just made the biggest mistake of your life."

Roberts kept his gun aimed directly at both of them and said nothing, slamming the large front door behind him on the way out.

"You were great," smiled Daniels as she quickly drove down the driveway from Canebreak and onto the main road, "and I'm duly impressed."

"Lucky, more than great. That's the only move I know, but...well that and kicking somebody in the nuts first, and then kicking him in the face."

"Who were those people?"

"I have no idea, probably just some white trash that washed up here from across the river. I'll tell Bill about them and he can send somebody over to pick them up on whatever charge he deems appropriate. That's the good thing about small towns, any town I guess. If you know who's in charge you can get things done immediately. I guess that at this stage in my life, whatever that is, I'm just no longer inclined to put up with anybody fucking with me, or anybody else, for that matter."

"You sound angry."

"I guess I am. I'm tired of stupid, violent people. They're everywhere, always trying to cause somebody a problem. Life's hard enough for most people without having to deal with unnecessary extra crap. If they'd made any real move at all I'd have shot both of them on the spot. I know enough about human nature to know what was going to happen next. They'd insult you, seek to belittle and cower me, and then get around to actually trying something. By then they'd have the psychological advantage. There were two of them, and both were bigger than me physically, so they figured that they could take me. I'm sure they could, if I'd given them the chance, but nothing, and I repeat nothing gets somebody's immediate attention like unexpected violence. Suddenly their world is upside down and everything is different. You don't have to be overly perceptive to read a situation like that. It's always the same, just different actors, and when you recognize the script, you always strike first, and hard, something really physical that disorients them. That's the thing they aren't expecting."

“Well, you taught them a lesson.”

“Maybe, but probably not. Next time they might be more prepared as a result of me striking first. So I probably just made the situation worse for somebody else they’ll bother, sooner or later. I despise violence, but I hate the necessity of using it even more. On the other hand, like James Brown said, `don’t start none, won’t be none.’ I’m always armed and I assume everyone else is as well. Only a fool starts some shit with a stranger these days. It’s just asking to be killed.”

14.

The Short Drive to Jackson

The funeral for Miss Murdock took place at the Episcopal Church at 2:00 on Saturday afternoon, August 6. It was a solemn affair with an appropriate eulogy befitting one of her wealth and status, admirably delivered by famed southern orator Rev. D.R. Twine, a former executive of the L&N Railroad, and pastor in residence emeritus of the famed South Wind, which for decades ran the route between Chicago and Florida. There was but slight reference to the circumstances of Miss Murdock’s untimely departure, with particular emphasisupon her aristocratic lineage. The church was full, given the sensational nature of her death, and was filled with persons for the most part, unknown to the decedent. Pall bearers included city leaders, most of whom she hadn’t especially esteemed when she’d been alive. The fact of the matter was that she’d been reclusive, condescending, and arrogant, and wasn’t generally liked, but the funeral was a major Halcyon social event nonetheless, with many people attempting to appear closer to her than they’d ever actually been, in the interests of advancing their social status, as if she could somehow acknowledge them from beyond the grave. The funeral was in a way, the premier social event of the year in Halcyon, a place to see and be seen.

The police chief and district attorney scanned the crowd of mourners seeking to note either the conspicuous presence or absence of specific people, but nobody in particular stood out. A brief and minor debate had taken place within the ranks of the defense team as to whether defendants Toma and Dautery should attend Murdock's funeral. Given the actual lack of evidence, their appearance would seem to confirm their innocence, that they had nothing to hide. On the other hand, the enmity between themselves and the decedent had been highly publicized, and was generally known, therefore their presence might seem hypocritical and could actually work against them in the all-important court of public opinion. Ultimately, the defense concluded that it would most likely be counterproductive for the defendants to attend Murdock's funeral. Not so for the defense team, although Solomon and Daniels were the only members to attend. Their presence inoffensively conveyed the perception of their client's innocence and respect without any blatant show of force. Co-counsel Lucien Dale was also in attendance, having actually known and liked the decedent.

After the service Solomon and Daniels spotted Tom Roberts outside the church and approached him. "What are you doing, I mean right now?" Solomon asked him.

"I don't know. Why?"

"I'd like to drive to Jackson this afternoon. Believe it or not, I have an old friend there, Steve Reuther, a friend from Brooklyn and my days at NYU, and I don't really know where I am, or where I'm going. I thought we could hang out, shoot the shit a bit, and even talk some business. You know your client Benjamin Knight is planning to file a Chapter 13 bankruptcy. That is, he's asked me to petition the court on his behalf. If that is granted, it will negate any contracts he has with your agency as well as any outstanding projects you have with him."

"No, I didn't know anything of the kind," Tom replied.

"I have his permission to discuss his situation with you," Solomon replied. I don't think it's too late to stop things, at least not yet. Perhaps you can make some suggestions. I'm not in favor of this move, and I've told him so."

"Well, I don't....," Tom replied.

"It'll be just you, me, and Nikki. I know you don't have anything else to do, I mean really. There is nothing else you could do here, even on a Saturday night. Come on."

"Well, I don't know. When do you want to go?"

"How long does it take to get there?" Solomon asked.

"It's 115-120 miles, more or less, so you can figure around two hours, or more. Really, I don't want..."

"Oh, come on," Daniels said, smiling at him. "Mark's right, there really isn't anything to do here. Besides, I need someone to keep me company."

"When do you want to go?"

"Now.That is, as soon as we can get on the road," Solomon said. "We'll go in my car. You can leave yours here at the church and we'll pick it up later. Let's go by the hotel garage, dump this rental and get my Bentley."

"I thought you sent it back to L.A.," Tom said.

"Well, I intended to but, I changed my mind. I don't want to sound like an elitist, but the fact is that I enjoy driving, as you know, and in L.A. I don't have much opportunity for that, I just thought I might find a nice two-lane road somewhere while I was here, smoke a big fat cigar, and just drive for awhile and see where it might lead, but I decided to go to Jackson."

"You could drive north to Natchez and take the Natchez Trace from there," Tom suggested.

"No, that's too slow, what's the speed limit, 50? No thanks."

The ride to Jackson passed more quickly than expected, and there was surprisingly little talk of the murder case. "This place is bigger than I remember," Solomon observed with some irritation, upon reaching Jackson. It has more exits than an illegal gambling joint. Tom, do you mind driving? I'm going to pull over. Nikki, turn on the navigator. You tell Tom where we need to go to get to the King Edward Hotel. Do you know where that is?"

"Yeah, I know where it is, but it's been closed and sitting there unoccupied since before I was born. Unless you're looking for ghosts, or just want to ride by and look at a boarded-up building, there's nothing there."

"It's been restored and is now called the Hilton Garden Inn," Nikki said, "but everybody still calls it the King Edward. I looked it up last night on the web. It's located at the corner of Mill Street and West Capitol. Take the High Street Exit."

"Really, that's great. I love old hotels."

Daniels and Roberts dropped Solomon at the hotel and rode around Jackson, stopping for dinner at some local place, talking, and getting to know each other better. By the time they retrieved Solomon at the King Edward and began their return trip, it was nearly 10:00 p.m., meaning that they weren't likely to be back in Halcyon before midnight. By the time they were twenty miles from Hwy 61, with Roberts at the wheel, Solomon was asleep in the back seat, having had too much to drink. Roberts, in the meantime had learned a lot about Nikki Daniels. In the first place, she wasn't involved with Solomon in anything other than a strictly business relationship. "We're both too smart for that," Daniels told him. "Mark lives for his work. Work is his bitch," she laughed. "Many women find him attractive, given his wealth, celebrity status, and contacts, but…well, as he put it, and I quote, he's `not about to get his...you know...caught in the cash register drawer.'"

Tom laughed. "That's an expression he frequently uses with me in regard to some of our mutual clients. It's appropriate."

"Well, anyway, it's great working for him as his assistant...legal manager, whatever you want to call it. I have a law degree myself, and that comes in handy in that I know what he's talking about all of the time."

"Really?" Tom asked. "Don't you want to practice law?"

"Good lord no," she laughed, "though I do assist. He does all of the heavy lifting, well Mark, and his two brothers. I stand in for him on occasion, in court, and handle a lot of his lesser business, but the truth is, he pays me more than I'd make working as an attorney, either on my own or at another firm. I'm licensed to practice in California, Nevada, and New York. Mark handled a high-profile case in Biloxi, Mississippi involving bank fraud a couple of years ago, so he went through the necessary steps to become licensed to practice law in Mississippi. I had to petition the court to be allowed to practice in this case, through what's known legally as `pro hac vice.' It's pronounced `pro hack veechie.' Basically, a local lawyer serves as the main counsel and a visiting attorney operates under his banner with the approval of a judge. And that's what's happened with this one, a judge had to approve me. It's for this case only, but since Mark is licensed to practice in Mississippi already, I'm working under his banner so to speak, rather than through a local attorney, as is usually the case. But Lucien Dale is officially co-counsel. Anyway, what was I saying? Oh yes, lawyers are as common as flies in L.A. I have a great office, an expense account, and lots of perks which I wouldn't have working either for myself or another firm. The only problem is that I'm on call pretty much 24-7. At least Dracula sleeps during the Day. Mark never sleeps, I swear. He has more energy than anybody I've ever known. But what about you? Hollywood is a long way from Halcyon, Mississippi. Why did you leave home?"

"There was nothing for me here. I didn't intend to go to law school like my brother, or my father, and I really didn't know what I wanted to do, but I had sense enough to know that whatever it was, I wouldn't be able to do it here. I drove to Los Angeles and rode around downtown for awhile and checked into the King Kong Hotel on West Sixth Street, you know, downtown. Anyway, the joint was a fleabag back then, though I think it'sfixed up now. Anyway, I didn't have much money and, didn't really know where I was, just somewhere downtown. I had no idea what I was going to do, either, at least not at first. There was a lobby, that is, the hotel had a lobby and there were some old copies of *Variety*, and the *Hollywood Reporter* lying around. I read through every copy I could find my first night at that joint, stayed up all night, actually. But by the time I went to bed I knew that I wanted to be an agent. I slept for the next two days. The drive had been arduous in that 1970 Cadillac convertible. The car did fine and never overheated, but I didn't know it would make it when I left Halcyon. It was a white-knuckle drive all the way.

"Anyway, I made it. I got to L.A. in October. By January, I had a job in the mailroom at Fire Intergalactic. I think they hired me to get me off the street, mainly to stop me from hanging around by the front door. But, they could've just as easily had security tell me to beat it, and that probably would've been the end of the matter, but for some reason they didn't. After that, I worked hard and got lucky. The harder I worked the luckier I got. I attended plays in small theatres at night, or went to shithouse clubs by myself, seeking to find actors, singers, and comedians who were hungry, like I was…am. Eventually, I was unofficially put in charge of my own division. Nobody else wanted to do what I was doing, because there wasn't any money in it, yet, but I wasn't making any money anyway, at least not back then, and somebody in the hierarchy thought that being young, I might stumble upon something established agents might not know about or want to fool with. Like I said, I wasn't making any money, but I wasn't costing anything much either, so the financial risk to the company was minimal. I started booking unknown acts in small theatres, you know, bands in clubs and listening rooms, sometimes for $50 a night. I was paying my way, but nobody was getting rich. After two years of that kind of late night work, I found a band that I really believed in, `The Cans,' and worked with them for nearly a year before I felt that they were ready. I signed them to a major record label deal at Capitol first my time out. It was more or less luck on my part. I called the head of A&R, who didn't know me from Adam, and actually got him on the phone. He agreed to a meeting and that's how I really got started. He decided in principle to sign them then, that day, after I'd played him a rough, homemade CD. Of course, he had to see them first on stage, live. I made sure that night that the small club was packed with screaming women. It's something Col. Tom Parker, Elvis Presley's manager, would have done, but it worked, and they were signed. Of course they went multi-platinum with their first album, and have stayed so ever since. At that point they were plugged into the agency's fair and concert department, and became an international act. That was eight years ago. Based upon that, I was allowed to do my own thing with other singers and bands, and then actors I'd developed, but of course always under the protective umbrella of the Fire Intergalactic Agency. They're all under contract to Fire, my singers, bands, comedians, and actors, but their loyalty is to me. It's worked out well for everybody. I like discovering and developing new talent, but I can't be stuck in an office all day every day. I serve as an unofficial manager for all of my clients, both actors and singers. I say unofficial because in California, at least, there's some law prohibiting an agent from being a manager as well, so the term `manager' isn't used at all, ever, although I approve all dates and contracts for any engagements of any kind brought to me by any agent from any branch of the company for my acts. I think it had something to do with the breakup of a monopoly of some sort there several decades before I arrived, MCA or something. I really don't know. Technically, I'm the `responsible agent.'"

"Do you ever think about going out on your own, you know, starting your own agency?"

"Not really," Tom answered. "Like you, I don't think I could make as much money working somewhere else. And anybody who starts any kind of business in this economic climate is asking for trouble. I don't want the responsibility, or the potential for expensive and frivolous lawsuits. And besides, they've been in business since 1924. There's no way I could do what they do for my clients on my own. More than that though, I like everybody over there. Also, I consider loyalty to be a virtue. Like respect, it's something that is earned, over time. They brought me to the dance, and I'm not leaving with anyone else."

"Mark said to tell anyone in Halcyon, who might ask, that you're a mailman. What's that about?"

"Well yes, I told him to tell anyone who might ask him about me, you know, anybody in Halcyon, especially my brother, how we happen to know each other, that I'm a mailman. I've never actually been a mailman though. I just don't want anybody here to know what I'm doing in California. I'm really a very private person. In the south, hell, maybe everywhere, I don't know, but in Halcyon at least, everybody thinks they have unlimited access to everything you happen to be involved in. Nobody here gives a damn what some mailman in California is doing, so nobody asks me any questions. So far it's worked well for me."

"But I'd think your friends and family would be proud of you for being the responsible agent for some of the most famous movie stars and singers in the world."

"They probably would be, but it might make my brother Bill jealous. For some reason, he needs to think of himself as the patriarch of the family, and that's alright with me. We've been getting along fine recently, and I want to keep it that way. Family dynamics are complicated, especially in the south."

"I hope you won't think me forward," Nikki ventured, "or nosey, but...well," she hesitated, "I heard that the reason you left Halcyon was...well, I heard you were `left at the altar' so to speak."

"I wasn't actually left standing at the altar in the classic sense," he laughed, "but that was part of it, I guess. But that was ten years ago, why are you asking me this?"

"The truth is, I'd like to get to know you better, and you're sort of," she paused, "mysterious."

"I'd like that myself," Tom replied, "but I figured that you were already `taken.'"

"That's a common misperception," she said, "given that I'm so frequently seen in the presence of Mark, but it is a mistaken one. In L.A., as you know, people make assumptions, and they just assume that I'm his mistress. Those who actually know Mark, know otherwise, but people are afraid of him, so anybody who does business with him is reluctant to ask me out."

"Do you see that car behind us?" Tom asked, suddenly changing the subject as he glanced in the rearview mirror. "I wish he'd dim hislights. It's probably nothing, but it's annoying. I think I'll pull over and let him go around us. Those bright lights will give me a migraine sooner than later. For some reason my eyes are highly sensitive to light, especially at night."

Roberts slowed the car, looking for a place to pull over. The car following him slowed as well, hanging back about a hundred feet or so. When Tom pulled off the road and stopped in front of an abandoned fruit stand, the car behind him stopped as well, right in the middle of the road. It was a dark stretch of road on a pitch-black night in the middle of nowhere. This wasn't good.

"What are they doing?" Nikki asked, craning her neck as she looked in the passenger side door mirror.

"Just sitting there."

"Well, we are on a curve, maybe they're afraid to pass until we reach a straightaway."

"Yeah, you're probably right," he said, pulling slowly back onto the road. But she wasn't right, and he knew it. This was something else altogether. He resumed his speed, while slowly withdrawing the Walther PPK from his pocket, flipping up the safety lever on its way out, and placing it under the edge of his right thigh, out of her sight, but accessible. In another couple of miles, they reached a straightaway, and the car behind them accelerated, presumably to pass, which it did. It slowed briefly as it pulled alongside, then moved ahead quickly and was soon out of sight around the curve ahead. It was a black late model Mercury or Ford sedan, Tom noted, with a loud exhaust, and its windows tinted nearly black. So much for that. False alarm.Still, caution was a natural thing for Tom, the same way a cat hesitates before stepping out the back door. It's a survival thing, an instinctive awareness of everything and everybody in one's environment.

As Tom approached another straight spot on the two-lane highway he again had a sudden intuitive sense that something wasn't right, and looking in his rearview mirror, noticed that there was a car behind him, following closely with its headlights off. Tom most likely wouldn't have noticed it at all if not for a quick flash of reflection on its hood from the Bentley's brake lights. It appeared to be the same Ford or Mercury sedan that had passed him a few minutes earlier. The car suddenly sped up and pulled alongside the Bentley, parallel, still with its headlights off. Its darkened passenger window lowered just enough for the barrel of a shotgun to extend, its glistening black surface illuminated by the car's instrument lights. Tom immediately hit the brakes, but not before the occupant of the sedan's passenger seat managed to fire a shot. Tom's rapid reflexes kept him from being hit by the pellets, but they struck the forward end of the Bentley's side window and windshield, sending balled glass shards across the dash and into the seat. But expecting another blast, Tom had already slowed the heavyBentley just enough to position it behind the black sedan's rear wheel. He turned hard to the left, crashing the Bentley's left front bumper into the sedan's right rear quarter, causing the sedan to lose traction and cross immediately in front of the Bentley, which hit it broadside. Tom stomped the accelerator and the V-12 surged to life, smashing the black sedan hard, grinding it sideways to the right and off the road, where it careened backwards down a ravine, struck a tree and exploded. The blast flashed in the rearview mirrors and lit up the surrounding darkness as flames from its ruptured gas tank raced up the trunk and branches of the tree.

It had all happened very quickly, in a matter of seconds, but seemingly in slow motion. Tom had acted instinctively, completely oblivious to the terrified screams of Nikki Daniels, the crash of grinding metal, or even the sound of the shotgun blast.

By this time, Solomon was fully awake, his intoxication gone in an instant. His shouts fully returned Tom to the present again as time resumed its normal speed. Tom brought the Bentley to a rapid stop on the side of the road, fearing an impending deployment of the air bags.

"Whoever that was recognized your car and assumed it was you at the wheel, Mark," Tom said. "They passed us a few minutes ago and then got behind us with their head lights off. They pulled up beside me, lowered the window and stuck a gun out and fired. At that point I hit the brakes, cut to the left and forced the driver to lose control, then I pushed the car off the road. I guess they hit a tree. Is everybody all right?"

Daniels was borderline hysterical, rapidly brushing her hair and face with her hands, sweeping glass chunks onto the floor. "It's OK Nikki," Tom said, grabbing both of her wrists and shouting. "You're safe! We're safe! That's glass. Stop that or you're going to cut yourself. Are you all right back there Mark?"

"Son of a bitch! I can't believe this shit. Somebody was actually intending to kill us. It's a good thing you were on top of things. They were after me. Someone's definitely after me, and it wouldn't have mattered whether they got both of you in the process. They were definitely trying to kill me, but why?"

"You're right about that," Tom said, as he turned on the car's interior lights, revealing a shattered side window and glass pellets from the windshield atop the dash, seats, and floor, as well as drops of blood on both his and Nikki Daniel's clothes.

"You're bleeding," she said, calmer now, touching his face.

"I'm OK, but we'd better call the police. I imagine whoever that was is dead."

"That's terrible," Daniels, said, "what a horrible way to die, to burn to death."

"They intended to kill us," Tom said passionately, "and would have if they could have. They got what they deserved. I'm so loaded on adrenalin I'm probably not going to be able to sleep for a week."

"Well," said Solomon, regaining his composure, "if I'd had any doubt about the innocence of Toma and Dautery, this would've removed it. They're still in jail. Somebody obviously doesn't want us on the case, and it certainly isn't the defendants."

Within fifteen minutes several local police cars and two highway patrol cars arrived along with a fire engine and an ambulance. Solomon, Daniels, and Roberts were questioned at the scene, and the sheriff, upon finding out that Tom Roberts was the Black County District Attorney's brother, transported them personally to the Halcyon police station, where they were met by Tom's brother and

Chief Bowman when they arrived, at around 2:00 a.m.

Solomon's car was examined at the scene of the accident, photographed, and towed back to the Black County police outdoor impound lot.

The following week at a hearing, Solomon secured the release of the defendants over the strenuous objections of the prosecution, despite the fact that they posed no potential flight risk or danger to anyone. Solomon and his staff took advantage of the international publicity the attempt on his life had generated for himself and his case, doing literally dozens of interviews for FOX, the three alphabet networks, *USA Today, the WallStreet Journal,* and other major newspapers.The `Animal house Murder' story was now even bigger than it had been before the attempt on Solomon's life. The prosecution's case was unraveling before its eyes, despite the D.A. having secured an indictment from a grand jury, but the D.A. wouldn't drop the charges. The case was going to trial.

Solomon didn't care one way or the other. The burden of proof was on the prosecution, not the defense. Sure, the murder weapon had been found in the defendant's house, Cypress Hill, but it had clearly been planted by someone else. The murder weapon was the only tangible evidence the D.A. had, but it wasn't owned by either of the defendants and couldn't be connected to them. Immediately after the hearing, Solomon and his entire crew then boarded his Gulfstream jet, with Tom Roberts in tow, and returned to Los Angeles. This case was a done deal as far as Solomon was concerned. They'd all return to Halcyon the day before the trial, whenever it might be scheduled. It wasn't up to him to do the job of the police. Who the real killer or killers of Miss Murdock might really be, wasn't his problem. He'd get the defendants exonerated for good, and that would be the end of his work in Halcyon. In the meantime, there was other legal business awaiting him at home, the kind that paid.

15.

Demonbreun P. Tchoupitoulas

"Tom, it's me," Nikki said. "Mark wanted me to call you and let you know that the trial has been scheduled for the first week of February. What? No, just now. Mark said you can ride on the plane with us. Hold on, he wants to talk to you."

"Hey Mark, what's up?"

"We've got a trial date. I want you to go with us. Are you free? Yes, the first week of February. It'll probably take two weeks or less, besides, you're being called as a witness by the prosecution. Your brother will probably call you later today, but there's more. Miss Murdock's will was probated. Yeah, right after we left, in August. It was fast, but in a town the size of Halcyon there probably isn't that much red tape. No, Mark Delgado got everything. If he wasn't rich before, he definitely is now. Your brother Bill called me this morning to give me the trial date, but he also told me that they got some more information on the people who tried to kill us, there were two of them. They were driving a stolen car, a 2012 Mercury. It had been taken from that black college near Port Gibson two days prior to the incident. Acorn, Alcorn? Yeah, both of them were fried, but there were two pistols, a twelve-gauge shotgun, and something called an MP-40 in the car, apparently some type of 9 mm German submachine gun from World War II. Yeah, it was illegal and unregistered. I know that southerners are gun-crazy, but I can't believe that you guys have guns like that lying around. Where does somebody get something like that? Yeah, I know there are machine guns in L.A. OK, you're right, never mind. Anyway, they've identified one of the would-be assassins. He was nobody either one of us would have had ever heard of, but he was well known to the police. His name was Deon Washington. He'd done ten years hard time at Parchman as an accessory to murder, but had been pardoned by the last departing governor of Mississippi on his way out, God knows why. He had an extensive criminal history prior to that though. Armed robbery, domestic assault, fraud, auto theft, etc., a rap sheet as long as my right arm. No, they haven't been able to identify the other man. Both were burned beyond recognition. Your brother…Tom, I know he's your brother and I'm not going to speak ill of him, but…he thinks that those two were intending to rob us, that they just happened to see a Bentley with California plates and thought we'd probably have some money on us. He considers it to be an attempted robbery that went wrong. He sees absolutely no connection or link to the trial at all. As far as he's concerned, the case of the would-be assassins is closed. The perpetrators are dead and that's the end of the matter, just another robbery attempt that didn't work out.

"I really don't understand that, but anyway, and I need you to keep this confidential, I'm sending Demonbreun P, Tchoupitoulas to Halcyon. He's a detective, a Louisiana native who speaks your lingo down there, so he'll fit right in. Demonbreun grew up in one of those decaying mansions of the Garden District in the Big Easy. I've used him before. He and his partner are brilliant. He'll be in Halcyon as an author and photographer who will ostensibly be in town to write and photograph a book on the great homes of Halcyon. An extensive and credible online resume has been created for him by my staff, including a list of his previous books, and some of his photographs, etc. Actually, he was a B movie actor in the late 1980s and early 90s and was a supporting actor in a number of particularly unremarkable films before becoming a detective. He'd done still photography for Paramount and other studios, so he's a real pro. In fact, I secured him a book deal from a New York publisher, now headed by a friend of mine from my days at NYU, so there really will be a book. My researchers tell me that there hasn't been a really good book on Halcyon homes since the book `Classic Halcyon,' nearly twenty years ago, so it's past time for another one. Contact is now being made from New York with the individual owners and organizations that own the main mansions in Halcyon to schedule him. This will insert him immediately into the loop, where he can do the real work I'm sending him to do, that is, to find out who wanted me off the defense enough that he wanted to kill me, and why.

"I'm convinced now that the murder of Miss Murdock was a crime of passion, that her killer was known to her, and that he, or she, is none the worse for the experience, and is still living and moving freely in Halcyon or the vicinity. He or she was probably there at the funeral, and isn't even remotely suspected. That the trial is proceeding as scheduled will give the real killer a false sense of security. Tchoupitoulas will flush him out and force him to make a mistake sooner or later. That's the way he works.

"Tchoupitoulas will, of course, have no direct link to me or our firm. As far as anyone down there is concerned, other than yourself or Lucian Dale, I don't know him and have never met him or even heard of him, so this must be kept on the q.t. I trust I can count upon your silence in the matter. I don't want to blow his cover."

"Sure," Tom replied, "I think that's a good strategy. Obviously there's more to this story than appears on the surface. I'm not a lawyer so I can't say for sure, but it seems to me that you should be able to get Toma and Dautery off easily enough the way things stand now."

"Your brother is every bit as stubborn and hard-headed as you are. He's convinced that Toma and Dautery are the murderers. Hell, he could be right, given his very high conviction rate, but I just don't think so in this instance."

Back in L.A. things returned to normal for Tom Roberts, though he'd been spending increasingly more time with Solomon's assistant Nikki Daniels, and enjoyed her company. Solomon was involved in a high-profile tax case, seeking to extricate studio head Max Bealmere from the clutches of the IRS. Consequently, Roberts and Solomon had only played racquet ball once in the month of October. The impending trial in Halcyon had been placed on Solomon's back burner. As far as Solomon was concerned, they could go to trial now. The prosecution had nothing, and the defense was ready.

Toma and Dautery, having been released from jail pending their trial, had become internationally famous based upon the worldwide news coverage of their decadent lifestyle, and had opened their decaying mansion to the public five days a week, with guests coming from literally around the world to meet them and tour the house. The $8.00 cover charge was considered by those who paid it, to be one of the best entertainment values in Mississippi. Toma entertained their visitors by playing a mix of classical, old time country music, and ragtime on a decrepit Chickering upright piano, while Dautery read selections of her own poetry to their many guests. Solomon was aware of the situation and felt that it was a good public relations move for the defendants who'd been instructed in no uncertain terms not to discuss their case or anything about it, with anyone at all. The house had been thoroughly cleaned and fumigated with some much-needed repairs made due to safety concerns, but its overall character remained mostly unchanged, with animals moving freely about the house as before, and goats still permitted to eat anything they found desirable. The only difference now, was that the animals' excrement was continually removed by a roving yardman on constant patrol. The kitchen had been cleaned as had the bathrooms, but the rest of the house, including the bedrooms remained the same, and sheets of peeling wallpaper still hung in tatters from the walls, and there was still junk nearly everywhere. Toma and Dautery had cleaned up as well, with Dautery flaunting an exaggerated beehive hairdo, and Toma dressing in a formal, but moth-eaten dinner jacket with raised collar and an ascot.

While the Halcyon old guard were outraged by this audacious and blatant display of aristocratic decadence, the defendants weren't, and neither were the local merchants and hotel operators, who successfully opposed the frequent attempts at legal wrangling seeking to stop Toma and Dautery from opening their house to the public. On most days, there were more than several dozen visitors to Cypress Hill, many having made the trip from Jackson, Baton Rouge, and New Orleans, but gawkers literally arrived from everywhere to see the decaying Civil War era mansion. That there was an impending murder trial awaiting Toma and Dautery, made the visit even more exciting to Cypress Hill's many guests. The fact of the matter was that Toma and Dautery were good for business in Halcyon.

The District Attorney, however, was not pleased by the circus like atmosphere generated by the visitors and unsuccessfully sought a change of venue, sensing that his case was evaporating due to the contamination of the potential jury pool. In light of the denial of his motion for a change of venue, he determined that it would be in the best interests of the state for the case to go to trial as soon as possible. The first open date on the docket was in February.

Solomon's detective Demonbreun P. Tchoupitoulas, had descended upon Halcyon and immediately found himself feted royally by the Halcyon old guard. Being a native southerner, he was comfortable with the climate, and the tempo of Halcyon, and easily ingratiated himself with the older ladies who ran the various garden clubs. He was frequently accompanied about town by his `assistant,' as he referred to Pommerly, a sixty-five year old black man from Tennessee, who'd been his best friend for most of Tchoupitoulas' fifty-five years. The two were a study in contrasts, with Tchoupitoulas being exceedingly refined, educated, and well-mannered, and Pommerly, generally more colorful and totally uninhibited. Tchoupitoulas was clearly gay, eccentric, and generally considered to be an expert on antebellum architecture, French and American Empire furniture, and Sevres porcelain, in particular. He also understood women in a way that no straight man ever could, and genuinely enjoyed the lost art of conversation, taking keen and sincere interest in the observations and opinions of Halcyon society women, most of whose husbands had `gone to glory.'

Pommerly, on the other hand was possessed of a high degree of what is commonly referred to as `street smarts,' that is, he had an inherent and immediate grasp of the gist of any situation. He was anything but gay, totally unpretentious, and an expert on nothing other than basic human nature, a subject which he understood thoroughly as a result of his own varied life experiences. Like Tchoupitoulas, Pommerly was also well-mannered, but unlike his boss, frequently lapsed into brief periods of drunkenness, usually the result of bad association. It was this easy comfort with and among certain black elements of the socio-economic strata that allowed him to gather information which no white man in the south would ever be able to obtain. When he emerged from his descent into inebriation the next day, seemingly none the worse for the experience, he would invariably have gleaned significant knowledge totally unsuspected by outsiders, or even insiders, for that matter.

Despite their obvious differences across the spectrum, each considered his partner to be extremely competent, and together they made a great team, and a really good living. Within less than a week of his arrival, Pommerly had bedded one of the waitresses at a local Halcyon restaurant patronized mainly by the bon ton. The information he'd gathered from her was common knowledge within the black community, but completely unknown to the white population of Halcyon, or evenly remotely suspected.

Pommerly's newest conquest, Miss Vergella Stone, worked as a hostess at Clifford, a Greek revival mansion that was open only for lunch. In a fortuitously synchronistic twist of fate, her aunt happened to be Hattie, the late Miss Murdock's maid. Pommerly had gleaned from their pillow talk that the reason Hattie had probably hexed `that Murdock woman' was due to the fact that she'd violated one of the most significant although unspoken rules of commerce between white employers and their black domestic help, specifically that the latter were to be provided for in some measure by the will of their deceased employer. Apparently, Miss Murdock's will had fallen from beneath the piano where it had been hidden. Hattie had read it and discovered that she'd been left absolutely nothing by her long-time employer. This, combined with the fact that Miss Murdock had talked down to Hattie and treated her like a dog for nearly thirty years, despite what Hattie had regarded as her faithful service, was the precipitating factor in the recent and rapid disintegration of their long-term relationship.

"The bitch wadn't gonna leave her nothing Mista," Pommerly reported to Tchoupitoulas. "The hoo doo is the real cause of that woman's murder, no matter who pulled the trigger."

"You don't believe any of that foolishness do you Pommerly?"

"Yeah, that's right D.T. I'm a black man so I naturally believe in Voodoo? I got skeleton heads in my luggage. Sometimes you...."

"Well, I know that you carry a little red bag inside your shirt all the time. I've seen it. If that's not Voodoo, then what is?"

"That ain't no Voodoo, it's just a little good luck charm."

"Then what's in that thing?"

"It's got a lodestone, for drawing money, and it's got a John the Conkeroo root which gives me extra power over women."

"Well, it certainly seems to work for you, so what else did you ascertain?"

"I bet you don't know this. Miss Murdock had an illegitimate baby, a boy child...father was some musician sideman she met at the Newport Jazz Festival. A jazz musician if you get my drift. Dig it Demonbreun Pontious Tchoupitoulas. A black man, a Negro! She done had a baby by a black man Mista."

"That is absolutely absurd," Tchoupitoulas answered with an audible sneer. "Sometimes you talk such absolute rubbish. That's just crazy talk, a classic example of what I can only refer to as non-logic. She was one of the most respected, feared, and richest people in town. Something that significant would have never escaped the notice of the populace here. True to form, you've dickmatized some poor woman, driven her crazy, and got her talking out of her head. I do declare, you simply aren't right."

"Is that so Mister wiseass? Well, for your information, that dead woman's son done came down here from that Catholic orphanage they stuck him in up in Boston when he done found out who his mother really is. He'd been hitting the dead woman up for money for years, blackmailing her, I guess."

"If that's as you say," Tchoupitoulas replied, "then why wouldn't he come forth with some sort of claim against what I can only presume to be a rather large estate? A simple DNA test would substantiate any claim he might make."

"I ain't got no answer for that now, and I agree that it don't make no sense, but if I was him, I'd bite that estate like a snapping turtle, put the lock jaw on it, and wouldn't let go `til it thundered, or `til I was rich."

"Setting aside, for the moment at least, the distinctly unlikely plausibility of the account you've just related, let's say, purely for the sake of argument, of course," Tchoupitoulas speculated, "that what you've just told me is true…"

"Ain't no argument involved. Ain't no speculatia neither. The man lives over in Jackson right now, about a hundred miles from here and I got his name and address, though you ain't gonna like what I'm about to say. His name is `John Doe.' That's right, John

Doe. Before you start talking shit, let me repeat, to clarify it for ya. You heard what I done said. The man's real name is John Doe. That's his legal name. He done had it changed to that, and I do mean legally, soon as he got to Jackson."

"But that doesn't make any sense at all," Tchoupitoulas replied.

"No, what you mean ain't that it don't make sense, what you mean is that it's above your knowledge box, or in your lingo, beyond your comprehension. You don't understand it. It makes perfect sense if you understand it. The somitch was stuck in a orphanage from day one. He don't know who his father is, but he ain't stupid. He's figured out that his parents weren't killed in some plane crash in Ethiopia or someplace, or murdered in some made up robbery like what happened to young Bruce Wayne on Batman. He probably suspicioned that whatever name he had was something somebody dropped on him at the orphanage. He might as well be who he really is, somebody unknown and unwanted, a high yella, neither Negro nor Caucasian, not black or white, too much of one, and not enough of either. I guess he could have named himself `X the Unknown,' after that space monster that was on some movie. Naw man, I respect him for that. What else is he supposed to do?"

"What, might I inquire, is the source of your information?" Tchoupitoulas asked, now genuinely interested.

"Now, you're the one talkin' shit. You should know by now that I'm every bit as efficient as you are, and just as thorough. Our methods are different, that's all. Yeah, I sexed that woman down, and she sang like a bird. I done told ja repeatedly that I'm a `pipester.' My daddy was a plumma and he taught me how to lay pipe. Now I'm through with that. For your information though, Hattie wasn't Miss Murdock's first maid. Do you dig what I'm sayin'? When Miss Murdock went to Paris, France for a year to `study,' if you get my drift, her maid Tantalus went with her, to France. Do you dig what I'm sayin? When Miss Murdock got back to Newport she arrived by herself. It wasn't but a short while later that Tantalus showed up in Boston, Massachusa with a dark-skinned baby boy child, and a big donation for the orphanage. And that was that. The onliest thing is that there was plenty of speculatia and talk in Newport. Miss Murdock and Tantalus cleared out of Newport and moved back to Halcyon where her cousin Delgado lived. Do you see where I'm coming from? Where this is leading?"

"Please continue."

"Well, Tantalus the maid didn't have no family, leastwise none she especially liked in Newport. She and Miss Murdock was best friends, despite their different social standings. That didn't make no never-mind to either one of them. Everything was fine for four years and the maid lived in her guest house at Eldorado, then the maid had a stroke, and that was that. She was big and fat and had a stroke and just conked out, but she'd gone to church at the Zion Tabernacle in Halcyon, every time the door opened, and you know how women talk in church.

"So Hattie Livingston became the new maid, and that was around thirty years ago. This is a matter of local record. It may not be written down anywhere, but everybody in hatchietown knew it, and nobody cared one way or the other. It was white folks' business."

"You've certainly done your work well, as usual, Pommerly. That's the difference between you and me. I'd never have been able to acquire that information, ever, and I know it. I believe that everything you've told me is probably accurate. But John Doe? I want you to run over to Jackson, spend a few days and tail him. I want to know what he does for a living, who he associates with, and where. Find out all you can about him. I'm not sure that any of this has, or will have any bearing on Solomon's defense case, but I'm certain that he won't be expecting any of this. This really is great work. Why don't you meet me over at the Thai jointat around 7:00 tonight? Let's have a really good meal. Then tomorrow I want you to go over to Cypress Hill and take the tour. I think it's $8.00 to go through the joint. I want your opinion on the two defendants. They're Solomon's problem, of course, and not ours, but I'd just like your gut instinct about them. And don't tell them who you are. I'm going to go over there myself, sometime this week, you can count on that. This is an interesting case. You can go over to Jackson after that."

"That's cool with me, D.T., and I could certainly use a big lobsta supper, but what have you found out by hanging out with all those rich folks?"

"Nothing of any particular value. I'd forgotten how gracious people are here, but I can't say that I've learned anything that isn't already common knowledge. Nobody especially liked Miss Murdock. She knew it and didn't care. Mark Delgado was indeed her boyfriend in the traditional sense, as well as her cousin, but there are no records of any marriage anywhere in Mississippi, Louisiana, Newport, Rhode Island, or anywhere else, for that matter. They never lived together, but he went over to her house nearly every day. Delgado is apparently as rich as Miss Murdock was, not that it particularly matters. He has a reputation of being cheap, despite his wealth, and is generally considered unpleasant and arrogant, and isn't particularly liked either.

"The town is buzzing with anticipation of the trial. It's obviously the biggest thing to happen here in anyone's memory. Speculation regarding the guilt or innocence of the parties is about equally divided on either side of the issue. Solomon thinks he's got the case locked down and that he's going to drop down out of the sky from California in a golden chariot surrounded by the heavenly hosts, like some big shot, embarrass the district attorney, get his acquittal, and then just flashlight back to Hollywood in a blaze of glory. He doesn't know it, but he's got his work cut out for him. You know how manic he is, so I don't ever try to give him anything other than an impartial presentation of the facts. If he wants my opinion he'll ask for it, and I'll give it to him."

"Me either," Pommerly agreed. "I don't like the somitch, not that he needs to know that. When you and I go to meet him at his office, or if I run into him somewhere, you know, a high tone restaurant or something in L.A., he's just as likely to act like I'm his long lost army buddy just back from the war, or to pretend he's never seen me before. The somitch is unpredictable. That's how he keeps people off balance. All I know is that every time I look at him, all I see is a big old sack of money in a fancy suit and nothing else. He's a big wind bag, inflated with hot air and horse shit. Let's hope nobody puts a tack in his chair in the courtroom or he'll fly around the room like a balloon with the stopper pulled out. But still, if I needed a lawyer to beat a murder rap, I'd want him. He could get charges dropped on the devil. He's a slippery little son of a bitch, but I think that's part of being a good lawyer. You've pretty much got to be a bad person to be a good defense lawyer. The slate of my life may not be entirely clean, but I ain't never done anything that somebody would go to hell for, leastwise, I hope not. Solomon has gotten brutal murderers off the hook, and one of them later murdered some poor girl working at a 7-11. She wasn't doing anything to anybody. Just working some crappy job, probably at minimum wage so she could take care of her baby daughter. And some no-good hooligan who Solomon got off for an earlier killing, shot that girl. Solomon would sell his mother for a shiny dime. He's pure evil."

"That may be a bit harsh Pommerly. He's a defense attorney, and everybody is entitled to a good defense. He's just good at what he does."

"A defense should be nothing more than that. It should not consist of tricking a jury into thinking that some no-good son of a bitch is just a poor, misunderstood somebody who'd been beaten down by life. If you's in a bank with a loaded shotgun stuck in somebody's face and it `accidentally' goes off, it ain't the victim's fault. If you kill somebody in any manner, for any reason other than self-defense, you deserve to fry. Now I'm through with that. Solomon is the devil's henchman. I'm not a religious man, as you of all people know, but there is a God, and he ain't mocked, leastwise not for long. All I'm sayin' is that I wouldn't want to be Solomon on judgment day."

"Well, me either," Tchoupitoulas agreed."Hell, I don't want to be me on judgment day, but I damn sure don't want to be him. We should both cross ourselves every time we see him. New Orleans, Baton Rouge, Los Angeles," he laughed, as he made the sign of the cross.

"Amen Holy Ghost!" Pommerly agreed.

16.

Jury Selection

The first week of February in Halcyon was colder than normal, but it didn't stay that way long. On day one of jury selection, the defense team was in court and in place at the left side of the courtroom facing the judge's bench twenty minutes before the trial was scheduled to begin, as were most of the potential jurors. An immaculately clad and groomed defense team consisting of Mark Solomon, Nikki Daniels, and Halcyon attorney Lucien Dale were in place at the defense table.

A primitive but adequate mobile belt scanner, similar to those found at airports had been wheeled into place, as well as a vertical walk-through scanner for the first day of the trial, and a group of several dozen had gathered early in the upstairs corridor waiting to be cleared for entry and hoping to secure a seat. Crowds in high profile murder cases are always expected, and this one was no exception. It was doubtful that everyone would find a seat. At 9:00 am, punctually, a door swung open at the front of the room and Judge Brock was announced by an officer of the court, ascended the few stairs to the bench and took his seat. He was a strange, weaselly looking fellow, approximately forty-five years or so old, who immediately looked across the courtroom from his perch, scanning the audience with beady, rodent-like eyes. He appeared to be smirking, but it was more of an impression than an actual fact.

The judge laughed quietly as he spoke to a woman seated at his right, who passed him several small stacks of papers pertaining to the trial. He then explained to the jurors that the trial would probably last around two weeks. Apparently, some sort of preliminary jury selection had already been agreed upon by both sides prior to today.

Solomon noted the formal appearance of the courtroom and felt strangely at home, despite the presence of six black cast iron Hunter ceiling fans, which looked like relics from another era. One of them emitted a loud but comforting buzz as it turned slowly overhead. They looked heavy, he thought, unlike the lightweight Chinese made ceiling fans he was used to in California. This was what a courtroom was supposed to look like, he noted quickly, thick wood panels around the room at eye level, an elegantly paneled witness box, and heavy wooden arm chairs at both the defense and prosecution tables, each massive and constructed of dark oak which showed wear and stains from many decades of use. No plywood or particleboard with plastic veneer here. This courtroom was worthy of the seriousness of the matter about to be considered within.

The prosecution began the proceedings with District Attorney Bill Roberts addressing the jurors and the courtroom. "Members of the jury, we are here today to try a pair who have been charged with murder. I'm going to stress that given the nature of our criminal justice system that the burden of proof rests entirely on the prosecution. The defendants are innocent until proven guilty `beyond a reasonable doubt.' The charges are First Degree Murder, of which there are two types. The first is Premeditated Murder, that is, the defendant intended to kill the victim to begin with. He thought about it, planned it, and then carried out that plan. That's Premeditated Murder. The second type of murder is known as Felony Murder, that is, any murder committed as part of another crime, such as robbery. In this case, the state is not seeking the death penalty, so your responsibility is simply to determine the guilt or innocence of the defendants. Should you find them guilty, the sentence will be imposed by the judge, so even though some of you might be personally opposed to the death penalty, that issue would not apply in this instance, as this is not a death penalty case. Do any of you know the defendants or the decedent? Do any of you have any prejudice toward any law enforcement official or agency? Are all of you comfortable with the laws? Would you have any problem enforcing them? Good.

"Ladies and gentlemen, the home is the one place above all else where everybody has a right to be safe and secure? Would y'all agree with that? One's home is a `sacred' place, for lack of a better word. It's been said that a man's home is his castle. That's part of the American dream, and the same applies to a woman. A woman's home is supposed to be her castle too. Isn't that true? Does anyone here think that a woman shouldn't be safe in her own home? Now, you're going to hear testimony about the decedent, the victim, Miss Murdock. We are probably going to be told that she was `rich' as if that's a bad thing, as if somehow she was less of a person because she was rich, and therefore might not deserve the same considerations that any of us might expect, specifically the right to be safe in her own home. I'm not rich myself, but I was raised to believe that if I worked hard enough, I might be rich someday. I still believe it. The victim was indeed rich by my standards, and probably by most of yours as well. She didn't have to work like most of us do, but that's no reason to resent her. Is there anyone among you who feels that the victim's wealth and social status might influence you in such a way that you couldn't be impartial? You might hear that she was rude to some people, that she looked down on others, that she thought she was better than everybody else, and that may be true. She was nice to me the few times I met her, but let's say she wasn't nice to most people, just for the sake of argument. Does that mean that she should be robbed and murdered in her own home? Did she deserve that fate just because some people thought that she was mean, or rude, or had a high opinion of herself?

"Your honor, I'm going to read the list of witnesses," Roberts said as he stood at the podium facing the jury box. After completing the list, he again addressed the jury. "Are any of these witnesses known to you?"

One juror raised her hand and said, "I know the chief of police?"

"Do you feel that could prejudice you in any way?"

"No sir."

"I went to school with one of the other jurors," number 7 said.

"Again, can you be fair and impartial and follow the laws of the court?" Roberts turned to the judge and said, "I pass the jury at this time your honor," and took a seat.

All eyes were on Mark Solomon as he rose from his chair and strode toward the podium which faced the jury. He was dressed in a light blue seersucker Brooks Brothers suit which had been tailored to fit perfectly. It wasn't flashy, and the 18-karat gold Patek Philippe watch which usually adorned his wrist had been replaced with a more subdued stainless Omega Speedmaster. His trademark brown alligator loafers had been abandoned temporarily in favor of more conservative brown wingtips. There was an air of expectation which preceded his opening remarks and prospective jurors listened intently.

"General Roberts has just told you the defendants are innocent until proven guilty, that it's up to the prosecution to build a case which clearly proves these defendants are guilty. That's the way it's supposed to be. I can tell by looking at you that you are more sophisticated than jurors were say, thirty years ago. You've seen enough crime dramas and courtroom scenes and trials on television and at the movies, that you know how the process is supposed to work. And yet, each of you, like myself, like each defendant, is a product of a lifetime of experiences, each of which have in some manner colored or shaped the way in which you…we see the world. The court merely seeks to make certain that your experiences aren't such that you would be unable to make a determination of guilt or innocence in this case, beyond a reasonable doubt. The district attorney has mentioned the term `reasonable doubt.' Are all of you clear on exactly what that means? Is there anyone who doesn't fully understand that? To recap, reasonable doubt means that an average, intelligent person, like any of you, would doubt something, whatever it might be. The prosecution must prove that the defendants are guilty beyond reasonable doubt. The defendants are not required to prove their innocence. Do all of you understand that?

"The defendants are not required to answer any questions of any kind at all. They don't have to testify on their own behalf. They are not guilty of anything, they've merely been charged. It's not up to them to say anything. They aren't in any way required to prove their innocence. Do you understand that they are not required by law to say anything in their own defense? Should either of them not appear as witnesses in their own defense, this is not to be considered to be indicative of guilt in any way. Are we all clear on this point? Good. Murder is a serious charge, but their guilt or innocence is not based upon the seriousness of the charges.

"Now, as jurors, would you think that, say, the sheriff or chief of police…that their testimony would mean more than that of any other witness? Would the chief's testimony possibly have more, or less weight than that of any other witness? The law presumes that everyone is telling the truth, and the testimony of one witness should be considered as accurate as that of any other witness. In other words, the testimony of a government official does not have more validity than that of any other citizen. It will be up to you to determine for yourself whether the witness is telling the truth, based upon your own experiences.

"I'll be asking you some questions and they are nothing personal, though they might seem so. By that, I mean that we are here to determine the guilt or innocence of the defendants, and some of you may be disqualified as jurors based upon your responses to some of my questions. Again, I'm not seeking to embarrass any of you, but we want to eliminate anyone who might have any bias toward the defendants on preexisting personal grounds, whatever the reason. You might have some bias of which you're not even aware, perhaps we all do to some degree. I think that all of you genuinely want to be objective, and given the seriousness of the charges against my clients, your fellow citizens, your neighbors, I honestly believe that each of you seek the same outcome as I do, a fair trial. You've all seen the statue of `Justice,' a blindfolded figure holding aloft a pair of scales. The blindfold means that justice must be impartial. The law must be impartial. No matter how remote you might feel the possibility could be as you sit here today, it might be you sitting in that box over there someday, snatched from the sanctity of your own home in the middle of the night and charged with some crime of which you're innocent. It might be your own son or daughter, wife or husband, who is charged. I want you to be as impartial as you would want…expect…any juror to be who might hold your fate, or that of a loved one in his or her hands. So, I'm asking you if there is anything in your background which could hinder you from being impartial?

"How many of you are hunters?" Solomon continued, sticking his hands in his pants pockets, and attempting to appear casual. Several jurors raised their hands. "Well, what types of guns do you have?" he asked as he visually scanned the jury.

One juror raised his hand and when called on replied, "What do you need?" which was followed by laughter.

"Well that's good. The 2nd Amendment of the Bill of Rights grants us the right to keep and bear arms. It is an affirmation of our God given right to protect ourselves and our property. Is there anyone here who thinks that...well, let's put it this way, is there anyone here who doesn't like guns? Who doesn't think that we have the right as citizens to keep and bear arms, whatever the reason? Thank you," Solomon said, and returned to his seat.

"Turn in your slips," the judge said, and the bailiff collected them from both attorneys and handed them to the judge. After a moment the judge addressed the jury. "Mr. Thompson, Miss Fowler, Mr. Smith, you are free to go." They rose and left the courtroom.

The judge shook a small cage with numbers in it and called three more names from the juror pool in the courtroom. "Numbers 351, 22, and 206 please step forward and take your seats in the jury box."

Finally, after a day long process which had been divided by an hour and fifteen-minute lunch recess, and three fifteen-minute breaks, a jury had been seated along with two alternates. Tom Roberts was surprised both by how many potential jurors there had been, and how many actually sought to avoid jury duty, despite the sensational nature of the case. Some of their excuses as to why they were unable to serve sounded lame, while others seemed more legitimate. It seemed to him that many of the judge's decisions as to whether to let some of them go or force them to serve appeared arbitrary. Tom was already casting the movie version of the proceedings in his own mind as the day's legal wrangling unfolded. Of course, he had an innate desire to see justice done, and didn't wish to see the innocent punished, but unbeknownst to his brother, and the prosecution team, Tom had brought in two screenwriters from Hollywood to surreptitiously follow the proceedings.

The judge then read the charges: First Degree Murder, Felony Murder, and Aggravated Robbery. He then addressed the attorneys and said, "I believe the jury is qualified." The judge then dismissed the rest of the potential jurors, thanked them for coming and said,"You're free to go." They rose en masse from the general courtroom audience and left the building, having basically been there all day. The judge then ordered the jury sworn in. Six guards were sworn in as well and the judge addressed the jury. "These guards will be with you during the course of this trial, which as I explained, may run as long as two weeks, although it could be less. You will be sequestered, and during that time, are not to discuss the trial, or any testimony from any witnesses, with anyone, even among yourselves, among fellow jurors. The reason is that the court does not want you to form any opinion regarding the guilt or innocence of the defendants until all testimony has been heard. We don't want any member of the jury influencing any other jury member, consciously or otherwise. It's your job to hear all of the evidence and then reach your own conclusions. Any opinion as to the guilt or innocence of the defendants prior to the conclusion of the trial would be premature, and therefore prejudicial."

Tom Roberts sat in the third row behind his brother, the district attorney on the prosecution's side of the courtroom. It wasn't that he had any preexisting opinion as to the guilt or innocence of the defendants, just that the courtroom was full, and the district attorney had reserved three rows of seats. Tom had never been to any trial of any sort where a jury had been involved. Sure, he'd testified in disputes between his clients and others in breach of contract matters on occasion, but he'd given his testimony when called, and then left the proceedings. He'd never attended a murder trial, and was surprised that there were that many jurors who'd been called initially, and he was actually appalled by their casual attire. Granted, they should be comfortably dressed, but some of them were downright slovenly. On the other hand, perhaps they'd been advised earlier in the judge's chambers that they were likely to be there all day and told they should dress comfortably. It wasn't that Tom was especially concerned with how they dressed, but respect for the court in and of itself would seem to demand that they'd be at least somewhat well-dressed rather than in gym shorts or polyester knit pants. Again, maybe this was just for today. He'd have to ask his brother about this, as it was curious, and it definitely wasn't his imagination.

17.

District Attorney Roberts for the State

The actual first day of the trial began promptly at 9:00 am. "All rise" the bailiff announced stepping through a door near the bench at the front of the courtroom, ahead of the judge. "The Court of Black County in the state of Mississippi is now in session. Anyone having business with this court draw nigh and ye shall be heard. God bless this great state and county. You may be seated."

Judge Brock surveyed the courtroom and then faced the jury. "I'm going to give you some instructions," he said. "Witnesses generally remain outside the court until after they've given their testimony. You may take notes, but these must be limited, and you may not write down the specific testimony of any witness. The state will present its evidence first, and then the defense may respond if so desired. Questions are not considered to be evidence, they are merely questions. There are two types of evidence to be considered, and they are known legally as direct evidence, and circumstantial evidence. One type of evidence is not necessarily `better' than the other. So, to recap, the state goes first, then the defense, and the state. The reason the state closes the trial is that the burden of proof is on the state. Again, you are not to receive any outside information about this case and you may not discuss any aspects of the trial with each other until the jury deliberation phase. Do not speak to any of the attorneys or any parties to this trial, including any witnesses, or to myself. To do so will result in a mistrial, and we'll have to start the entire process again from scratch.

"I reiterate that the defendants in this case start with a clean slate. Neither of them are required to say anything. The venue is Black County in the State of Mississippi."

The district attorney stood and said, "The defendants in this matter were duly indicted by a grand jury docket number 4725 convened in Black County, Halcyon in August of last year. Count 1.The defendants did exercise control over property by the use of violence. Count 2. On or about August 2 of last year, the defendants did kill Miss Jeannie Murdock in the perpetration of a crime against the peace and dignity of the State of Mississippi."

"How do you plead?" the judge asked.

Solomon stood addressing the bench and stated, "Not guilty," Your Honor, and took his seat.

The district attorney whispered something to his co-counsel, then stood, and walked toward the podium facing the jury. "Let's start with the day before the murder. The decedent, Miss Jeannie Murdock was at home minding her business as she always did. She was a private person, someone who asked nothing from anyone. She didn't cause anybody any problemsand expected none herself. Like most of you, she considered her home to be her castle, a place of private refuge, a peaceful oasis in this land of intense heat, humidity, and swarming mosquitoes, somewhereboth restful and familiar, and above all, a safe place. And yet there was one problem which she was forced to deal with repeatedly, and against her will. Neighbors. Some of us have had problems with neighbors ourselves. Maybe they allow their dog bark all night, or they let their yard grow up and won't cut it. Perhaps they leave trash in the yard, or they refuse to keep their animals properly tethered and restrained. Or maybe they play loud music all night. It could be anything. In most instances, these annoyances are seldom more than that, mere annoyances, and we generally try to address these issues in a courteous manner, since we have to live next door to these people, and they must live next door to us. Usually these matters resolve themselves, over time, but sometimes they don't, despite our sincere, courteous, and repeated attempts.

"Sometimes, the problems just continue. In the case of the murdered woman, Miss Jeannie Murdock, she'd been harassed repeatedly by animals owned by the defendants, roaming into her yard and destroying her property. This had been going on for several years. The defendants, responding to numerous complaints indicated both in words and by their actions, that `it wasn't their problem.' Basically, they didn't care. Miss Murdock didn't like their animals trespassing on her property? Too bad, it wasn't their problem. You might ask yourselves, `OK, what's the big deal, really? So some animals roamed into her yard from time to time.' But it was a big deal to Miss Murdock. She'd always kept her lawn mowed and her house and yard immaculately clean. She was a good citizen, and took pride in the appearance of her property. She paid her taxes, minded her own business and caused no problems for anybody. The defendants' hogs were allowed to roam wild, and frightened Miss Murdock to the extent that she'd actually become afraid to go outside in her own yard. They uprooted expensive shrubbery and bushes, destroyed her careful landscaping, and devalued her property. The same for the goats that wandered over, ate the flowers out of her garden, as well as the tomatoes, peppers, and other plants she'd so carefully tended. Her beautiful garden had been ruined, her plants and shrubs uprooted by foraging hogs, and she no longer felt like she could even go outside in her own yard safely. She'd essentially become a prisoner in her own house.

"But it gets worse. The rampaging goats also entered her garage and stomped and dented her car with their hooves, basically destroying the hood, top, and trunk, all the while excreting, urinating and defecating upon the paint, ruining its finish. Her gentle requests turned into impassioned pleas, all unheeded. Eventually, she called the police.In short, she did everything within her power to legally put a stop to this abuse at the hands of her neighbors, but to no avail. The police gave the defendants a warning and threatened them with a citation. Again, the defendants could not have cared less. The rights of their neighbor to live in peace were of absolutely no consequence to the defendants," he said, pointing at them. "What was Miss Murdock supposed to do? She'd asked them, begged them, and called the police. She'd done everything within her power to resolve the matter peacefully, courteously, in the same way she would expect, and deserve to be treated herself. She'd even spoken with me about the situation. She wasn't the perpetrator of these offenses. She wasn't the offending party. She just wanted to live in peace in her own house and on her own property. Was that an unrealistic expectation? Was it too much to ask?

"At length, and weary from fruitless attempts at stopping what had become open, hostile, and ongoing aggression and abuse at the hands of the defendants, she decided to take matters into her own hands. She shot one of the neighbors' goats. Should she have shot the animal? Maybe not, but what else could she have done at this point, given the circumstances? Hopefully, she reasoned, that would be the end of the matter. Maybe the defendants would finally decide to put their animals in a pen or some sort of enclosure where they belonged. Not at all. On the contrary, Mr. Toma and Miss Dautery were outraged, not by the fact that their animals continued to roam at will, not that they had destroyed Miss Murdock's car, or ruined her landscaping, or eaten the flowers and the vegetables from her garden. No, they were outraged that Miss Murdock had the audacity to defend her own person and property.

"Her neighbors, the defendants, on the other hand, had willingly let their property deteriorate to the extent that it had become an embarrassment not only to themselves, but a disgrace to this community, an eyesore. More than this, however, the defendants seemed to feel a sense of arrogant entitlement based upon some misguided sense of their own self-importance, as though somehow the basic rules of proper deportment did not apply to them. They felt no need for any courtesy, explanation, or restraint, and in fact, considered Miss Murdock tobe the problem, not themselves. The state will show that the very day before Miss Murdock's murder and robbery in her own house, that the defendants had come onto her property, as trespassers, confronted her face to face, and threatened to kill her. The prosecution will prove beyond reasonable doubt that it was this arrogance and exaggerated sense of self-importance which finally persuaded the defendants to enforce their intentions at the end of a gun barrel. They had the motive, the means, and the opportunity, and did indeed rob and murder Miss Murdock, in cold blood, within her own house. This was premeditated murder, pure and simple. The defendants knew Miss Murdock's schedule. They knew when her maid left, and they knew when her cousin Mr. Delgado arrived. These events were daily occurrences and you could set your watch by them. The defendants picked their window of opportunity, conspired to, and did rob, and murder Miss Murdock in cold blood, within the sanctity of her own home.

"The defendants will likely be portrayed by Mr. Solomon as `damaged.' He would have you believe dear friends, that Mr. Toma was incapable of handling his own affairs, that he was weak and simple-minded, childlike, in fact, incapable of perpetrating any crime of any kind. Mr. Solomon would hope to have this court believe Toma was passive and lacked both the mental and physical strength to conceive or execute any type of violence. In fact, he's a frail man," Roberts said, pointing at the defendant, "incapable, the defense will seek to have you believe, of any activity which requires any sustained physical exertion, the type that would be required to move a body.

"Don't believe it. Mr. Toma, in fact, regularly killed and butchered hogs, chickens, and cattle, single handedly, brutally slaying them in cold blood, beating their brains in with a hammer, slitting their throats, draining their blood, and then dismembering their bodies with an axe and a saw. And Miss Dautery, by her own admission, is an expert marksman, who'd been visited by the police on several occasions for illegally discharging a firearm within the city limits, shooting at `trespassers,' as she called them.

"Mr. Toma," the D.A. continued, "was indeed capable of, and did in fact, move the body of the decedent, Miss Murdock, from her home, after they had shot her, in an attempt to cover up the murder, a crime which had been instigated by the other defendant Miss Dautery, who in popular lingo could be considered to be `the brains of the operation.' Her jealousy and hatred for the decedent was indeed a long standing one, as we shall show. The two had once upon a time been friends, and had travelled in the same social circles, but as the fortunes of the two defendants waned, they became hostile toward the decedent whose wealth continued to increase, seemingly effortlessly. The state will prove beyond reasonable doubt that the defendants did willfully and intentionally rob and murder Miss Murdock," the district attorney concluded, and took his seat.

Defense attorney Solomon stood, and approached the podium facing the jury. "Good morning my friends, we're here today to determine the guilt or innocence of these two people, your neighbors, and, quite literally, their fate lies in your hands. We start proceedings today with facts, and that's what I will be presenting you with, throughout the course of this trial, facts. The district attorney, Mr. Roberts seems like a nice enough man. He's from your fair city, and I must say, this is indeed one of the most beautiful places on earth, and many would think this gives him sort of a home field advantage, and perhaps it does. Now in my case, I'm admittedly an outsider. I would love to have been born here, but that's just not the hand I was dealt. I'm what some of you refer to as a Yankee, but be that as it may, I have no doubt that you'll listen to the testimony that will be given here, and will be able to separate fact from fiction, based upon an impartial consideration of the evidence, and your own good judgment.

"Now, some of you are no doubt wondering, why has this Yankee lawyer come all the way out here from California to defend these two people? It's a logical question, and I want to answer it directly so that you can look beyond me, and my presence here, and cut straight to the facts. I believe these two people are innocent. That's the long and short of it. I've been fortunate, blessed in life. I don't deny it, but like many of you, I've worked hard, and now, I feel like I need to give something back. If I didn't believe that these two people, Bill Toma, and Miss Olivia Dautery weren't absolutely innocent, I wouldn't be here.

"They are, what some people might consider to be peculiar, that is, despite their family history and pedigree, they don't seem to fit in with the image some people of this city wish to put forth. Some might even call them an embarrassment, based upon their appearance and lifestyle, and yet this is America, and we have the right to dress and live as we please, and aren't we glad for that freedom?

"Now let's start with the reason we're here today in the first place. The fact is that Miss Murdock is dead, that she was murdered. She didn't die peacefully in her sleep of old age, but was robbed and murdered in her own home. That's a fact, a matter of record upon which we all agree. The next fact, upon which we can all agree is that this crime, murder, is the worst, the most despicable criminal act possible, the intentional taking of another person's life, in cold blood. It's bad enough to be robbed in one's own home, but to be murdered on top of that, to lose one's life by violence is horrible. It's also true that someone committed this crime. Miss Murdock was murdered by somebody.

"Mr. Roberts over there, believes that the two defendants are responsible for the death of Miss Murdock, and he will attempt to persuade you that they killed her. Now Mr. Roberts is not a bad man, he's just mistaken. There were, in fact, many people who could have killed Miss Murdock, and one of them did, but it wasn't Bill Toma or Olivia Dautery. All they've ever done is to attempt to live in peace. I am passionate about these two, I admit it, but I…" he paused for effect, "I know innocence when I see it, and these two people have done nothing. You've often heard that the truth will set you free. The truth will indeed set the defendants, your neighbors, free. I thank you again for your service." Solomon returned to his seat and Bill Roberts rose to begin the prosecution's case in chief.

"The prosecution calls as its first witness, Sgt. Bob Farrel." Farrel was sworn in and seated in the witness box. "Where were you on the night of Thursday, August 2, of last year Sgt. Farrel?"

"I was the officer on duty at the police station that night."

"Who else was there?"

"Several officers were also there who were off duty, including

Gary…I mean, Chief Bowman, yourself, and your brother from California, as well as Sgt. Davis, who was also on duty, and several other officers on duty."

"Can you tell the court what happened that night?"

"It was a typical summer Thursday night. It was hot outside. Several of us were at the station passing time and shooting the breeze. At around 8:00, or near that time, Sgt. Taylor brought in Rabbit Poteet and another man, from Port Gibson, I believe, who'd been involved in a minor altercation behind Fat's Chicken Shack. They'd calmed down and were released. Sgt. Taylor took Poteet back to his house in his squad car."

"And then what happened?"

"Well, at 9:05 p.m., the phone rang, and I answered it. It was Mr. Delgado calling. He said that he was at Miss Murdock's house, Eldorado and that there had been a murder, he thought."

"What do you mean, `he thought?'"

"He said that there was blood at the scene but that there was no body, that she was missing, and that we should get over there right away."

"And what did you do then?"

"I told him to stay put, and not to touch anything, that we'd be right over. I then handed the phone to Chief Bowman, who spoke to Mr. Delgado briefly, and then we loaded up and went over to Eldorado."

"Who all went to Eldorado?"

"I drove a squad car, and Walter Smith rode with me. Chief Bowman, yourself, and your brother, rode in the chief's car. Upon the chief's orders I stationed a patrol car at each end of the street to keep traffic from coming into the area. The street was secured immediately. I was stationed outside the victim's house to see that nobody entered. You, Chief Bowman, and your brother, entered the residence along with Mr. Delgado, who'd been standing on the porch when we arrived."

"No further questions, Your Honor."

"You may cross examine the witness," Judge Brock directed the defense.

"Sgt. Farrel," Solomon said, standing, and looking at a sheet of paper to be sure he had the witness's name right, "you say that the phone call from Mr. Delgado was at 9:05. How can you be sure about the time?"

"Well, anytime I answer the phone, I always look up at the clock on the wall and note the time, just in case the call turns out to be important, as it was in this case. It's a habit."

"No further questions, Your Honor."

"The prosecution calls Chief Gary Bowman." Bowman was sworn in and seated in the witness box. "Chief Bowman, would you please give the court some of the highlights of your history in law enforcement?"

"I've been the Chief or Police in Halcyon for eight years now, but before that I was the head of security for Pelgram industries for five years, and prior to that I was a homicide detective in Jackson, Mississippi for nearly a decade. My formal…"

"You have a degree in criminology from Mississippi State, is that correct?"

"Yes."

"Your Honor," defense attorney Solomon interrupted as he rose, "the defense will stipulate that Chief Bowman is an expert witness."

"Very well," the district attorney continued, "how many murders would you say you've investigatedin your career as a homicide detective? Approximately?"

"Several dozen, at least."

"Thank you. Now tell the court what you found on the night of the murder when you arrived at Eldorado."

"I arrived at Eldorado in my car along with yourself and your brother, at approximately 9:10 p.m. Mr. Delgado was standing on the front porch, smoking a cigarette, and waiting for us. He told us that he'd arrived at 9:00, as usual, and found the front door unlocked and most of the house lights on, but that Miss Murdock wasn't anywhere to be found. He showed us the blood which he'd discovered in the house as well as on the back porch and the driveway. He was concerned about Miss Murdock and felt that she'd met with violence."

"Why would he have thought that?"

"Because there was a substantial amount of blood, as well as a bullet hole in the wall and another in a window frame, consistent with a shooting. His concern was justified, given the scene."

"In your opinion, as the Chief or Police, did you think at this point that there had been a murder?"

"Objection, Your Honor," Solomon shouted, "this calls for a conclusion on the part of the witness."

"I'm going to allow the witness to answer the question. As the Chief of Police, he's expected to draw conclusions from evidence at hand. Proceed."

"Yes, there was no question in my mind that there had been a murder, even though there was no body at the scene of the shooting, and one wasn't immediately located."

"Did you express this opinion to those present?"

"No, I didn't."

"And why is that?"

"Opinions are frequently superseded d by facts, and given the fact that Mr.Delgado was generally regarded as Miss Murdock's closest relative, I thought it best not to discourage him if there was the possibility that she might still be found alive."

"Now Chief Bowman, you visited the defendants on August 2, last year, the night of the murder, at their house at Cypress Hill, questioned them, and took them to the station for further questioning. They were held and subsequently charged with the murder of Miss Murdock. You returned to Cypress Hill with a search warrant later, accompanied by Sgt. Carl Draper, did you not?"

"Yes, I did."

"The defendants were in custody at the time, is that correct?"

"Yes, they were."

"Precisely what were you searching for at that time Chief Bowman?"

"Any evidence which might have some bearing on the crime."

"And will you tell the court what you found?"

"Sgt. Draper and I found ourselves in a very dangerous situation considering the condition of the property. There were boards missing on the porch, wagon wheels lying on their sides, exposed nails, broken glass, and animals wandering about in and out of the house. It was unsanitary in the extreme…"

"Objection."

"Overruled. The witness may continue."

"The place was absolutely filthy, with roaches and mice running across the floor. There was clutter, litter, and garbage everywhere."

"But you did manage to find two guns did you not?"

"Yes, we found a nickel-plated .32 caliber Smith & Wesson pistol, and a model 1911 Colt .45 pistol."

"Your Honor, the prosecution would like to introduce these two items into evidence at this time as exhibits 1 and 2. I show you this .32 caliber pistol, Chief Bowman, and ask you now if it was one of the pistols you discovered at Cypress Hill on the night of the murder?"

"Yes, it has my mark."

"What happened with the two pistols you and Sgt. Draper found at Cypress Hill?"

"They were both sent to the MBI crime lab in Jackson. This .32

was determined through ballistics tests to have been the murder weapon."

"The weapon you found at Cypress Hill, the defendants' house on the night of the murder is the murder weapon?" Roberts asked loudly, as he faced the jury.

"Yes, this .32 Smith & Wesson is the murder weapon."

"Thank you. No further questions your honor."

"You may cross examine Mr. Solomon."

"Tell me, Chief Bowman," Solomon asked, "you say that you arrived at Eldorado and found Mr. Delgado there, casually smoking a cigarette, and that he showed you what he'd found, including multiple bullet holes inside the house, is that correct?"

"I did not use the word `casually.' I said that Mr. Delgado was standing on the porch smoking a cigarette when we arrived. Yes, there was a bullet hole in a bedroom wall and a .32 caliber bullet lodged in a window frame, which he'd discovered."

"Well, how would you describe Mr. Delgado's demeanor? Did he appear calm to you, or agitated?"

"He was neither."

"Come now, Chief Bowman, surely he must have been one or the other, given the circumstances."

"Objection," Roberts shouted. "Counsel is leading the witness."

"I withdraw the question, Your Honor. Now, Chief Bowman, would you consider that the crime scene was properly secured?"

"Yes, I would."

"You were more concerned with finding Miss Murdock than you were with finding the killer. Is that safe to say?"

"No, I wouldn't say that was the case. Although I said nothing to Mr. Delgado at the time, I'd concluded, as I've already testified, that based upon my own past experience, that is, given the presence of the amount of blood at the scene, Miss Murdock was already dead, even though her body wasn't on the premises."

"So who exactly was in the house initially? On the night of the murder? Mr. Delgado, yourself, the district attorney, and his brother, Tom Roberts, is that correct?"

"Yes."

"Did you consider Mr. Delgado to be a suspect?"

"No, there was no reason to. He'd said that…."

"Let me continue.Why didn't you consider Mr. Delgado to be a suspect?"

"Well, he just wasn't, there was no reason that… I mean…he and Miss Murdock…."

"In other words, Chief Bowman, based upon Mr. Delgado's statements atthe time, you'd already concluded that the defendants were the prime suspects, and did not feel it necessary to follow the basic standard police procedure that would apply in the investigation of any murder case," Solomon sneered.

"Well…I…"

"Did you perform a gunshot residue test on Mr. Delgado?"

"No, I didn't."

"Wouldn't it have been prudent to perform a gunpowder residue test on Mr. Delgado? Isn't it possible that Mr. Delgado could have killed her?"

"He wasn't a suspect," Chief Bowman repeated.

Solomon stepped back from the witness stand and approached the jury, turned again to Chief Bowman, and said, "Since Mr. Delgado was the only person at the scene of the crime, it would seem obvious even to a layman, that there should've, as a matter of standard police procedure, been a gunshot residue test performed on him, just as a matter of course. Wouldn't you agree?"

"Mr. Delgado was never a suspect, at any time, but technically, yes. If I had to do it over, I would have checked him for gunshot residue, as a procedural matter, not that it would've proved anything."

"Quite the contrary, it might have proved, beyond reasonable doubt that he had not fired the shots which killed Miss Murdock. I'm merely saying that there was an obvious rush to judgment on the part of law enforcement to pin the blame on the defendants, and that there was no attempt... there was no intention to look elsewhere, to even consider any other possibilities. This is bad police work. By your own admission, you were careless, even reckless in not testing Mr. Delgado for gunshot residue.

"Did you search his person?"

"Again, he wasn't a suspect."

"His car? His residence?"

"No. I repeat. He wasn't a suspect."

"I ask you Chief Bowman, in front of this jury of your peers if you consider that to have been proper criminal investigation?"

"Mr. Delgado was not a suspect. There was no reason to investigate him."

"Your honor, I move for a dismissal of the charges against the defendants, and that they be released at once," Solomon petitioned the judge.

"Counsel, approach the bench, both of you," the judge demanded. "Mr. Solomon, I'll grant that this oversight was an error on the part of Chief Bowman, however, Mr. Delgado is not the defendant in this case. A grand jury has handed down an indictment according to the laws of this state, and I'm not prepared to end the trial this at this juncture. I'll allow the prosecution to proceed with the presentation of its evidence. Mr. Solomon, you may continue."

"Regarding the guns found at the home of the defendants by yourself and Sgt. Draper, that night, it would appear that from the cluttered conditions you've described that it would have been extremely difficult to have found any evidence of any sort at Cypress Hill, and yet you easily managed to find two pistols. Where were they?"

"They were sticking out from under a rug near the front door."

"In plain sight?"

"They weren't in plain sight, and in the darkness, nobody could have seen them."

"But you and Sgt. Draper found them easily enough. With all the mess, disorder, and disarray that you've described in that house, doesn't it seem strange to you that the guns were so easy to find? In other words, Chief Bowman, if the defendants were seeking to conceal the murder weapon wouldn't it have been likely that they would have, given their intimate knowledge of that house, been able to find a more secure location in which to hide them?"

"Objection."

"Overruled."

"Was the front door at Cypress Hill locked when you arrived?"

"No."

"Were any of the doors in or out of the house locked?"

"Not to my knowledge."

"In other words, Chief Bowman, nearly anyone could have wandered into that house, and placed the pistols there, isn't that so? As the defendants were being detained at the police station, practically anyone could have placed the murder weapon in that house, couldn't they?"

"I suppose it's possible, but there was a patrol car parked in front of the house, so it's doubtful."

"Were the lights on inside the house while the patrol car was parked outside?"

"No, I don't believe so."

"Were the lights on inside the house when you and Sgt. Draper arrived to search the house later that night?"

"No."

"So, Chief Bowman, while the defendants were being detained at the station, their house was unsecured. Is that right?"

“There was an officer parked in front of the house with his light bar on.”

“Was he patrolling the perimeter, or just sitting in his car?”

“He was in his car.”

“In his car. I see. How many doors are there in Cypress Hill, on the first floorthat someone could have entered the house through? Three? Four? Five?”

“I don’t know,” the chief replied.

“For your information Chief Bowman, Cypress Hill has seven doors to the inside, and from the patrol car it would have been impossible to see more than one of them. No further questions Your Honor,” Solomon stated, and returned to the defense table.

“Redirect?”

“No, Your Honor.The prosecution now calls Mark Delgado.” Delgado was sworn in and seated in the witness box. “State your name for the court.”

“Mark Delgado.”

“Mr. Delgado, what was your relationship to Miss Jeannie Murdock?”

“She was my first cousin.”

“Does that make her your closest living relative?”

“Yes.”

“She was also your best friend, wasn’t she? Would that be an accurate statement?”

“Yes, it would.”

“It would also be accurate to state that she…that you probably knew her better than anyone, isn’t that so?”

“Yes.”

“Mr. Delgado, was it unusual for Miss Murdock’s door to be unlocked?”

“She never left her door unlocked, given the fact that she was afraid of the neighbors,” he said, pointing directly at the defendants.

"I object," Solomon shouted.

"Sustained. The witness will confine his answers specifically to the District Attorney's question, and refrain from any additional embellishment."

"Very well," Delgado replied, casting a dismissive glance at the judge. "Miss Murdock's doors were always locked, without exception. Whenever she left the house, even to go to the garage, or to get her mail, she always locked the door behind her, and carried her key with her, a prudent course of action, given her circumstances," he observed, looking first at the jury, and then nodding in the direction of the defendants.

"Mr. Delgado," the D.A. continued, "Would you please tell the court your activities on the day of the murder, up until the police arrived at Miss Murdock's house?"

"Well, I was up at around 8:30 a.m., dressed and ate breakfast. My maid Chantelle was already there, having arrived, as usual at 8:00 am, and let herself in with her key. I retired to the library where I read until approximately noon. It was impossible to remain focused given the noise of the lawnmower outside, since the yardman was mowing my lawn. I got into my car and proceeded to the The Kitchen at Lady of the Lake, where I ate lunch. After that, I went to the main post office and retrieved a package I'd been sent from New York which contained some cigarettes I'd ordered. I then drove to the Exxon station and had my car washed and polished. After that, I returned home, read the paper, ate dinner, and then left for Miss Murdock's at around 8:55."

"How can you be so certain about the time? Did you visit Miss Murdock every day?"

"Yes. I visited her every evening at 9:00, stayed for one or two hours, and went home."

"Was there ever any variation in your schedule?"

"Certainly. If either of us didn't feel like getting together we'd call and put it off until the following day, but this was rare. On Saturdays and Sundays, I'd have lunch over there and stay the afternoon, or we would upon occasion, have lunch or dinner out. Sometimes we'd drive to Jackson for the day, or even to Walnut Hills in Vicksburg, or the Carriage House in Natchez, although that was infrequent. But that was, generally speaking, the schedule on weekdays, her house at 9:00 p.m., punctually."

"On the night in question, the night of the murder, you arrived at 9:00 p.m., as usual, is that correct, Mr. Delgado?"

"Yes."

"Would you please tell the court what happened then?"

"I parked in the driveway in front of the house, where I always parked. I ascended the steps and knocked on the door. As soon as I knocked, the door swung open slightly, indicating that the door was unlocked. I opened it the rest of the way and stepped in, calling for Miss Murdock. There was no answer. I stepped into the front room, fully into the house. I was immediately assailed by a strange and pervasive smell, which I recognized as gunpowder. I noticed blood on the floor in the dining room, a blood trail from the dining room to the bedroom, and out to the back door, which was also unlocked and open. There was more blood on the side gallery steps, with a larger pool of blood at the base of the first step."

"Your Honor, I move that this architectural diagram of the house be placed in exhibit. Mr. Wiltz, if you please." A line diagram of Miss Murdock's house appeared on a large screen to the left of the bench.

"Mr. Delgado, please continue."

"I followed the blood out onto the side gallery and downstairs into the driveway. At that point there was no further blood that I could see. It was dark outside, that is, beyond the driveway and there are no street lights, just that one pole-mounted security light across the driveway by the side of the house. I immediately returned to the house and called the police station."

"In other words, you quickly searched the house for Miss Murdock, did not find her, and then immediately called the police. Is that correct?"

"Yes, I called the police."

"And then what did you do?"

"I searched the house again, entering each room and calling for her, but she wasn't there. I concluded that she'd been abducted or kidnapped, although given the presence of that much blood, I feared the worst."

"You mean you feared that she was already dead."

"Yes, I thought that she was dead."

"Mr. Delgado, did you think that there'd been a robbery?"

"I object," Solomon shouted. "It calls for a conclusion on the part of the witness."

"Let me rephrase the question. Did you notice anything missing?"

"Not at that point. I was more concerned with finding Miss Murdock, wherever she was."

"Was it subsequently determined that her jewelry box was missing?"

"Yes, she had a small security box which she kept under her bed, which was later discovered to be missing."

"Were you aware of the contents of that box?"

"Objection! Your honor…"

"It's a yes or no question. You may answer the question Mr. Delgado."

"Yes, I was familiar with the contents of the box."

"Would you describe the box and its contents for the court, Mr. Delgado?"

"The box was rectangular and approximately 14" long, 12" wide, that is, if viewed from the end, and probably 8" deep. It was rosewood and had a lock on the front surface, to which Miss

Murdock had the key, which she always kept around her neck."

"What did the box contain?"

"Jewelry, mainly, as she kept her valuable papers in a safe deposit box at the bank."

"Would you say that the contents of the box were valuable?"

"Objection! The witness is not a jeweler," Solomon shouted.

"Sustained."

"The box contained several large diamond rings," Mr. Delgado replied, ignoring Mr. Solomon's objection, "as well as a half dozen antique rose gold pocket watches, several heavy, multi-strand diamond necklaces, earrings, various large ruby, emerald, and sapphire rings, and bracelets, that I knew of. These were family heirlooms which she treasured. Some of them had belonged to her mother and grandmother."

"Why would she keep these valuable items in a box under her bed?"

"Objection!" Solomon shouted. "This calls for a conclusion."

"She kept them under the bed," Delgado answered, not waiting for the judge to respond to the defense attorney's objection, "because she frequently wore them around the house, and she enjoyed getting them out and admiring them. They were too valuable to wear in public, and she enjoyed looking at them. And sir, do not interrupt me again!" the witness replied, directing a cold glance at Mr. Solomon. "Do you understand me?"

"Your objection is overruled, Mr. Solomon, and Mr. Delgado," the judge ordered. "You are not to address anyone in court unless I instruct you to do so. You will confine your answers solely to the questions asked. Is that clear?"

"Yes, Your Honor."

"Continue, General Roberts."

"What's the value of the contents of that box?"

"Objection! Your honor, the prosecution is again calling for conclusions on the part of the witness and…"

"Your Honor," the D.A. interjected, "the prosecution is attempting to prove that this homicide was the result of a robbery. We are seeking to establish that there was ample motive for robbery based upon the value of the contents of the missing box."

"Yes, Your Honor," Solomon replied, "but unless the witness is qualified as an estate jewelry appraiser…."

"Mr. Solomon, I'm going to allow the prosecution to pursue this line of inquiry to establish motive. You may continue General Roberts."

"Mr. Delgado do you know the value of that box's contents?"

"I can't say specifically, but I know that her jewelry was insured for around $1 million by some company in New York, and that she kept all of her favorite jewelry in that box."

"Your Honor, I submit this insurance policy to the court for exhibit. It contains a list of the jewelry covered by the policy, which was issued by Manheim Trust Mutual Insurance in New York, showing Miss Murdock as beneficiary. The amount of the policy is $1,250,000. Now Mr. Delgado, let's continue. Would you consider that amount to be a sufficient motive for robbery? Or murder?"

"Yes, I would."

Tom Roberts expected his friend Solomon to object to the last question and was surprised when he didn't. Apparently, Solomon was going to let the D.A. establish robbery as the motive for the murder. He couldn't see how that benefited the defendants.

"I'm going to change the subject now Mr. Delgado. The defendants are known to you, is that correct?"

"Yes."

"How long have you known them?"

"A long time."

"Can you qualify that? Ten years? Twenty years? Longer than that?"

"More than twenty years."

"Were you and the defendants formerly friends?"

"We weren't friends, per se, but we did travel in the same social circles, and were frequently in each other's company, although these arrangements were always undertaken by Miss Murdock."

"Were the defendants frequent guests at your house?"

"No, I lived with my mother until her death, at Oakmont, and she did not wish tobe disturbed by visitors. Most gatherings took place at Miss Murdock's former house, Marble Hall, but yes, the defendants were frequent visitors, among others."

"So, you were at one time on good terms with them, is that correct?"

"Yes, they were generally pleasant enough, and we enjoyed their company, as there were so few of us left."

"Few of whom?"

"Persons of our class."

"I see. At some point, the relationship between the four of you took a turn for the worse, is that right?"

"Yes, you could say that."

"Was there any single incident which caused that to occur, or was it more of a gradual disintegration?"

"Things were fine until Jeannie, that is, Miss Murdock sold Marble Hall and moved to Eldorado. Eldorado was a much smaller house than Marble Hall. At that point Miss Murdock more or less stopped entertaining, although the defendants would come by Eldorado for tea or a cocktail from time to time. Everything was fine between all of us until Bill Toma moved into Cypress Hill."

"Your honor, I again refer to the third exhibit. Mr. Wiltz, if you please. This aerial map on the screen over there shows the proximity of Miss Murdock's house, Eldorado, in relationship to Mr. Toma's house, Cypress Hill. There would seem to me to be enough land between the two houses that there should've been no problem, at least in terms of their physical separation. What happened?"

"To be explicit, Miss Dautery began dropping in on Miss Murdock unexpectedly, and frequently, without having been invited, presuming upon a familiarity which did not exist...well, it existed, but not to the extent that Miss Murdock ever wanted anyone dropping by unannounced, without phoning first, to make certain that it was convenient. Miss Murdock was courteous and cordial, initially, but at length the visits by Miss Dautery became a nuisance, and she asked Miss Dautery to call first, rather than just dropping by uninvited. Miss Dautery reacted with hostility, apparently incensed at what she interpreted to have been some sort of `high-hatting' or personal slight on the part of Jeannie, that is, Miss Murdock."

"In other words, she felt like she had been snubbed by Miss Murdock?"

"Yes, although that hadn't been Miss Murdock's intention at all. She'd merely asked Miss Dautery to call before coming over, in case Miss Murdock might be otherwise occupied. There had been no intent whatsoever to offend Miss Dautery, but after that, from that point forward, Miss Dautery refused to speak to Miss Murdock, or to acknowledge her, even if they encountered each other in public."

"Had the decedent done anything else which might have offended either of the defendants?"

"Absolutely not."

"So, what had actually been merely a misunderstanding, a misinterpretation, was construed, or I should say, misconstrued by Miss Dautery to have been an overt act of hostility, if not actually aggression."

"Objection!" Solomon shouted. "The witness has already stated that it was a misunderstanding."

"Sustained."

"Yes, but there was no real, tangible, reason for Miss Dautery's overreaction whatsoever."

"If that had been all there was to it, it would seem that there was no reason that Miss Murdock and the defendants could not live in peace with each other, even if in silence, so there must have been more," the D.A. observed. "Was there something else?"

"Yes, it came back to Miss Murdock that the defendants, specifically Miss Dautery, had been speaking ill of her."

"Objection. Hearsay, your honor."

"Sustained. The jury will disregard Mr. Delgado's answer."

"Was there anything more?"

"They began letting Cypress Hill basically fall down."

"By `they,' you mean the defendants, the owners of Cypress Hill. Is that correct Mr. Delgado?"

"Yes. Cypress Hill was one of the most beautiful homes in Halcyon, that is, it was until Bill and Olivia, that is, until the defendants moved over there."

"And when was that?"

"Approximately twenty years ago, maybe less."

"How did they let the place `fall down,' as you put it?"

"They began to fill the yard with refuse, old tires, rusty car wheels, empty bottles and Coke cans. I don't know where they managed to find that junk, but find it they did. There were old wagon wheels, saw horses, bits of scrap wood and metal, car parts, rusty bicycles, basically trash. God knows what they wanted with that garbage. They put that sort of refuse mainly on the front porch, in plain sight. The house needed a coat of paint, which it never received, and railing on the front gallery began to rot and detach. They'd leave the rails just suspended there, neither repairing nor removing them, until they eventually fell down by their own weight. Window sashes simply disappeared. There one day, gone the next. Who knows where or why? Basically, the house started to disintegrate the day they moved in."

"They kept the yard mowed, didn't they?"

"They did at first. Your brother, Tom Roberts, used to mow their lawn at the same time that he mowed Miss Murdock's. When he went away to school Miss Murdock got a new yardman, the defendants did not."

"In other words, the defendants' house, Cypress Hill, began to fall into disrepair, becoming increasingly dilapidated with every passing year. Is that correct?"

"Yes, it grew worse with each passing year, at first, but I would say that the destruction ultimately became month to month, rather than year to year."

"And why was that, Mr. Delgado?"

"Because they," he said, pointing to the defendants, "began acquiring animals."

"What kind of animals? Dogs? Cats?"

"Yes, cats. All crazy people start with cats."

"Objection!"

"Mr. Delgado, you are instructed to answer counsel's questions. Confine your answers to the questions, without embellishment. You may proceed General Roberts."

"So the defendants began getting animals. Were there animals besides cats and dogs?"

"Cats, dogs, geese, goats, hogs, chickens, cattle, and an abundance of cockroaches, mice, rats, and God knows what else," Delgado replied disdainfully, with a dismissive flourish of his hand in the direction of the defendants, as the courtroom audience erupted in subdued laughter.

"And why was this a problem?"

"Objection! Calls for a conclusion."

"Your Honor, the state intends to establish motive. It's a matter of record that the decedent filed a complaint on April 14, last year with the police department," Roberts stated, holding aloft a copy of the police report. "Mr. Delgado is listed on the complaint as is the decedent. Therefore, he is qualified to answer."

"Overruled. I'm going to allow the state to continue along this line. Do you wish to introduce that police report now?"

"The prosecution intends to question the officer who took the report, but, yes, Your Honor, this is as good a time as any," Roberts replied, handing the document to the judge, who looked at it briefly and passed it to the woman seated at a small desk to his right.

"The problem was that the defendants allowed their animals to roam the neighborhood freely, and their goats and hogs destroyed Miss Murdock's expensive shrubbery, flowering plants, and garden, uprooting eating, and trampling them."

"You did in fact, contact the defendants, did you not, Mr. Delgado, on behalf of Miss Murdock, and ask them to kindly keep their animals on their own property?"

"Yes, I called them on several occasions by telephone, visited them more than once at Cypress Hill, and asked them politely to please keep their animals on their own property."

"This was prior to the filing of a formal complaint. How did they respond to these requests?"

"From the outset, Miss Dautery displayed a hostile and dismissive attitude, basically indicating…well, at first, she denied that her animals had strayed from Cypress Hill, and said that any possible damage had no doubt been the result of somebody else's animals, that is, if any damage had actually occurred."

"Mr. Delgado, I direct your attention, and that of the jurors, to the aerial photo on the screen over there at the front of the courtroom. Are there any other houses on Cypress Hill Lane other than the defendants' house, Cypress Hill, and Miss Murdock's house, Eldorado?"

"No, those are the only two properties on the street."

"Are there any other houses nearby, on adjacent streets or properties, from which animals such as goats or hogs could have ventured onto Miss Murdock's property?"

"Absolutely not. No other houses in the neighborhood had animals other than cats and dogs. The goats and hogs clearly came from Cypress Hill."

"Your Honor, I submit this photo as the prosecution's next exhibit.Mr. Delgado, let me continue. If you will again turn your attention to the screen. Mr. Wiltz, if you please. Mr. Delgado, please tell the court what you see, and can you identify it?"

"It is a photo of Miss Murdock's car, or rather what's left of it."

"Do you see any damage to the car in the photograph which was caused by the defendants' goats?"

"Objection."

"Mr. Solomon, I'm going to allow the witness to answer the question since damage to Miss Murdock's car was part of the original complaint, and because the witness is listed on that complaint along with Miss Murdock. You may answer the question Mr. Delgado."

"The car has an aluminum hood, and trunk, which you may clearly see here, have been dented by the hooves of the defendants' goats."

"What kind of car is this Mr. Delgado?"

"It was, and I emphasize was, an Aston Martin Lagonda."

"Would it be accurate to suggest that it would be expensive to repair the damage to the car caused by the defendants' goats?"

"Expensive is a relative term."

"Would you, yourself, personally consider the repair to be expensive?"

"Yes, I would, although I couldn't speculate what it would actually cost in this instance. I know first-hand that previous repairs to that car were expensive. The damage caused by the goats made the car unusable. The goats ruined it altogether. I don't think the car could be repaired at all now."

"Your Honor, at this time I wish to introduce these receipts for landscaping at Eldorado as exhibits," the district attorney said, handing the receipts to the judge.

"Mr. Delgado, you were very much involved in Miss Murdock's day to day life, including her business affairs, is that correct?"

"Yes, I handled many of her day to day matters."

"These receipts for landscaping in May of last year were the result of what?"

"Objection!"

"Overruled. Answer the question Mr. Delgado."

"This was...it was necessary to have a professional team of landscapers come from Jackson to clean up the mess caused by the foraging and rampaging hogs and goats from Cypress Hill. The goats had literally eaten many of Miss Murdock's flowering plants down to the ground, stripped them of any flowers and leaves, essentially killing them. The hogs, as if in league with the goats, uprooted many of her prized boxwoods and other shrubbery."

"How often did these landscapers have to come to her house to repair the damage caused by the defendants' rampaging animals coming over to Miss Murdock's from Cypress Hill?"

"I'm not sure, frequently over a period of several weeks."

"Was this work expensive?"

"You have the receipts there, you...yes, the work was expensive, but I don't remember an exact amount, what it was, how much it cost."

"Well, let me refresh your memory. One of these receipts from this past May is for $2,700. Here is a second receipt from the same company for $1,700. Also from May. That's $4,400. That's a lot of money for replanting a garden. Was that the end of the matter?"

"It should have been, but no, it wasn't. It was incessant. Toma and Dautery had no regard for boundaries, private property rights, or proper deportment."

"Would you say they were bad neighbors?"

"Objection!"

"Overruled. Mr. Solomon, I'm going to allow this line of questioning. Answer the question Mr. Delgado."

"They weren't neighbors at all, but rather hostile antagonists."

"In light of the ongoing problems with the defendants, did you have any recommendations for Miss Murdock in terms of a solution to the situation?"

"Yes, I suggested that we, that she, buy a professionally trained police dog to keep the foraging animals at bay."

"No further questions, Your Honor."

"Defense?"

"Yes, Your Honor," Solomon, replied as he rose and proceeded to the witness stand. "Were the defendants personally hostile to you, or merely to Miss Murdock?"

"I object, Your Honor. Hearsay."

"Mr. Roberts, it is a matter of police record that Miss Murdock complained about the defendants. However, Mr. Delgado can't answer for the decedent. He may answer the question solely as it pertains to himself. Answer the question Mr. Delgado."

"Yes, Your Honor. On the times that I complained to the defendants, I was speaking specifically to Miss Dautery, the brains of the operation, if I may use the word `brains' in any context with regard to either of the defendants. I would certainly say that she was openly hostile to me. Yes."

"Mr. Delgado," Judge Brock interrupted, "this is the third time I've had to instruct you to answer the questions you've been asked without embellishment or speculation. You will confine your answers specifically to the questions asked. Now, Mr. Delgado, answer the question."

"Yes, Your Honor. Miss Dautery was hostile to me."

"Was this before or after you attempted to evict them from their own house and have them thrownonto the street?" Solomon asked loudly.

"I object to this Your Honor."

"I withdraw the question. Now, Mr. Delgado, you told the court that Miss Murdock never left her door unlocked, but that her door was unlocked when you arrived on the night of her death. Is that correct?"

"Yes, she…"

"Was her door unlocked when you arrived on the night in question? Yes or no?"

"Yes."

"So, since her door had not been forced, it appears that she did leave her door unlocked. Thank you. Do you have a key to Miss Murdock's house?"

"Yes."

"To your knowledge, does anyone else have a key to Miss Murdock's house?"

"No, not to my knowledge, other than her maid, Hattie."

"Now, Mr. Delgado, you further testified under oath, that goats from the defendants' house had destroyed Miss Delgado's car and made it unusable? Is that correct?"

"Yes, that's what I said."

"Would you like to amend your statements regarding the car Mr. Delgado?"

"No, the photographs clearly show the damage caused by the goats from Cypress Hill. I stand by what I said."

"Isn't it true that Miss Murdock had already abandoned the use of her car in favor of a bicycle?"

"No, she used a bicycle on occasion, but kept her car in good order."

"I think you must be mistaken Mr. Delgado."

"I'm never mistaken about anything, sir."

"It would seem that, in this instance, that you are mistaken Mr. Delgado, either that, or you are deliberately seeking to mislead this court. According to state records, the registration on that car expired eight years ago in June and was not renewed. Obviously the car had mechanical issues which made it unusable as opposed, to merely cosmetic ones allegedly caused by rampaging animals."

"Well..."

"We'll just accept that you are simply mistaken, rather than intentionally attempting to deceive the court Mr. Delgado, but let's continue. You have indicated by your testimony that you and Miss Murdock were best friends, and more or less inseparable, would that be an apt description of your friendship?"

"I said that we were best friends."

"Yes, Mr. Delgado, you did. You also stated that you handled many of her day to day affairs, is that correct?"

"Yes. What about it?"

"Then you must have been aware of the terms and conditions of her will. Is that correct?"

"No, I wasn't aware of her will until after her death...murder."

"Who stood to benefit financially from her death?"

"Objection. Your Honor, this...."

"Sustained."

"I withdraw the question. Mr. Delgado, as the sole heir of the decedent, you did in fact benefit financially from her death."

"Objection. Your Honor..."

"Your Honor, it is a fact that Mr. Delgado, as the sole heir of the decedent did, indeed benefit greatly financially from her death. That's a matter of public record."

"Overruled. Continue Mr. Solomon."

"What was Miss Murdock's estate worth? How much did you inherit Mr. Delgado?"

"I don't know an exact amount. There were stock certificates, some land and a house in Louisiana, a building in New York somewhere…I really don't know. It was a substantial amount, if that's what you're seeking to establish."

"Would you say $15 million would be a close approximation?"

"I really wouldn't know. You should probably check with her attorney and her accountant. I don't know."

"Well Mr. Delgado, if I'd just inherited somewhere in the neighborhood of $15 million, I believe I'd know a little bit more about it. But since it doesn't seem like that much money to you, I guess the court can understand that you wouldn't necessarily know an exact figure, so in light of that, and I won't hold you to it, but as an approximation, would $15 million sound about right?"

"Yes."

"Objection. Your Honor, Mr. Delgado is not on trial in this court, the defendants are. This entire line of questioning has nothing whatsoever to do with either the facts in evidence, or Mr. Solomon's defense of his clients."

"Mr. Solomon, where are you going with this line of inquiry?"

"Your Honor, the prosecution introduced an insurance policy in the amount of $ 1.25 million, insuring the decedent's jewelry, attempting to establish a motive of robbery. Mr. Delgado was the beneficiary of that policy. Mr. Roberts has opened this door, and it is my intention to show that, if robbery was indeed a motive for the defendants, it could have equally been a motive for other persons, including Mr. Delgado. The defense acknowledges that Mr. Delgado is not on trial, but merely seeks to establish reasonable doubt, and if, as the prosecution contends, robbery was the main motive for the murder of Miss Murdock, there are other people who stood to benefit more from a robbery than either of the defendants."

"Mr. Roberts, since you introduced the insurance policy as evidence, and have posited robbery as the primary motive for the murder, Mr. Solomon will be allowed to question the witness about these matters."

"Thank you,Your Honor," Solomon continued. "Now Mr. Delgado, since you are the beneficiary of the insurance policy underwritten by Manheim Trust Mutual on Miss Murdock's missing jewelry, I ask you, have you been paid by the insurance company yet?"

"Yes, I have."

"And how much did you receive from the insurance company?"

"I can't recall."

"Well, let me refresh your memory. General Roberts entered into evidence a certified copy of that insurance policy valued at $1.25 million less than ten minutes ago. Is that the amount you received from the insurance company? Yes or no."

"I suppose it was."

"You suppose? You stated to the court under direct examination from General Roberts a few minutes ago that you considered robbery to be the underlying motive for Miss Murdock's murder, did you not? In other words, you felt that $1.25 million dollars was sufficient cause for robbery and murder, is that correct?"

"Yes."

"Miss Murdock's death then has enriched you by more than $16 million. Mr. Delgado, following that line of thought, would you consider $16 million to be sufficient cause for robbery and murder?"

"I object!" The D.A. shouted as Mark Delgado stood up in the witness box, his normally serene face contorted in anger at the implications suggested by the defense attorney.

"No further questions, Your Honor."

"Sit down Mr. Delgado. I order you to take your seat. Redirect, General Roberts?"

"No further questions, Your Honor," Roberts replied as Mark Delgado stepped down from the witness box, and in passing the defense table, cast an angry glance at Mark Solomon. Nikki Daniels remarked, "He doesn't look too happy with you."

"Like I should care, already. We came to town to shake things up," he replied. "I'm just getting started."

"It's getting close to noon," Judge Brock said, as he looked at his watch. "Court will recess for lunch now and will resume at 1:15."

The jury left the courtroom through the door by the judge's bench at the front of the courtroom, followed by the defendants. At precisely 1:15 Judge Brock resumed court.

"The prosecution calls Sgt. Stephen Davis," Roberts announced when court had resumed. Sgt. Davis approached the witness box, was sworn in and seated.

"Sgt. Davis, I call your attention to an aerial map of the crime scene, showing the house of the decedent, Eldorado, and its relation, to Cypress Hill, as well as the site where Miss Murdock's body was found. You can see that the property lines have been drawn on the map with a marker indicating the boundary between the Murdock property and that of the defendants. You were the first at the scene when Miss Murdock's body was found. Is that correct?"

"Yes, I found the body."

"What time was that?"

"It was around 5:30 a.m. Friday morning, perhaps 5:45."

"Please describe what you found."

"Miss Murdock's body was face up in a thicket of weeds and brambles."

"Would you describe the scene for the court?"

"There were blood stains on her clothing, and the weeds surrounding her had been trampled by whoever had placed her there. She'd obviously been there for quite awhile," Sgt. Davis concluded.

"Objection," Solomon shouted, "The witness is not a medical examiner or coroner, does not know how she arrived at the scene, or how long she'd been there."

"Sustained," the judge, agreed. "Sgt. Davis, please confine your answers to specifically what you observed."

"Yes, Your Honor."

"I repeat the question."

"Miss Murdock was lying on her back. She appeared to be fully clothed, although her feet were bare. Her legs were exposed below the knees. I observed that there were no scratches or cuts on her legs or feet of the type that would have occurred if she'd walked there from the house. The brush was flattened or depressed on both sides of her body. There was a path of sorts that had been created by whoever dragged or carried her body to that location."

"Objection," Solomon shouted.

"Your Honor," District Attorney Roberts called, addressing Judge Brock, "Sgt. Davis is reporting what he observed. Miss Murdock was not dropped there by a flying saucer. She was transported there by somebody."

"Your point is indeed well taken," General Roberts. "Objection overruled. Continue Sgt. Davis."

"I noticed that the weeds and brush, which were generally between three to five feet tall in the surrounding area had been recently flattened on the property between the edge of the house, that is, the driveway, and where I found the body."

"Can you show us on this map?" Roberts asked.

"Yes, this is where I found the body," Davis explained, using a pointer to indicate the spot on the map. "This entire area of several acres is overgrown with weeds, scrub brush, and thorns. The brush in the area leading from Eldorado which runs from the side of the driveway toward Cypress Hill has been disturbed, that is, knocked down. The weeds and brush are bent over leading from the driveway to the spot where I found her. The rest of the area except for that is overgrown and undisturbed."

"You mean that that stretch between the driveway of Eldorado and Cypress Hill is the only part of this large area that has been disturbed, that this disturbance of the foliage in this stretch is recent. Is that correct Sgt. Davis?"

"Objection, Your Honor," Solomon shouted.

"Answer the question," the judge instructed.

"There was no preexisting path or trail, if that's what you're asking."

"Sgt. Davis. If you would, please tell the court if the spot where the body was… where you found Miss Murdock's body, was on the property of Miss Murdock's house, Eldorado, or on that of Cypress Hill, the defendant's residence."

"It was here," Davis said, touching the pointer to the spot on the map indicating the location of the body. "It was on the defendants' property, not Miss Murdock's."

"But it was clearly on the defendants' property, Cypress Hill."

"Yes, it was on the defendants' property, Cypress Hill."

"Thank you. No further questions, Your Honor."

Solomon's assistant Nikki Daniels stood and approached the witness. "Sgt. Davis, how long have you been on the police force in Halcyon, Mississippi?"

"Almost seven years."

"How many murders have you investigated during that period of time? More specifically, how many other bodies have you discovered, other than Miss Murdock's, during the course of your work in Black County?"

"None. Hers is the first body I've ever found."

"How was the body transported to that location?"

"I'd say it was carried there."

"Looking at the diagram again, how far would you estimate the body of Miss Murdock to have been carried?"

"I'd estimate the distance to be around three hundred feet, more or less."

"That would be a good guess Sgt. Davis. The actual distance as measured was three hundred and twenty-seven feet, to be precise. Would you also say that whoever carried it, that is, whoever moved the body from the actual site of the shooting would have to have been fairly strong?"

"Yes."

"You seem like you are pretty strong yourself, Sgt. Davis. How tall are you?"

"Right at six feet."

"Do you lift weights?"

"Objection," the D.A. shouted. "I don't see that whether or not Sgt. Davis lifts weights, or that his height has any relevance to the location of the body on the property at Cypress Hill."

"Overruled. The court is going to allow the defense the same latitude it granted the prosecution. Sgt. Davis may answer the question."

"Yes, I work out regularly."

"Theoretically speaking, then Sgt. Davis, would you have been able to move a body of that weight and size that distance through brush that high in what was on the night of the murder, basically total darkness?"

"It would have been possible inasmuch as someone did transport the body that distance under those circumstances, but it would've been difficult, even for me, and I can bench press 180 lbs."

"I see. Following that reasoning, and in your opinion as a professional law enforcement official, would it have been possible for a woman just slightly over five feet tall and of slender build, say someone the size of Olivia Dautery, to have moved that body?"

"Objection. Your honor that question calls for a conclusion from the witness."

"General Roberts, I'm going to allow the witness to answer the question as he is a police officer and expected to draw conclusions based upon evidence he has observed during the course of an investigation."

"No."

"So, in your professional opinion, as an officer of the police department, would the defendant Olivia Dautery have been able to have moved Miss Murdock's body from Eldorado to the location where you discovered it?"

"No."

"What about Bill Toma, Sgt. Davis? He's of slight build, do you think he would have been able to have moved Miss Murdock's body to the location where it was found in almost total darkness?"

"Objection. Your honor," Roberts shouted, rising. "Sgt. Davis has no idea whatsoever whether or not either of the defendants could've moved her body."

"I withdraw the question Your Honor," Daniels answered. "No further questions."

"The witness may step down."

The D.A.'s brother, Tom Roberts was understandably impressed by Nikki Daniels exchange with Sgt. Davis, a witness for the prosecution. She had basically used him to establish that neither of the defendants would have been able to move Miss Murdock's body. His thoughts were interrupted by the voice of his brother.

"The prosecution calls Tom Roberts," the district attorney said as he stood and moved toward the witness stand.

"Mr. Roberts, you were known to both the decedent and to Mr. Delgado, is that so?"

"Yes, I had cut Miss. Murdock's yard several summers, when I was in junior high, and until I graduated from high school, but that was more than twenty years ago."

"So, how long had you known the decedent?"

"All of my life. She is...was a friend of my mother's, and my...our father did some legal work for her from time to time."

"So, she was a family friend, is that correct?"

"Yes, I'd say she was a family friend."

"When did you see her last?"

"I visited her on August 2nd, the morning of her murder."

"Mr. Roberts, you are originally from Halcyon but moved to Los Angeles approximately ten years ago, where you are currently employed as a mailman, a letter carrier, and you were in town for your, our father's funeral. Is that correct?"

"I moved to Los Angeles ten years ago," Roberts answered, not wishing to lie in court by saying he was a mailman.

"Why did you, how did you chance to visit Miss Murdock on that Thursday morning, the day she was murdered?"

"My mother speaks…spoke with her a couple of times a week, you know, just to check up on her. Miss Murdock hardly went out in public anymore, so she wasn't going to attend my…our father's funeral, but she wanted to see me, so Mom insisted that I visit her and said she'd be expecting me."

"Why would she want to see you? You were just her yardman, and that was, you say, around twenty years ago."

"Well, she'd liked me, I suppose. Mom had sent me a thousand dollars after I'd moved to Los Angeles, to help me get settled. It was actually Miss Murdock who'd sent me the money, though I didn't know that at the time. She'd given it to Mom and told her to send it to me, but not to say that it was from her."

"Why would she send you money?"

"Just nice, I guess."

"How long were you there, at her house on the day of the murder?"

"Not more than an hour, if that."

"Did she at that time express any fear regarding her neighbors, the defendants?"

"Objection," Solomon shouted. "Hearsay."

"Well then, tell me in your own words your conversation, what you talked about."

"She asked me about California and how I liked it. I asked her what had happened to Cypress Hill. It looked to me like the place was falling down. I wondered if Mr. Toma and Miss Dautery had sold the house to somebody else. It had really deteriorated since I'd seen it last. I used to cut the yard over there when I was a kid, generally on the same day that I cut Miss Murdock's yard, but not always."

"Please continue."

"Well, she told me that Mr. Toma and Miss Dautery still lived there but that they'd let animals run wild and that the animals had wrecked the house. She said that she'd complained to them repeatedly about their animals coming over to her house, Eldorado, and tearing up her garden and uprooting her bushes."

"Did she say that they had threatened her?"

"Objection, any answer would be hearsay," Solomon stated, "since the decedent is not available for cross examination. In fact, Your Honor, I ask that the entire testimony of this witness be removed from the record. This is all hearsay and nothing but. It's inadmissible."

"Counsel, approach the bench. I'm going to allow the witness to answer the last question under the Mississippi Rules of Evidence subsection 803, exception 2, `excited utterance.' If the witness states that Miss Murdock was excited at the time of her comments to him, I will allow the testimony. I won't allow his testimony otherwise. You may proceed." Turning to the witness the judge said, "Mr. Roberts, you may answer the question."

"Miss Murdock said that she had shot one of the roaming goats, and that when Miss Dautery had come to collect the dead goat that she'd been threatened by Miss Dautery, who said that she would, and I quote `blow her head clean off.' She was worried that they...the defendants, would try toburn her house down, or kill her."

"So, based upon what she said to you, in a state of excitement, on the morning of her murder on the day of the murder, she was genuinely and immanently afraid of the defendants?"

"Yes."

"What happened next? Did she express any more fears regarding the defendants?"

"Well, suddenly Miss Murdock produced a .45 automatic, seemingly out of nowhere and showed it to me. She said that she was ready for them."

"Ready for whom?"

"Miss Dautery and Mr. Toma."

"I now show you this .45 automatic pistol, a 1911 model Colt which was previously entered into evidence by the prosecution. It was recovered by Chief Bowman and Sgt. Carl Draper at the defendants' home, Cypress Hill, on the night of the murder. Mr. Roberts, is this the gun you saw at Miss Murdock's?"

"It looks like the pistol she showed me. That is, she showed me a Colt .45 and this one looks like it. It's an earlier 1911, as you can tell by the shorter thumb guard beneath the hammer, hers was like that, but is this the same gun that she showed me? I can't say for sure. I think it is, but I can't say for sure."

"I object," Solomon blurted, "this pistol has nothing to do with the proceedings under consideration here. The district attorney can't prove that this pistol ever belonged to either the decedent, or the defendants. That being the case, I ask that this .45 caliber pistol be withdrawn as evidence and that all testimony regarding it be stricken from the record. It has no bearing on this case whatsoever. This is nothing more than some ill-conceived fishing expedition on the part of the district attorney."

"Your Honor," the D.A. replied, "the witness has testified that Miss Murdock admitted to shooting three of the defendants' goats, and that she showed this .45 caliber pistol to the witness, and this testimony by the witness has been allowed by the court. The prosecution is certainly within its rights inseeking further clarification in regard to the defendants threatening to kill Miss Murdock. And given that this specific pistol was found along with the murder weapon at the defendants' house, on the night of the murder, and entered into evidence by the state, it has some bearing on this trial, even though it was not the murder weapon."

"Mr. Solomon, I'm going to allow the prosecution to pursue its questions regarding this pistol, inasmuch as it was found at the defendants' house."

"Thank you, Your Honor," the district attorney replied and resumed questioning the witness. "Now, Miss Murdock told you on the morning of her murder that she had showed a gun that looked like this one to the defendants, didn't she? In fact, she actually ran back into the house and instructed the defendants to wait until she returned with the gun, didn't she? I'm asking you specifically about this pistol, and not any speculation you may have had about anything beyond that. What, exactly did she say regarding this pistol? Did she threaten the defendants with it?"

"They threatened her, and Miss Murdock threatened them."

"No further questions, Your Honor."

Solomon stood and walked toward the witness stand. "Mr. Roberts, we really don't know whose gun this is, do we? You've said yourself that `it looks like the gun' Miss Murdock showed you, but you really aren't sure, are you?"

"No."

"No further questions, Your Honor," Solomon said.

"Nothing on redirect, Your Honor," the D.A. said.

"You may take your seat, Mr. Roberts. Prosecution, call your next witness. No, on second thought, let's take a fifteen-minute recess."

The jury exited through the judge's door at the front of the courtroom and those remaining milled around in the courtroom and in the corridors. The trial resumed in fifteen minutes.

"The prosecution calls Lt. William Thompson to the stand. Your Honor, I submit this police report for state's exhibit number 5. Now, Lt. Thompson, according to this report, you were dispatched to Cypress Hill on the night of April 14, last year, weren't you?"

"Yes, I was."

"Would you please tell the court the reason for that call?"

"I was dispatched to Cypress Hill as the result of a report of shots fired."

"Do you remember the circumstances?"

"Yes. I arrived at Cypress Hill at around 8:15 p.m. and found Miss Dautery standing in front of her house in possession of a 12-gauge shotgun."

"Do you recall what type of shotgun it was?"

"Yes. It was a Remington automatic."

"In other words, it held more than one round at a time, is that right?"

"Yes."

"Had the weapon been fired?"

"Yes, the weapon had been fired."

"How did you determine that?"

"There were multiple spent 12-gauge shells strewn across the driveway, and Miss Dautery openly stated that she'd been shooting at trespassers."

"What did you say to her?"

"I told her to hand me the weapon, and asked her why she was discharging a weapon within the city limits."

"What happened then?"

"She complied, passing me the weapon. I asked her if she knew that it was unlawful to discharge a weapon within the city limits."

"She said that she appreciated my concern but that she didn't have time to wait for the police to arrive, and that she had a right to defend her property."

"Do you remember her specific wording?"

"She answered something to the effect that when seconds count, the police arrive in minutes," a remark which was immediately followed by laughter in the courtroom.

"How would you define her attitude?" the D.A. asked loudly over the muffled laughter of the courtroom audience.

"Defiant."

"Why do you say that she was defiant?"

"I object," Solomon shouted.

"Answer the question Lt. Thompson."

"She said that the Constitution granted her the right to keep and bear arms in the defense of her person and property, and that she `didn't have to justify her actions to me or to any so-called authority.'"

"Did you issue her a citation?"

"No."

"Why not?"

"For one thing, she was on her own property. For another, there was nobody in sight, that is, no other persons nearby who could be considered to be a target. I didn't think that she would continue shooting, so I let her off with a warning."

"But you were dispatched to Cypress Hill again, approximately three months later, were you not?"

"Yes, I was."

"And what, Lt. Thompson, was the reason for that subsequent call?"

"Gunshots."

"So you were called to Cypress Hill again due to another report of gunfire from one of the defendants, is that what happened?"

"Yes, I was again dispatched on a 911 call to Cypress Hill and Sgt. Tanner and I arrived at around 5:30 p.m."

“Your Honor, I submit this second police report from July 22, of last year as state’s exhibit number 17.”

“So it was still daylight outside?”

“Yes, it was still light.”

“And what did you find when you arrived?”

“The defendants were on the upstairs gallery at the front of the house. Mr.Toma was seated in a rocking chair with his feet propped on top of the porch railing, and Miss Dautery was reloading a pistol.”

“Did you personally hear any gunshots at that time?”

“Yes, she was in fact in the act of firing her pistol across the street when Sgt. Tanner and I arrived.”

“What happened then?”

“I told her to put the weapon down and to come downstairs and to the front door.”

“You said that she was holding a pistol. Did you see the pistol?”

“Yes, both of us saw it?”

“Can you describe it for the court?”

“It was a small caliber nickel-plated revolver.”

“I show you state’s exhibit number 9, a .32 caliber Smith and Wesson revolver, which was found at the home of the defendants on the night of the murder, during August of last year. Do you recognize this pistol?”

“That appears to be the pistol that Miss Dautery had in her possession when we arrived.”

“The murder weapon?”

“Yes, the murder weapon?”

“No further questions.”

Defense attorney Mark Solomon stood and then approached the witness stand. “According to these reports Lt. Thompson, you were called to Cypress Hill on two occasions due to reports of gunfire, is that correct?”

“Yes sir.”

“And yet you declined to give Miss Dautery a ticket either time, wouldn’t you say that was unusual on your part?”

“Yes, it was not in accordance with standard police procedure, but on the second occasion she addressed me by name from the porch, and apologized for shooting within the city limits. She explained that she wasn’t actually shooting at anybody, just in the general direction of a trespasser who she said had been `digging for treasure.’”

“So, she was again merely defending her property? Is that correct?”

“She thought she was, at any rate.”

“Isn’t it true that she had filed police reports herself on several occasions regarding trespassing, specifically, during the year preceding your first visit to Cypress Hill regarding the report of gunfire?”

“Yes, there had been several reports of trespassers on the property at Cypress Hill, mainly teenagers, kids drinking beer and parking on the far side of her property, across the street from her house.”

“But in fact, persons other than Miss Dautery had also reported trespassers on Cypress Hill property, is that correct?”

“Yes, Gale Lane borders the property directly facing Cypress Hill. Kids congregate there and basically play music, drink beer, and let off steam.”

“Lt. Thompson, I again refer to the aerial map showing the proximity of Eldorado at the left, and Cypress Hill at the right side of the map. Please take this pointer and indicate the location where the trespassers have been sighted, both by Miss Dautery and others in the area, that is, on Gale Lane, which borders the front of Cypress Hill’s property. Now, how far would you estimate the distance to be between the front of Cypress Hill and Gale Lane?”

“I’d say it’s at least 600 feet.”

"Thank you. Now, would you please tell the court why you declined to cite Miss Dautery a second time?"

"I didn't consider her to be a threat to myself or anyone else. I'd told her that if I had to come out here again over her shooting any kind of firearm that I'd have to arrest her and charge her with disturbing the peace. Besides that, she might accidentally kill or injure somebody. I'd also told her that if she had any further concerns, all she had to do was call us, and somebody would be over here in a matter of minutes. I promised her we would increase patrols on the Gale Lane side of her property and instruct the patrol officers to keep an eye out for any trespassers. This seemed to satisfy her and she promised me that she wouldn't shoot anymore. And that was that."

"So there have been no additional calls with regard to gunfire from Cypress Hill?"

"No sir."

"She was courteous and non-combative, and you didn't consider her to be a danger to herself or anyone else. Is that correct?"

"Yes."

"Now Lt. Thompson, I want to ask you about this weapon which was found on the night of the murder at the defendants' residence. I show you state's exhibit number 9, the murder weapon. Is this the same revolver you saw in possession of Miss Dautery upon your second visit to Cypress Hill, or merely one which resembles it?"

"I cannot positively identify this particular revolver as the same weapon I saw in Miss Dautery's possession on my second visit to Cypress Hill."

"If someone were standing on the ground in front of Cypress Hill it would be difficult to distinguish a nickel-plated .32 caliber from any other nickel-plated or bright stainless steel revolver that someone on the second-story gallery might be holding. Would it be safe to say, in your professional opinion as a law enforcement officer, that from that distance it would be nearly impossible to state with certainty that the pistol Miss Dautery was holding wasn't, for example, a nickel-plated H & R .22, a .32, a Ruger .38, or even a Taurus .357. Is that correct Lt. Thompson?"

"I didn't actually examine the gun in Miss Dautery's possession. Like I said, I instructed her to put the pistol down and to come downstairs, which she did. She left the pistol somewhere upstairs."

"In other words, you never actually saw that pistol any closer than from, say, twenty or thirty feet away, and then, only for a duration of a few seconds, is that correct?"

"Yes."

"Given the fact that Cypress Hill faces west, and you arrived at 5:30 p.m., is it possible that the bright afternoon sun reflecting off the barrel during the brief period that you saw the pistol might have only made it appear to be nickel-plated, and it might not have actually been nickel-plated at all? Isn't that possible?"

"Yes, I suppose it's possible."

"More specifically, Lt. Thompson, since you can't identify either the manufacture, or the caliber of the pistol Miss Dautery was holding, the only thing you can say with certainty regarding the weapon is that it was shiny. No further questions, Your Honor."

"The witness may step down. As it's nearing 5 o'clock, court will adjourn for the Day. Court will resume at 9:00 a.m. tomorrow morning. In the meantime, I'll remind you again, no member of the jury is allowed to discuss this case with anybody, including other members of the jury. You're dismissed."

18.

The Prosecution Rests

"All rise. Court is now in session. The Honorable Judge W. C. Brock is presiding. You may be seated," the bailiff ordered.

"The prosecution calls Dr. John Deering.Dr. Deering, would you please tell the court a little about your qualifications as a medical examiner. First of all, you are employed by a private firm which has been hired by the state of Mississippi, is that correct?"

"Yes, I'm employed by Forensic Medical Pathologists, Ltd., a U.K. based organization which provides forensic services to the State of Mississippi, among others. I am currently actively licensed in Mississippi, Tennessee, and Arkansas. I am based in Jackson, Mississippi."

"You have been previously qualified as an expert witness in forensic pathology. What are your specific qualifications as a forensic pathologist?"

"I have a medical degree from the University of Tennessee, did my residency at Parkland in Dallas, and went from there to study surgery at Vanderbilt. I subsequently studied pathology for four years at the University of Tennessee, that is, subsequent to medical school."

"Dr. Deering, would you please tell the court, just exactly what pathology is?"

"Basically, pathology is that branch of medicine which deals with the study of illness. Forensic pathology deals with the legal issues of pathology. A forensic pathologist determines the cause of death, and the manner of death."

"Dr. Deering, how were you brought into this case?"

"The Black County medical examiner requested an autopsy and I was called to perform that function."

"The autopsy is the chief tool of the forensic pathologist. Is that correct?"

"Yes, it allows us to establish both the cause, and the manner of death."

"Dr. Deering, if you please, would you explain to the court, the difference between the terms `cause of death' and `manner of death?'"

"Cause of death indicates what physical injury actually caused death, specifically, wounds, as in this case. The manner of death could beaccidental, as in a car crash, a fall, electrocution, or through some other agency. In this case, the cause of death was multiple fatal gunshot wounds, and the manner of death was homicide."

"What exactly is involved in an autopsy?"

"First of all, the body of the decedent is removed from the bag in which it arrives. There is a detailed external examination and there are photographs taken. The clothes are then removed, marked, photographed, and bagged as evidence. There are subsequent tests, a toxicology report, additional photos, X-Rays and diagrams. The body is then opened, organs removed and weighed. We are looking specifically for illness and injury. We take specimens, tissue samples, etc. and publish a report. The autopsy report has an injury section. In this case there were two wounds, labeled A.& B. There was blood in the chest cavity and stomach."

"Dr. Deering, I call your attention to the photograph of the decedent on the screen to your right. I presume that you took these photographs, is that correct?"

"Yes, I took these photographs."

"Just what do these wounds indicate to you Dr. Deering?"

"The wounds indicate that the decedent was killed while in a sitting position and that there were two bullet wounds."

"Were both wounds, that is, both A.& B., fatal wounds?"

"Yes, both A.& B. were fatal wounds, both individually and corporately."

"Were there any defensive wounds?"

"No, the first wound, A., was a chest wound, and obliterated the heart."

"Do you mean the heart stopped as a result of wound A.?"

"Yes, at that point there was no longer any blood pressure, and no more than five or six seconds of oxygen left."

"What does this mean in practical terms?"

"It means that there would have been little bleeding at the scene of the shooting, at least until the body was moved. Blood always takes the path of least resistance, and the position of the body determines blood flow."

"In your estimation, Dr. Deering, how long would Miss Murdock have lived after wound A.?"

"She was dead in a matter of seconds."

"Wound B. was an abdominal wound. It was also fatal?"

"Yes."

"Your Honor, I submit these photographs as state exhibits 65. and 66. I ask that 65, and 66 be posted to the jury. Now Dr. Deering, if you would, please describe wound C. for the court."

"Wound C. on the decedent's back is the exit wound from shot B."

"Mr. Wiltz, place 67 and 68 on the screen. Now Dr. Deering, what to these images show?"

"The body has been cleaned both to see and demonstrate the wounds."

"What happened to the decedent's clothes?"

"They were removed from the body, photographed, bagged and tagged, and sent to the MBI lab in Jackson for additional tests."

"Now Dr. Deering, you come to us as an expert witness in

forensic pathology. You are also a ballistics expert, is that correct?"

"I'm not specifically a ballistics expert, per se, I'm a terminal ballistics expert, that is, an expert about when bullets hit the body."

"I ask Your Honor that Autopsy Exhibit 104 be shown to the jury. Now, Dr. Deering, what is this?"

"It is labeled `bullet fragments from right chest,' and is marked with my initials and the date I sealed it."

"Now, Dr. Deering, was there a muzzle to garment test performed, and if so, would you describe that to the court?"

"Yes, there was a muzzle to garment test performed. This consists of firing a weapon of the type and caliber of that used in the murder. Shots are fired onto papers which, when compared to the autopsy, determine the distance from which the shots were fired."

"Was Miss Murdock's body tested for drugs?"

"Yes, that's standard procedure in a murder case."

"What were the results in this instance?"

"Negative. There were no reportable levels of any drugs."

"Thank you. No further questions Your Honor."

The judge looked in the direction of the defense. "No questions Your Honor," Solomon said.

"The witness may step down."

"The prosecution calls Michael Bayne to the stand. Now Mr. Bayne, you are a firearms examiner for the state of Mississippi, for the Mississippi Bureau of Investigation, is that right?"

"Yes, I am."

"Would you please tell the court your qualifications for this job?"

"I have a Bachelor of Arts in Forensic Chemistry, two years of on the job training, and hundreds of hours with a microscope at the BATF Academy lab. I have also undergone training in this field with the FBI at Quantico, Virginia."

"You've been qualified as an expert in your field as a firearms examiner and a forensic chemist.Is that right Mr. Bayne?"

"Yes, I'm an expert and have testified as such in thirty-five trials to date."

"Mr. Bayne, is this a submission receipt?"

"Yes, it is a receipt for evidence brought to the lab."

"Did you generate a firearms report?"

"Yes."

"Do you recognize this report?"

"Yes, it has my initials."

"I submit this report as exhibit 110, Your Honor. Now Mr. Bayne, would you go through the list of the items that were delivered to you?"

"Yes, I received a .32 caliber Smith & Wesson revolver, two unfired .32 caliber bullets, several .32 bullet fragments, a fired .32 caliber bullet, three spent, that is empty .32 caliber shell casings, a dress, an undershirt, a pair of socks, and various undergarments."

"Did you test fire the pistol, and if so, what were the results as far as its operation and capacity?"

"The revolver loaded and fired as designed. It was functioning normally."

"Now, please describe this sealed envelope and its contents."

"It is marked with my name, the subject, and the victim's name, and contains two spent, that is, fired .32 caliber shells."

"You also received bullet fragments removed from Miss Murdock's body, as well as one bullet removed from a window frame in the decedent's house, is that correct? Have these bags been marked for this trial?"

"Yes, as Exhibits 86 through 94."

"Now, Mr. Bayne, what tests were you asked to perform?"

"I test fired .32 caliber shells of the same manufacture as those from the weapon, and then compared them microscopically with the spent shell casings taken from the same gun."

"Were these shells fired from the murder weapon?"

"Yes."

"Are these bullets, then, the ones that killed Miss Murdock?"

"Yes, they are."

"No further questions, Your Honor. Mr. Solomon, you may cross-examine this witness."

"Now Mr. Bayne were there any fingerprints on the shell casings, or on the pistol?"

"Nothing identifiable. Everything had been thoroughly wiped clean."

"So, neither of the defendants' fingerprints were found anywhere on the murder weapon, is that correct?"

"There were no fingerprints on the weapon at all, or on the spent cartridges, that is the empty shells."

"So, actually, anyone could have fired the fatal shots, isn't that so?"

"Theoretically, yes."

"Since the spent shell casings had been removed from the pistol at some point and wiped clean, isn't it possible that the spent shells could have been inserted into the wrong, that is, into different chambers within the cylinder after the murder? That is, isn't it possible that the spent cartridges could have been replaced into different chambers of the pistol's cylinder than those from which the bullets were originally fired?"

"Yes, it's possible, not that…"

"Thank you, Mr. Bayne," Solomon said, cutting him off mid-sentence. "No further questions Your Honor."

"Redirect?"

"No further questions, Your Honor."

"Thank you, Mr. Bayne, you may step down."

Tom Roberts had listened with amusement as Solomon basically invalidated the testimony of the prosecution's witness, Mr. Bayne, by establishing that there were no fingerprints linking either of the defendants to the murder weapon. He'd made that absolutely clear to the jury, while at the same time, confusing them with that business about the chambers of the cylinder in which the spent shells were replaced. It didn't matter one way or the other, as the spent shells had been fired from the murder weapon. It was basically double-talk. Tom was surprised that his brother let Solomon get away with it, that his brother didn't question the relevance of Solomon's cross examination of Bayne.

"The prosecution calls Sgt. Carl Draper. Now Sgt. Draper, on last August 2, the night of the murder, you accompanied PoliceChief Bowman to search the defendants' house, Cypress Hill. You subsequently returned the following day during the daytime hours to continue your search for evidence, accompanied by Walter Gardner, a police photographer.What did you find on that second occasion?"

"We found a handwritten diary belonging to Olivia Dautery."

"Your Honor the prosecution would like to introduce this diary into evidence. It has been examined by the MBI lab in Jackson, compared with writing samples from the female defendant, and the entries were, indeed, written in the hand of the defendant, Olivia Dautery. Mr. Wiltz, if you please. I direct the jury's attention to the screen to page 451 to the entry dated July 2 of last year. Now, Sgt. Draper I'm going to ask that you read that entry to the court precisely as it's written."

"I've had it with that insolent bitch, and her useless cousin. She's brutally murdered another one of the innocent members of our animal family, and she will pay the ultimate price for her cruelty in due course. In the meantime, I watch and wait. She'll get what's coming to her, and I'll live to see it."

"No further questions, Your Honor."

"Mr. Solomon?"

"Sgt. Draper, regarding this diary that you found which is purported to belong to Olivia Dautery, and referring again to page

451, to the section you've just read to the court, there are no specific names mentioned in it anywhere, are there? This entry could literally refer to anyone. No further questions."

"Redirect, Mr. Roberts?"

"No further questions, Your Honor."

"Call your next witness."

"The prosecution calls Mr. Walker Turlock." After the witness was sworn in and seated, the district attorney questioned him. "Mr. Turlock, I ask you to examine this document and tell the court what it is."

"This is a certified copy of a marriage license issued to Olivia Dautery and Maxwell Burke."

"Your Honor, if it please the court, the prosecution would like to introduce this as State's exhibit 108. Now Mr. Turlock, you were on duty when this marriage license was applied for and granted, is that right?"

"Yes, but that was more than twenty years ago, and I'm retired now."

"That is your signature on the document though, isn't it Mr. Turlock?"

"Yes it is. I signed all of them during that period."

"I ask you sir, do you remember the particular circumstances surrounding this specific application for a marriage license?"

"Objection," Solomon shouted. "It's doubtful that the witness would remember the circumstances regarding this, or any otherspecific marriage license.He probably signed hundreds, if not thousands of them during his tenure in that capacity."

"Overruled. The witness may answer the question if he has direct knowledge regarding this document. Continue General Roberts."

"Yes, I remember this one in particular because Miss Dautery and Mr. Burke were so jubilant, almost giddy. Miss Dautery was positively radiant. She was a big deal socially, you know, prominent."

"Did you know her personally?"

"No, she was a member of the upper class, you know. I didn't know her personally, but I knew who she was. Everyone in town did."

"You must have issued hundreds of marriage licenses, how do you happen to remember this one?"

"Like I said, everybody knew who she was, and Mr. Burke was from New York. He was also well-dressed and elegant. They seemed to me to be a perfect match. I'd seen their pictures in the paper, you know. They'd been entertained by all of the owners at the big houses in town. When the announcement of their impending marriage hit the paper, it was big news. I remember that because it seemed that their pictures were always in the society section."

"Would you explain to the court how a marriage license works?"

"It's issued, and then the parties to whom it is issued, have six months to actually get married by a legal authority, a justice of thepeace, an ordained minister, you know. If that doesn't happen, then the license expires and a new one must be applied for. In other words, the parties aren't actually married until an actual marriage has taken place, that is, officially."

"That didn't happen in this case did it Mr. Turlock?"

"No, the license was never exercised."

"And why was that?"

"Objection.Your Honor, the question calls for a conclusion."

"Sustained."

"I'll withdraw the question. But the marriage never took place?"

"That's true, and the license expired."

"The reason that the license expired," Roberts shouted toward the jury, "was because shortly after this marriage license was issued, the would-be groom abandoned the defendant and ran away to Newport, Rhode Island with the decedent, Miss Murdock! Isn't that so?"

"Objection!" shouted Solomon, "the district attorney knows this question calls for a conclusion, and is therefore inadmissable, and he's also leading the witness."

"Sustained."

"That was the rumor around town at the time," the witness answered, "but I don't know that for a fact. All I can say with certainty, from my own knowledge, is that the license expired."

"Objection. Your Honor, I ask that this entire testimony be stricken from the record. Rumors aren't facts and despite the fact that the witness has denied personal knowledge as to why the license expired, the jury is left with the implication that the decedent somehow interfered and stole the would-be groom from the defendant."

"Objection sustained Mr. Solomon, but I'm not inclined to strike the testimony of this witness as the prosecution is seeking to further establish motive."

"I ask that this marriage license be published to the jury," Roberts continued. "Now Mr. Turlock, I call your attention to this newspaper clipping from the *Halcyon Star*. It is a fact, is it not, that Miss Dautery's former fiancé, Mr. Burke, took his own life after a failed reconciliation attempt with Miss Dautery?"

"Objection," Solomon shouted. "Your Honor, the question calls for a conclusion, and counsel is clearly leading the witness."

"Objection sustained."

"I withdraw the question, Your Honor. I introduce this newspaper clipping From the December 27 edition of *New York Times*, as prosecution's exhibit 112. Note the date. Now Mr. Turlock, would you please read this press clipping to the court."

"Wealthy New York socialite and well-known publishing heir Maxwell Burke died unexpectedly from an apparently self-inflicted gunshot wound to the heart on Monday, December 25, according to the coroner's report. His body was discovered at his Manhattan townhouse by his valet at around 9:00 a.m. the morning following his death. Sources close to the situation said that Mr. Burke had been increasingly despondent over a scheduled marriage to a Halcyon, Mississippi debutante which had been cancelled several months ago. Funeral arrangements are incomplete at this time. Associated Press."

"That was Christmas day of the same year the marriage license had been applied for, was it not Mr. Turlock?The defendant Olivia Dautery's true love had been stolen by her former close friend Miss Murdock, toyed with, and then cast aside. In sorrow over his actions, he killed himself with a bullet through the heart, on Christmas day! Thank you, Mr. Turlock. No further questions," Roberts continued, turning toward the judge.

"You may cross examine the witness, Mr.Solomon," Judge Brock stated.

"No further questions, Your Honor,"Solomon replied.

The court was suddenly interrupted by the loud and pitiful sobbing of the defendant, Olivia Dautery, who sat with her face buried in her hands, tears running between her fingers. Solomon placed his arm around the shoulders of the defendant, pulled her toward him, and held her as she cried, while Nikki Daniels directed an icy stare at the district attorney who held her glance briefly, then stood, addressed the judge and stated loudly, "The prosecution rests."

"Mr. Solomon, is the defense prepared to present its case?"

"Your Honor," the defense attorney said, rising to address the judge, "I'm going to ask for a directed verdict in this case, since the prosecution has clearly been unable to present sufficient evidence that the defendants are guilty of the crimes with which they've been charged. I ask that the court dismiss this case and release them at once."

"Mr. Solomon, I'm going to deny your request and allow you to proceed with your defense, but as it's late in the day, I think it will be better to start fresh. Court will resume tomorrow morning at 9:00 a.m. Court is now adjourned," Judge Brock shouted, striking his gavel.

19.

Solomon, L.A. Style

Over dinner, defense attorneys Nikki Daniels, Mark Solomon, and Lucien Dale, discussed strategy as well as the events of the day's proceedings. "I'm satisfied with the way things are going," Solomon observed. "They've done a good job so far. They've presented their case in a coherent, linear fashion without confusing the jury with too many dates, witnesses, or too much information. They've done a good job with what initially seemed to be a weak case. As you know, I always start by attempting to deliberately discredit any witnesses for the prosecution, seeking to create doubt about their testimony in the minds of the jury. Roberts knows this, and he's more or less stacked his witness list with expert witnesses. It's hard to undermine someone who is a recognized authority, like a medical examiner, or a coroner. These people have excellent credentials and know their jobs."

"The initial selection Sgt. Draper read from the diary was somewhat incriminating, I thought" Lucian Dale observed, "but more indicative, I think, of anger than intention. There was no direct threat involved. Still, I think it made an impression on the jury. The testimony regarding the marriage license, while seemingly cruel, certainly established a legitimate motive over and above the mere killing of a few goats. That line could prove problematic for us in that it indicates a deeper, long standing, and really legitimate motive for murder, one of revenge."

"Women can be ruthless at times," Nikki Daniels observed, "as the decedent must've been. Still, I think Roberts' introduction of that marriage license might have done the prosecution more harm than good, in that it might have created sympathy for Olivia Dautery, but I'm not sure. I tried to read the jurors' faces, to get a sense of their reaction, but I didn't get anything one way or the other."

"I don't know either," Solomon agreed, "but I think it worked in favor of the prosecution. If that isn't one of the strongest motives for murder, I've ever heard of, I don't know what else could be. That singular event was without doubt, the defining moment of Olivia Dautery's young life. It truly altered and ruined her, and her descent into her present squalid circumstances can be directly traced back to that event, and probably specifically to that date. She never recovered. The prosecution clearly established a strong and legitimate motive in the minds of the jurors. Roberts is every bit as effective as a prosecutor as his brother is as an agent and manager. Perhaps we've underestimated him."

"Well, what's next?" Dale asked.

"We're going after the maid, Hattie Livingston."

"Mark," Dale admonished him, "you aren't going to get a straight answer out of Miss Murdock's maid, unless you confine your questions strictly to her name and place of employment. I know these people, and she isn't going to answer anything. She's most likely unaware of the 5th Amendment, so she won't invoke its protection against self-incrimination. She just won't answer your questions, and she'll ignore any commandment from the judge to do so. What do you hope to gain from bringing her forward as a witness?"

"Chances are," Solomon replied, "that she won't answer any pertinent questions, but she will appear to be hostile to the court, and to the defense. In fact, I hope she doesn't answer anything I ask. I'm interested in showing the jury that there were many people who had the means, the motive, the opportunity, and above all, the intent to kill Miss Murdock. I simply seek to create reasonable doubt within the minds of the individual jurors that it was the two defendants who murdered her. I think the next few witnesses will clearly move the focus away from the two defendants."

"All rise, Court is now in session, the Honorable W.C. Brock presiding. You May be seated."

"Is the defense ready?"

"Yes, Your Honor. The defense calls as first witness Dr. Hypolite De Jean." A tall, imperially slim, and elegantly dressed black man stepped forward, was sworn in, and took the stand.

"Dr. De Jean," Solomon asked, what is your profession?"

"I am a houngan."

"Would you please tell the court exactly what that means?"

"I am a high priest of Voudau, or Voodoo, as it is more commonly called."

"Now, if you please, tell the court exactly what that is."

"Voudau is an ancient African religion which came with the slave trade to the Caribbean, particularly Santo Domingo, that is, the western side of the island generally known as Hispaniola, specifically, Haiti."

"Are you from Haiti?"

"Yes, Le Cap, that is, Cap Haitian, at the northern part of the island."

"And how long have you lived in the United States?"

"Since 1985."

"And where do you live now?"

"Metairie, Louisiana, near New Orleans."

"And what is your vocation?"

"I am the pastor of the Erzuli Temple. I am a high priest."

"Is there a seminary, that is, is there any formal training in Voodoo?"

"There is an oral tradition, as in Judaism, for example, and with other religions as well. This is particularly so with my religion in that slaves were forbidden to read or write in many areas, so the traditions and instructions had to be passed down orally."

"And where did you receive your training?"

"L'Universite Paris-Sorbonne."

"No, Dr. De Jean, I mean your training in Voodoo?"

"At the feet of the masters, both in Haiti, under the tutelage of the late Dr.Gatoa, the foremost authority on the religion in the western hemisphere."

"And how long did you study under him?"

"I spent fifteen years with him in the field."

"You have also written articles for the *Caribbean Review*, is that correct?"

"Yes, for that publication and many others."

"How many books have you written Dr. De Jean?"

"I've had fourteen published so far, with my fifteenth scheduled for publication this forthcoming spring."

"Would you please tell the court some of their titles?"

"Yes. My first book was `The Significance of African Religion in the Caribbean.' I also wrote `The Destruction of the Arawak Indians.' There were two volumes of `Haiti After the Fall of Christophe,' the first of which dealt with the immediate aftermath of the revolution. The second volume concerned the early Twentieth Century occupation of our nation by the United States Marines. And there were several books which examined the significance of Voodoo in post-colonial Haiti, and its continuation and evolution into the current era as well as its migration to the southern United States."

"Thank you, Dr. De Jean. Your Honor, I submit this altered photo of the decedent, Miss Murdock into evidence as defense exhibit number 1," Solomon stated, handing the photo to the judge. "It was discovered beneath a rug in the murder room by the police photographer at Miss Murdock's house, shortly after the murder. I direct the jury to the screen for an enlargement of the photograph in thehands of the witness. Now Dr. De Jean, I show you this photograph of the decedent Miss Jeannie Murdock, which was found beneath a rug at Miss Murdock's house by investigators on the night of her murder. In your professional capacity as a high priest in the religion of Voodoo, would you please tell the court its intended purpose."

"The clear intent of this altered image was to cause harm to the person pictured in this photograph. You will note that the eyes of the photograph have been obscured by painting them black. Additionally, coarse blackthread has been stitched vertically through the eyes in a zig-zag manner, to ensure that the victim will be blinded."

"Objection, Your Honor," the D.A. shouted. "It doesn't matter what anybody did to any photo of the decedent. She wasn't killed by Voodoo, black magic, or any other superstitious nonsense, but by a .32 caliber pistol."

"Mr. Roberts, I'm going to allow the defense to present its case. As thephotograph was found at the decedent's house on the night of the murder by the police, I'm going to allow questions about it. Overruled."

"Dr. De Jean, would this be a literal or a symbolic blindness?"

"The eyes are considered in Voodoo, as in other religions, to be the `windows of the soul.' The deliberate blackening and sewing of the eyes, as noted in your exhibit, is both literal and symbolic. On its own it would be an attempt to confound the victim, to make her confused, and unable to see clearly, that is, it would diminish her ability to make good and rational decisions...but when used in conjunction with the other maliciously altered features indicated on the screen, is indicative of the specific intention to kill the person in the photograph."

"Your Honor, I object," the district attorney called angrily, as he stood up. "This is a court of law, not of superstition. This testimony has nothing whatsoever to do with this case."

"Overruled. General Roberts, I'm going to allow the defense to present its case, but Mr. Solomon, I caution you that this line of questioning had better be moving in some sort of coherent direction."

"Yes Your Honor. Now Dr. De Jean, would the sewing of the eyes by itself, that is, without the other alterations seen in the photograph, be sufficient, in your professional opinion, to have caused the death of the decedent, Miss Murdock?"

"Your Honor, I must object to this entire line of questioning. It's offensive, unscientific, and more importantly, totally irrelevant. It's a matter of record that Miss Murdock was killed with a .32 caliber revolver, not through the agency of some ridiculous and juvenile attempt to `doctor' the decedent's photograph. In the absence of a legitimate defense, Mr. Solomon is clearly attempting to distract the jury with the hocus-pocus and theatrics he's so famous for, but this is a courtroomand not a carnival sideshow."

"General Roberts, I'm going to allow the defense to present its case, as did the prosecution. The stakes for the defendants in the matter now before the court are of the highest possible significance. Objection overruled. Continue Mr. Solomon. The witness may answer the question."

"No, not by itself. The blackening and sewing of the eyes is part ofa more comprehensive attack upon the victim. The blackened and sewn mouth and nose, in addition to the treatment of the eyes, is specifically indicative of a deliberate intention to kill the person in the altered photograph."

"In other words, Dr. De Jean, in your professional opinion, this was indeed a deliberate and premeditated attempt to murder the decedent, Miss Murdock, was it not?"

"There can be no doubt about it. This was a deliberate and premeditated attempt to kill the person in the photograph."

"Dr. De Jean, this altered photograph has been recognized by the court as a true image of the decedent Miss Murdock. In your professional opinion, was this amulet the cause of Miss Murdock's death?"

"Yes, it was a contributory factor."

"Objection! Your Honor, I object!" Roberts shouted over the roar of the courtroom audience. "Your Honor, the forensic pathologist has already clearly shown the cause of death to have been two gunshot wounds caused by a .32 caliber pistol. This is unscientific mumbo-jumbo, an obvious attempt to confound and confuse the jury."

"No further questions," Solomon interjected quickly, before the judge had a chance to respond. "You may cross examine the witness."

"Order! I want order in this court!" the judge shouted as he repeatedly struck his gavel. "This is a courtroom, not an athletic event. I will not have any disturbance. Any further outbursts and all of you except for those parties directly involved in this trial will be removed from this courtroom." After things had quieted down, the judge continued. "Mr. Roberts, you may cross examine the witness."

"But Your Honor, I…"

"You may cross examine the witness."

"Yes, Your Honor," the D.A. replied as he cast a dark glance at Mark Solomon."Now, Mr. De Jean, you just mentioned an oral tradition as the source of your alleged expertise. You are not licensed by the state of Louisiana, or any other official government body as a Voodoo priest, are you?"

"What is your name again, sir?" the witness inquired.

"I am Bill Roberts, the District Attorney of Black County, the prosecutor in this case, and am licensed by the state in that capacity.

I have a law degree, and am licensed to practice law in the state of Mississippi. Now I ask you again, Mr. De Jean are you licensed by any official state, local, federal, or any other legitimate government organization or authority as a Voodoo priest? Yes or No?"

"First of all, Mr. Roberts, you will refer to me as Dr. De Jean. I will not allow you to disrespect me personally, or my religion. I am every bit as qualified in my field as you imagine yourself to be in yours, probably a great deal more, but to answer your question specifically, there is not anyone, anywhere, in any government agency, who is even remotely qualified to examine or certify me. I am recognized by my peers not merely as an authority, but as the supreme authority in my field within the North American continent."

"But you still haven't answered my question `Dr.' De Jean. Are you licensed by any official state or federal authority?"

"No."

"No further questions, Your Honor."

"Redirect, Mr. Solomon?"

"Yes. Now Dr. De Jean, how many times, to the best of your recollection have you testified as an expert witness in American courtrooms?"

"I can't say precisely, but more than two dozen, at least, in states ranging from Florida, to New York, to California."

"Thank you, Dr. De Jean. No further questions, Your Honor."

"You may step down."

"Defense calls Walter Payton to the stand. Thank you. Mr. Payton you are a criminologist, fingerprint expert for the state of Mississippi, and the Mississippi Bureau of Investigation and based in Jackson, is that right?"

"Yes."

"So, you are an employee of the state of Mississippi, is that right?"

"Yes."

"All right Mr. Payton, I direct your attention to the screen to your right. I ask you have you seen this photograph before?"

"Yes, it has my initials."

"Would you tell the court what it is, and why was it brought to you and by whom?"

"It is the photograph referred to by the previous witness, an altered photograph of the decedent Miss Jeanie Murdock, and was sent to me by the Halcyon police department, Black County, for the purpose of determining whose fingerprints were on it?"

"What did you do with that image, Mr. Payton?" Solomon asked.

"I was given several sets of reference fingerprints with whichto compare the prints I found on the altered photograph of the decedent."

"And will you tell the court your findings, Mr. Payton."

"The prints I found on the photograph of the decedent were a match with those of a Mrs. Hattie Livingston."

"Were there any other prints on that photograph Mr. Payton?"

"There were partial prints of the decedent, Miss Murdock."

"Other than Miss Murdock's and those of her maid, Mrs. Hattie Livingston, were there any additional fingerprints?"

"No, but there were numerous other fingerprint smudges which were not identifiable."

"No further questions, Your Honor."

"Mr. Roberts?" the judge asked.

"No questions, Your Honor."

"Call your next witness."

"The defense calls as its next witness, Mrs. Hattie Livingston." Mrs. Livingston stood and walked toward the witness stand, where she stated her name and was sworn in. She was nicely dressed, Tom Roberts noticed, probably in clothes she normally wore to church. She was `stout' for lack of a better description, and probably around

60 years old.

"You may be seated."

"Now Mrs. Livingston," Mr. Solomon began, "you were a maid under the employ of the decedent Miss Jeannie Murdock, is that correct?"

"Yes."

"And how long did you work for her?"

"Almost thirty years."

"Did you like her?" Solomon continued.

"Not especially," the witness replied.

"I see. Mrs. Livingston. I now direct your attention to the screen, and show you defense exhibit number 1, the photograph of the decedent, Miss Murdock, the photo we've been talking about. Do you recognize it?"

"Yes."

"Now remember, Mrs. Livingston, you are under oath. Did you blacken and sew the eyes, nose, and mouth of Miss Murdock's picture?"

"No."

"Your Honor, I move that charges of perjury be brought against Mrs. Livingston and that she be declared a hostile witness. She is deliberately attempting to conceal crucial evidence in a murder trial. As stated by the previous expert witness, her fingerprints were found all over this photograph."

"Objection!" the district attorney shouted. "Your Honor, this entire line of questioning has nothing to do with the already established facts in this case. Mr. Solomon is deliberately seeking to confuse and bewilder this court and jury with this unorthodox detour to who knows where."

"I am inclined to agree with you, Mr. Roberts, and yet the court will not tolerate perjury. Mr. Solomon, would you ask the witness the question again?"

“Mrs. Livingston, you are under oath. That means you’re required by the court to answer the question honestly. If you do not do so, charges of perjury may be brought against you and you may face jail time, a fine, or both. Do you understand this?” She did not reply, so the judge repeated the question.

“Yes.”

“You will address me as Your Honor. Do you understand me Miss Livingston?”

“Yes suh, yo Honah, I sho does,” she answered mockingly.

“Now Mrs. Livingston, the court has ordered you to answer the question,” Solomon continued, “so I’ll ask you once again, did you blacken and sew shut the eyes, nose, and mouth of Miss Murdock’s photograph? Yes or no?”

“No.”

“Your Honor, I submit to the court that the witness did deliberately and maliciously alter this photograph of the decedent with the specific intention of killing her. An expert witness, Dr. De Jean, has testified that the intended purpose of this altered photograph was specifically to kill Miss Murdock. In light of his testimony that the amulet was a contributing factor to the death of Miss Murdock, the fingerprints upon the evidence are those of the witness, and the fact that the object of her malice did in fact die, I ask that the charges against the two defendants be dismissed and that the witness be bound over to a grand jury on charges of contempt, perjury, and First Degree Murder. Your Honor, I call for a dismissal of all charges against the defendants.”

The courtroom immediately erupted with a combination of laughter, applause, and dismay, as the district attorney shouted “Objection! Objection! I object Your Honor!”

“Counsel, approach the bench.”

“Mr. Solomon, I’m not going to allow your motion for a dismissal.”

"But your honor, an expert witness has clearly shown that the decedent's maid, Mrs. Livingston deliberately and knowingly attempted to murder the decedent, and that she did in fact die."

"Well, yes, perhaps she might have intended to harm the decedent, Mr. Solomon, but according to the rules of evidence, this isn't going to work for you. The court does not recognize Voodoo, or whatever it is, to be the cause of the decedent's death. In the first place, ballistics reports have already shown the actual murder weapon to have been the .32 caliber pistol already entered into evidence by the prosecution, and acknowledged as such by this court. As Mr. Roberts has mentioned more than once, there is no causal relationship that can be established between the murder weapon and this witness."

"Your Honor," Solomon interrupted, "The prosecution has sought to charge and convict the two defendants as the path of least resistance. The prosecution's evidence is flimsy, and purely circumstantial. The prosecution surely knows, or should know, that in any case based solely on circumstantial evidence, that if there is any other reasonable explanation at all, it must be considered to be more legitimate than strictly circumstantial evidence. It is one of the defining elements of the entire concept of reasonable doubt.

"The defense intends to prove that there is indeed a direct link between the murder weapon and this witness, that the doctored photograph of the decedent was merely the first part of an intricate plot which was instigated and brought to fruition by the actual murderer or murderers. The witness had ample motive for murder, as well as unfettered and total access to the residence of the decedent."

"Your Honor," the district attorney objected, "the witness is not on trial, the defendants are. This grandstanding is clearly an attempt on the part of Mr. Solomon to divert the course of justice by obfuscating the actual evidence and confusing the jury with wild and absurd ramblings totally lacking any factual basis. He is well known for disrupting numerous courtrooms with this type of Hollywood hi-jinx."

"I would be inclined to agree with the prosecution in this instance except that the witness is clearly hostile and about to be charged with perjury if she fails to answer the question honestly a third time. In light of that, and the fact that the prosecution has presented its case, I'm going to allow the defense the same latitude. It is not the court's desire to charge this witness with perjury...Mr. Solomon, under the circumstances, if you have no objection, given the time of day, I think I would like to adjourn until 9:00 am tomorrow morning. The court has determined that the witness is indeed hostile. Perhaps if the witness understands that she will be held in contempt and charged with perjury if she fails to answer the defense's questions, and what that will mean specifically, she might be more inclined to answer. In other words, she might be more compliant if she thinks about it overnight."

"That's acceptable to the defense, Your Honor. We have no wish to harass or intimidate this witness in any way,"Solomon said, casting a glance in the direction of the jury, "we merely want the witness to answer the question."

"Mr. Roberts?"

"I have no objections, Your Honor, but I reserve the right to cross examine the witness."

"But I warn you, Mr. Solomon," the judge continued, "the only reasonI'm allowing you to continue with this line of questioning at all, is that this witness is obviously concealing something which might have some bearing on your case. But as to your reference about circumstantial evidence necessarilybeing trumped by any other reasonable explanation, the key words are `reasonable explanation.' Inasmuch as we already have the murder weapon, and it is a pistol, not some altered photograph, your premise does not hold water."

The two attorneys returned to their respective tables and the judge addressed the witness and the court. "Mrs. Livingston, the court has deemed you to be a hostile witness, and has ordered you to answer the defense's questions. As it's late in the afternoon and we've all had a hard day, court will adjourn until tomorrow morning at 9:00 am, at which time you will retake the stand. If you fail to answer Mr. Solomon's questions again, or fail to answer them honestly, you will be charged with perjury as well as contempt of court. And you will be placed in detention until such time as you are prepared to answer. Is that understood?"

"I don't have to answer a goddamn thing in no white mens' court," she replied loudly, casting an angry glance at the judge. There was an audible gasp throughout the courtroom as she continued, "Do you understand THAT Yo' Honah?" she mocked.

"Bailiff! Take the witness into custody. She will be held until further notice. I will not allow the sanctity of the court to be disrespected by anyone. Mrs. Livingston you, will remain in custody overnight. Take her away. Mr. Roberts, charge the witness with contempt of court. I'll wait until court is in session tomorrow to decide whether or not to bring charges of perjury, depending upon her testimony." The witness was forcibly dragged out of the courtroom, struggling and cursing all the way.

"Court is adjourned!"

Later that evening, defense attorneys Mark Solomon, Lucien Dale, and Nikki Daniels, along with detectives Demonbreun P. Tchoupitoulas, and his partner, Pommerly, met for a drink and a strategy session at a Mexican joint on South 61. "That was a strange ending in court today," Tchoupitoulas laughed. "You've got the prosecution on the run."

"Run baby run!" Pommerly added.

"I don't know about that, but I do know that there is a lot more to this thing with that maid than meets the eye. I don't know what it is yet. There's no reason for Mrs. Livingston to lie other than that she doesn't want to be implicated as an accessory to murder."

"Well, that seems like a good enough reason to me," the detective speculated.

"Yeah," Pommerly interrupted, "she thinks that her amulet is what caused the real killer or killers to have shot that woman. If she says she doctored that woman's picture, she figures that she's liable to be charged with murder her own self."

"That's absurd," Solomon said. "She's been charged with nothing other than contempt of court. If she lies on the witness stand tomorrow, she'll be charged with perjury as well. The thing which I find most perplexing is that she surely knows that her fingerprints are on that photo. She must certainly know that it's a matter of record, that it's scientific evidence. What does she hope to gain by pissing off the judge?"

"Like I done said," Pommerly answered, "she'd much rather be charged with perjury than murder. Wouldn't you?"

"She's not going to be charged with murder, so her thinking is clearly flawed," Solomon answered with mounting irritation.

"Well, you can say what you want, but I'm just telling you what she's thinking now. The maid don't want to be charged with no murder. Now I'm through with that."

"Mr. Dale," Solomon asked, "Given that you are a Halcyon native, and that seven of the jurors are black women, how do you think the maid's outburst was perceived by the jury?"

"Well, since you laid the groundwork for the altered photograph of Miss Murdock with Dr. De Jean's testimony, and a fingerprint expert's prior to calling her as a witness, I think that she will be perceived by the jury to have been argumentative and hostile based upon her attitude. With a black assistant district attorney, and a majority of black jurors, I think her derogatory reference to a `white man's court' didn't win her any friends, even among her peers. Obviously, the black segment of the public has not been excluded from the legal proceedings in this or any other recent instance. If anything, I'd say that there is a perception among the jurors that she definitely intended to harm the decedent, who did in fact die. I'd say her testimony helped the defense."

"I agree, although I'm surprised that she was so haughty," Solomon speculated. "I'd anticipated that she would be a hostile witness, but I expected that she would answer the questions I asked her. I'll be curious to see how she handles herself tomorrow. It wouldn't surprise me at all if she shows up with her own attorney standing next to her on the witness stand, telling her what and how to answer."

"Yes," Dale agreed, "that wouldn't surprise me either, but basically all any attorney can do to avoid being held in contempt of court himself, is to instruct her to avail herself of the protections afforded by the Fifth Amendment."

"What happened with your investigation of John Doe, Miss Murdock's alleged bastard son?" Tchoupitoulas asked Pommerly.

"He apparently disappeared."

"Disappeared? What the hell do you mean disappeared? You're supposed to be watching him."

"Yeah, D.T. I done told you that."

"No, you didn't say he disappeared, you said that he hadn't shown up in a while."

"Now, ain't that the same thing?"

"The definition of the term disappear would seem to indicate a more permanent condition than he `hasn't shown up in a while,' which is what you told me. I assume that you are still monitoring his house?"

"Of course, but there ain't been much to watch. He hasn't been there, I mean at all. He hasn't even come back for his toothbrush."

"So how long has it been since he was there?" Tchoupitoulas asked.

"When was it you was here last Mark? I mean in Halcyon?"

"First week of August, last year."

"Well, that's just about how long he's been gone," Pommerly answered.

"You mean you haven't ever actually seen him?" Tchoupitoulas asked.

"Damn, D.T. don't you read the weekly reports I've been sending you? If you'd read the reports, you wouldn't be asking me stupid questions like that. I've never seen him, but to put in a capsule for you, I've spent a lot of time in Jackson and I checked with the property manager at the Spanish Trace Apartments. John Doe's apartment rent is paid a year in advance, that is, it's paid from June to June each year from a bank draft from his account at the First Bank of Jackson."

"So you were able to gain access to his bank records?" Solomon asked.

"I was able to gain access to the man who collects the rent, the apartment manager, the property manager. He said he didn't give a shit whether John Doe is there or he ain't. He told me it didn't make him no never-mind one way or the other since he don't never have to put a pistol on Doe to make him come up with the rent money. All of the subject's utilities are paid by automatic withdrawal from his bank every month, and the rent is paid until this coming June 1. But Doe's car is still parked in the garage at his apartment, all covered with dust, like he ain't been driving in a while. All that's in my reports."

"What kind of car is it?" Tchoupitoulas asked. "A Cadillac?"

"You damn racist!" Pommerly scolded him. "You just assume that a Negro with some money is going to buy a Cadillac, don't you? It would never occur to you that the man might have a Lincoln or a

Mercedes. You just assume that since the subject is a black man that he just has to have a Cadillac. Will we ever be done with stereotypes of the black man?"

"Well," Tchoupitoulas replied, "there's no need to take some high and mighty attitude and get yourself all puffed up. I asked you a simple question, and I don't believe that I especially care for your tone. What kind of car is it?"

"A Cadillac," Pommerly laughed. "Aw D.T., man, I'm just playing with you, but the fact is that he's missing, and has been missing. I ain't saying that anybody's been messing with his mail, or anything like that, but if you was to check his bank statements you'd note that the bank balance in his checking account ain't been reduced except for monthly service charges and utility payments inthe five, no, nearly seven, months that some third party, unknown to me, might've had an accidental look at them, if you catch my drift."

"Let's see," Tchoupitoulas speculated, "a man with a nice apartment, a nice car, and money in the bank disappears without notice, just leaves, doesn't call anybody, doesn't talk to anybody, and doesn't stop delivery of his mail. What does that tell you?"

"I don't know what it tells you, but I t tells me that either he's dead, or is gonna be, that somebody's after him. He has a reputation as a gambler, and not one who wins very often. He might be on the run, at least that's the rumor around town. He owes Jay Steiler big money, the kind you pay, one way or the other, if you dig what I'm sayin.' That piddly seven thousand dollars left in his bank account ain't enough to make a dent in what he owes, from what I've been able to gather. I went by the Big Wheel, that strip joint in Jackson owned by Jay Steiler, and God knows who else, and met Jay Steiler my own self. It was as spooky a place as I've ever been in my life, a strip joint with some well-dressed but rough looking employees, all packing heat. I had to go through three levels of security before I got in to see the man myself, and I was patted down by three different guys before I got into the inner sanctum. In fact, I was temporarily relieved of my traveling companion."

"Your what?" Solomon asked.

"My heater, my rod…"

"He means his pistol," Tchoupitoulas observed with some irritation. "Get to the story Pommerly, and try to stay focused."

"There was a couple of strippers just lying around in Steiler'soffice like cats. When I got back there he told them, the bitches, to beat it, and then his men sat me down in one of the chairs facing his desk. At both ends of his desk there was a man standing there like Napoleon with his hand on his heater inside his sport coat. They just looked at me the whole time with their zombie dead fish eyes. I didn't make any sudden moves, if you catch my drift.

"`What can I do for you?' Mr. Steiler asked me without looking up. "`I understand that you are an associate of Mr. John Doe.'"

"`The nigger owes me money,'" I said, "`and I ain't no `sociate of his. I was hoping you might use a little influence to find him for me. The word around town is that he owes you money too.'"

"`You're obviously an associate of his,'" Steiler said to me, "`and he sent you here on a mission of discovery to determine how serious we are about debt collection. When you report back to him, tell him he needs to step up and address the matter while that option exists, make some sort of payment arrangements, you know, like they do at the IRS. Like the IRS, we have collection agents throughout this great nation. I'm a busy man and I don't wish to expend the energy necessary to chase someone down to collect a legitimate debt. In the meantime, there are increasing interest and penalties associated with his debt. At this juncture, I'd rather have the money he owes me than consider other options, but you should inform him that, like the IRS, sometimes my interests are equally served by making an example of someone who refuses to honor his obligations. At some point soon, I may decide his debt is uncollectable, and write it off. At that time, I will no longer be willing to accept payment. This debt is an outstanding one and will be called in, in the very near future at an as yet undetermined date, one which is subject to my rapidly darkening mood. I've acted in good faith in this matter, Mr. Doe has not. His apartment is being monitored by my agents and I have issued an unofficial warrant to pick him up and bring him in. Tell him that he can run, but sooner or later he will have to deal with this matter, one way or the other, and so will I. Right now, a phone call can forestall further collection efforts. Thank you for coming by, Mr. Pommerly, you're dismissed.'" That's what he done told me. I knew that his use of the word `dismissed' meant for me to beat it. I've never been so glad to get out of any place in my life.

"The nitty gritty is that John Doe is hiding out somewhere dodging Jay Steiler. So far, I've been unable to find out how much he owes, or where he's hiding out. I'm under the distinct impression that his marker is about to be called. It probably would've been called in already exceptin' that they don't know where the somitch is. But just because they don't know where he is don't mean that somebody ain't looking for him, or that they won't find him, but I will say this. He's done one hell of a job making himself scarce. It ain't easy to just disappear these days, to just hide out without a trace, but if I was him, I'd call that gangster Steiler while he still has the chance, you know, and make a payment arrangement."

"Good work Pommerly," Tchoupitoulas praised him, "you mentioned something about his girlfriend in one of your reports, you see, I do read them. Nancy Wilson? Williams? What's the situation with her?"

"Yeah, Nancy Wilson, just like the singer, only white…a chesty white woman who used to work at the Big Wheel as a pole dancer. She's gone too, but she's only been gone for five months. She's at her aunt's condomania in Tupelo. I had someone tail her up there and she's under surveillance right now."

"Do you think she's meeting John Doe there?" Solomon asked.

"If she is, she's taking her own sweet time about it. I mean she ain't met him anywhere yet. I figure that Steiler's got somebody tailing her too, case she hooks up with Doe, at which time they'll plop down on him like a falcon, and he'll disappear for real, forever."

"So you have an address on her?" Solomon asked. "I'm going to need that. Given the circumstances I'd say the prospects for Mr. Doe don't look so rosy right now. I don't know what other sources of revenue might be available to him, if any, but one thing's for sure, he won't be able to seek financial relief from Miss Murdock, under the circumstances."

"In terms of the trial what do you intend to do with this information, specifically the alleged relationship of John Doe to Miss Murdock?" Dale asked Solomon.

"I'm not sure yet. I need something else, something more. Right now, all I have is hearsay, rumor, and innuendo."

"But if this so-called John Doe really is the illegitimate offspring of Miss Murdock I don't see how locating him has any bearing on this case at all, at least in terms of exonerating the defendants."

"He's the dark horse in this matter. Miss Murdock's will was probated in what I'd consider record time, leaving everything to her cousin Mark Delgado. A simple DNA test can establish Doe's relationship to Miss Murdock. He'd clearly be entitled to a large part of her considerable estate,and whatever gambling or other debts he's incurred could be quickly resolved. Things always ultimately come down to certain basic questions. Why hasn't Doe come forward to claim a large share of what he probably regards as `his' money? Especially given his underworld debt? I'd think if anyone had a genuinely pressing and plausible motive to kill Miss Murdock, it would be him."

“You’d think he’s the first person the police would be looking at, but still, ain’t nobody gonna kill his own mother under any circumstances, `specially not any black man, even a deadbeat,” Pommerly speculated. “Besides, the police don’t even know he exists.”

“He had the big three,” Solomon observed, “motive, means and opportunity. He was able to come and go as her yardman without creating suspicion, but thanks to your excellent work, we’re aware that the decedent probably has a son, a possibility which the prosecution doesn’t even suspect, and even if they did, wouldn’t mention. But I still need more information. Pommerly, I want you to go up to Tupelo and interview Doe’s girlfriend. She has to know where he is. I want to talk to him as soon as possible. If he’s afraid of anybody, tell her that I can arrange immediate security for him, at my expense, all that he needs. Tell her to have him call me. Tell her I’ll make sure he gets all of the money from his mother’s estate that’s rightfully his. If she’s in touch with Doe, and certainly she is, that will lure him out of the bushes faster than anything.

“There’s still something very perplexing and suspicious about the speed with which her will was probated,” Solomon said reflectively, almost as if talking to himself. “She was dead and barely cold and in the ground. This strikes me as curious. I know you told me that things move faster in a small town, Mr. Dale, but still, this seems hasty to me, especially in light of the fact that her death was a homicide. Common decency, and a basic general respect for the dead, seem to have been thrown out of the window in this case. Admittedly I don’t know much about the south, but given what I do know, it strikes me as very uncharacteristic of your long-standing reputation for southern traditions. I just wonder why there was some pressing need to execute her will so quickly, that’s all.”

“Well, nobody was especially surprised by the terms of her will,” Dale said. “Mark Delgado was the only person close to her, and everybody in town knew it. She might still have had relatives in Newport, Rhode Island, but if so, she wasn't on good terms with any of them, and as far as I know, hadn't communicated with any of them in years. Maybe she didn't want anybody she didn't like, or who didn't like her, getting any of her money. She can't be blamed for that, and it's not unusual. The fact is, she really didn't like anybody other than Delgado, and the district attorney's mother, whom she spoke with frequently, but seldom saw. She probably wanted things wrapped up quickly to make it more difficult to oppose her wishes. I really don't see anything unusual about that at all."

"I'm just not satisfied with that. It was still way too fast, under any circumstances. I imagine you know her attorney, Mr. Dale. If you don't mind, I'd like you to visit him and see if Miss Murdock had given him any specific instructions relating to a quick resolution and closing of her estate, or if it was Delgado's lawyer who was in a hurry to settle things."

"Yes, her attorney was Don Light, and I know him. I'll drop by his office at noon recess tomorrow and see what he has to say."

"There's one other thing that bothers me," Solomon remarked as an afterthought, "There is absolutely no security in that courthouse. There was a portable scanner in place the first day, but it has been pushed against the wall ever since. I know that you guys don't want some Yankee coming down here and telling you `that's not the way we do things in the big city,' but this lax security really is appalling."

"I don't think that you have anything to worry about. This is Halcyon, and everybody knows everybody else."

"Somehow, in light of our reasons for being here in the first place, I don't find that thought especially comforting," Solomon concluded.

20.

Tighten Up

"All rise. Court is now in session."

"Defense again calls Mrs. Livingston to the stand."

"Bailiff, escort Mrs. Livingston to the witness stand."

The witness was escorted by the bailiff to the witness stand along with an attorney who addressed the judge. "Your Honor, may I approach the bench? My name is Kelvin C. Johnson, and with the court's permission, I've been retained by the witness, Mrs. Hattie Livingston to represent and assist her in answering the questions necessary for her testimony in the matter here before the court."

"You are aware that the court has deemed her to be a hostile witness, and that charges of contempt of court and perjury are pending against her."

"Yes, Your Honor."

"Very well, Mr. Johnson, but let me warn you, that any further disruptive outbursts will not be tolerated in my courtroom. Is that understood?"

"Yes, Your Honor, the witness wishes to cooperate fully with this court."

"Very well. Mr. Solomon, you may resume your examination of the witness. Mrs. Livingston, you are still under oath. Proceed."

"Mrs. Livingston, I again show you defense exhibit #1, a photograph of the decedent, Miss Murdock. I also call the jury's attention to yesterday's testimony of state fingerprint expert Walter Payton, who told the court that your fingerprints, and those of the decedent were the only identifiable fingerprints found on the altered photograph. Now I ask the question again, Mrs. Livingston, did you alter that photograph of Miss Murdock?"

The maid's lawyer instructed to her to answer the question. "No," she replied.

"Your Honor," the district attorney shouted as he rose, "this is a deliberate attempt to intimidate and browbeat this witness. She's worked as a domestic servant in that house for nearly thirty years. I maintain that during the course of her employment she probably handled everything in that house on numerous occasions. The medical examiner has already testified that the cause of death was a .32 caliber pistol which has been entered as evidence as such. This entire line of questioning is irrelevant and nothing but an elaborate attempt to confuse and mislead the jury."

"I withdraw the question," Solomon said, suddenly seeming no longer interested in the line of inquiry which he had initiated the previous day with such fanfare. "No further questions."

"Anything on redirect Mr. Roberts?"

"Yes, Your Honor," the district attorney replied, casting a puzzled look at Solomon. "We're going to settle the question of the photograph once and for all. Now, Mrs. Livingston, you've repeatedly maintained that you did not alter this photograph in any way, although you do admit handling it, isn't that so?"

The witness had been instructed by her lawyer to answer the district attorney's questions, and finding him less abrasive than Mr. Solomon, complied readily. "Yes sir, I touched it. I dusted everything in that house all the time, but one time, I accidentally knocked that picture on the floor and it broke the glass out, about two years ago. Miss Murdock had me to take and go down to the Dollar General store and buy a new frame."

"So you reframed that picture yourself, is that right?"

"Yes, it was a regular size 8 by 10 inch frame. I took the glass out of the new frame and put it back into the old frame, the one that I knocked over. Miss Murdock told me to go and take the new frame and put in the trash. It was a new frame and she didn't want it, so I asked her could I have it, and she said to take it, so I did."

"Well, Mrs. Livingston, how did that photograph get altered and placed beneath that rug?" Roberts asked.

"I don't know."

"After you reframed the photograph, did you replace it in its former location?"

"Yes, I put it back where it was before I broke the glass. A couple of months later it wasn't there, so I suspicioned that Miss Jeannie had done moved it, and that was that."

"During the course of your long employment there Mrs. Livingston, did Miss Murdock frequently move things around?"

"She didn't move big things very much, like tables, or sofas, or chairs, but she'd take and move some lamps and pictures around. She'd have me take and get some out the closet and put some others back in. They was all framed pictures, you know. The picture that you been asking me about was just gone one day. I suspicioned that she'd put it in a closet somewhere, but it didn't make me no never-mind where she put it."

"Thank you, Mrs. Livingston. Your Honor, and members of the jury, I believe her testimony satisfactorily explains her fingerprints being on that picture," Roberts said as he approached the jury. "Mrs. Livingston was willing to stand by her testimony regarding the photograph, even though it meant spending the night in jail and facing a charge of perjury. One thing more, Mrs. Livingston, why didn't you just answer Mr. Solomon's questions yesterday Mrs. Livingston?"

"I did. He asked me and I said no. I told the truth, but that wasn't enough for him. If he'd just have asked me how my fingerprints got to be on that picture to begin with, I'd of told him, but instead he wanted to accuse me of taking and killing Miss Murdock with Voodoo or some kind of black magic or witch stuff. I'm a Christian woman and I had nothing to do with whatever was done to that picture, and I don't know nothing about no Voodoo, but that man over there just kept going and going. The truth was the last thing he was after. If he'd just've asked me like you did, I'd of told him the truth, just like I told you. He's not a nice man."

"No further questions, Your Honor. I move that the contempt of court charge against Miss Livingston be dismissed Your Honor."

"The witness may step down. It is so ordered."

Demonbreun P. Tchoupitoulas burst through the rear door of the courtroom and walked briskly down the aisle to the defense table addressing Solomon in a whisper before he could call his next witness. "Your Honor, I apologize to the court for my interruption," he called toward the judge in a thick Louisiana accent, as he handed Solomon a folded manila envelope which he removed from his coat pocket.

"A new will has been found which left John Doe half of her estate," Tchoupitoulas whispered to Solomon. "It was unknown even to her own attorney, I mean her regular lawyer."

"Where did it come from?"

"It was found by Delgado's maid, Chantelle. It's witnessed and notarized and takes precedence over the earlier will which has already been probated."

"How do you know that?"

"I read the son of a bitch."

Solomon seated himself, opened the envelope and quickly read the single page document, noticing as he concluded, the name of the notary, and the date of the document. "Where did you get this?" Solomon asked as he passed the document to Lucien Dale.

"Pommerly, of course. Delgado's maid found it stuffed under a cushion at Miss Murdock's house, Eldorado, where Delgado had sent her to clean up the place, since he intends to move over there in the near future. The maid thought it was significant and decided to give it to the police, but upon reflection figured that she might be arrested for having stolen it. Also, she didn't want to lose her job with Delgado."

"But the police had been over that place with a fine-tooth comb. How is it that they would have missed it?"

"Hell, the police aren't omniscient, and people usually tend to find what they're looking for. In other words, the cops weren't looking for a will in a sofa, especially since they already had one. Delgado has never been a suspect. He presented a valid will which had been given to him by the decedent, and that was that. The matter was closed because everybody thought it was closed."

"This is a valid, legal, and binding document according to the laws of the state of Mississippi, and it invalidates the will which has already beenprobated, as it is more recent," Co-counsel Dale said as he passed the document to Nikki Daniels. "It complicates things, but has no bearing on this case, at least in terms of the defendants. What are you going to do?"

"I don't know, but I'd better think of something, and fast. Does Delgado know about this new will?"

"No. She gave it to Pommerly as soon as she found it. She called him and he went right over and picked it up in person. He told her not to say anything to anybody about it, especially Delgado, or she might get in trouble."

"Why didn't she give it to Delgado?"

"Pommerly's been `entertaining' her, and she probably thinks she's in love with him, or rather, that he's in love with her…besides, she doesn't like Delgado."

"Mr. Solomon, may we continue?" the judge asked with obvious irritation, after more than a minute and a half of whispered conversations between Solomon, Tchoupitoulas, and Lucien Dale.

"Your Honor, may I approach the bench?" Solomon said as he stood facing the judge. "I have just received some crucial new evidence which has a direct bearing on this case. It will alter the entire basis of the defense's representation of these two defendants. I realize that court has just started session today, but I beg the court's indulgence in the form of an adjournment for the rest of the day while the defense considers this new and crucial evidence."

Solomon's request of the judge was interrupted by the district attorney who rose from his seat and angrily approached the bench. "Mr. Solomon, what are you trying to pull? You're wasting the court's time and the taxpayers' money. This should've been attended to before court was in session. I must protest."

"Counsel approach the bench," the Judge Brock ordered. "This is highly irregular," he agreed, "however, since this is a murder trial, the court intends to grant the defense as much leeway as possible, but I'm not going to delay this trial unnecessarily, and I'm not going to ask the jury to leave the courtroom. Counsel, both of you, proceed to my chambers and I'll consider the request. In the future, Mr. Solomon, please attend to such matters outside the courtroom. You were asked at the beginning of this trial if youwere ready and you indicated that you were. If you weren't prepared, you should have said so at that time. Court will recess for ten minutes," the judge ordered, striking his gavel loudly.

After fifteen minutes or thereabouts, the two attorneys exited the judge's chambers. The frowning district attorney walked briskly to the prosecution's table and quickly whispered something to his co-counsel before being interrupted by the bailiff's shout "All rise. Court is now in session."

The judge seated himself, turned to his left and addressed the jury. "Members of the jury, sometimes during the course of a trial, new evidence arises unexpectedly, which may have a direct bearing on the outcome of the case in question. In most instances when this occurs, there is a brief recess during which the new evidence is considered, and the trial then continues. New evidence has just now been presented to the defense, which Mr. Solomon has explained to the court. In the interest of providing the defendants the most thorough defense possible, court is going to be adjourned for the day. I realize that this, or any delay of the trial by even a day, is an inconvenience for each of you, and the court apologizes. Again, you are not to discuss the case with each other or anyone else. Court is adjourned until 9:00 am tomorrow morning."

After court at the Mexican restaurant, Nikki Daniels turned toSolomon."What did you tell Judge Brock that persuaded him to adjourn until tomorrow morning?" she asked, as she brought a cool glass of sangria to her lips.

"I didn't mention the will, if that's what you mean, but I certainly danced some sort of jig before the judge, with the district attorney raising hell all the while. Finally the judge granted my request for recess."

"What's the strategy now?"

"I'm not really sure. Does anybody have any ideas? Hold on," Solomon said, as he looked at his phone. "It's Pommerly. Just a minute. I'm putting you on the speaker phone, the hands free. No, it's a Mexican joint. It doesn't open for half an hour. Yeah, they let us in early. No, just go ahead."

"Delgado has a big ass gambling problem," Pommerly stated dryly, "one which is a lot worse since his mother croaked several years ago. I don't know whether she'd kept him in check prior to that, or that he just didn't want to piss her off by her finding out about it. She was the one with the money, and she wasn't the generous type. But he was the only heir and he got all her dough, and everything else. I don't have no specific amount, but it was plenty. During the last year or so, specially in the last several months, he's been unloading everything he owns, presumably to cover gambling debts which he has much less trouble getting than getting rid of, if you dig what I'm saying. He has a liking for private, high stakes card games hosted by Jay Steiler in Jackson. They let him win enough at first, to keep him hooked, but they've been slowly bleeding him dry…the long con game. He was just about out of money when Miss Murdock was murdered. He wasn't in debt as far as I can tell, exceptin' to Steiler. But it was constant. He'd run up a big bill and then they'd ban him from the games until his bill was paid, but it looks like he was running out of rope, and if she hadn't been killed, he might've ended up floating in the river at some point. Do you dig what I'm sayin'?"

"Well, that explains why he wanted the will probated so quickly,"Solomon speculated, "but still, Steiler isn't likely to kill the goose that is laying golden eggs."

"Oh, I got cha," Pommerly reconsidered, "you mean Steiler's running Delgado for the long con game."

"That's a likely scenario," Solomon concluded.

"Yes it is," Tchoupitoulas agreed. "Most of Delgado's holdings are out of state, and his financial manager is based in New York, so everything he might have disposed of would likely be totally under the radar here. He has a brokerage account in the big apple, but has allowed much of that money to flow into and through the bank here, in Halcyon, probably as a matter of convenience. What are you going to do with this information?"

"I don't know yet, but this is bringing some things into focus. Thanks Pommerly, good work."

"What now?" Lucien Dale wondered aloud.

"Is there anywhere you have to be today?" Mark asked.

"Not especially."

"In that case I'm prepared to stay here all day, if necessary. I hate to do the prosecution's work, but it's clear to me that the district attorney is in way over his head. As a Halcyon native, I think he's too impressed with the aristocratic pedigrees of the people involved to be able to see beyond that, but I'm not. We're used to dealing with rich people and high-profile cases. The defense can rest now, as far as I'm concerned, and as soon as the doors to the courtroom open tomorrow morning, I'll present our closing arguments. But the press expects a show, and they'll get one. Our reputation is at stake, so the three of us are going to solve this crime right now. Everybody in this town is just too close to the facts to see them clearly. Now, all we have to do is to convince the jury. Let's get to work."

21.

The Best Defense

As Mark Solomon and his defense team entered the courtroom the following day, they passed the metal scanner pushed into a corner of the corridor, unplugged and unused, again. Solomon simply shook his head at the incompetence and lack of security but said nothing. Still, it made him uncomfortable. Everybody in the state of Mississippi has a gun. He already knew that much, and the thought that some maniac could just walk through the door and start shooting made him extremely ill at ease.

"All rise. Court is now in session. You may be seated," the bailiff stated.

"Is the defense ready?" Judge Brock asked.

"Yes, Your Honor, the defense is ready."

"You may call your first witness."

Solomon's right hand man Nikki Daniels, rose and addressed the court. "The defense calls Nancy Wilson. Your honor, this witness is testifying under subpoena, and is here against her will. I ask that the court declare her to be a hostile witness."

"It is noted."

"Mrs. Is it Miss or Mrs. Wilson?"

"It's Mrs. although I'm now divorced. Wilson is my married name."

"Very well, Mrs. Wilson. You are now, that is, currently a resident of Jackson, Mississippi, is that correct?"

"Yes."

"Are you living there at present?"

"I still have an apartment there, but I've been staying at my aunt's in Tupelo."

"And why is that? Is your aunt ill?"

"I'd rather not say."

"And why is that?"

"I'm afraid."

"Afraid of what?"

"The witness will answer the question," the judge directed.

"My boyfriend has disappeared, and I believe he was murdered. I think he was killed in a car wreck back in August."

"I object. Your honor, this line of questioning is running so far afield that it's confusing the jury. It's certainly confusing me. Whoever her boyfriend is," Roberts said dismissively, "certainly has nothing to with the matter now before this court. This is yet another of many attempts on the part of Mr. Solomon to bewilder the court."

"Miss Daniels, while the court wishes to provide the defendants the opportunity to present an adequate defense, I'm inclined to agree with the district attorney."

"Your Honor, I ask the court's indulgence. The defense will show that this witness's testimony has a direct bearing on the case, and further establishes motive."

"The defense has sought to establish motive in several different directions, by attempting to implicate persons not even connected to the issue before this court. Unless you can somehow tie all of this together in a coherent fashion, and fairly quickly, I'm going to sustain the district attorney's objections."

"Yes, Your Honor, I believe that I can do that if the court permits."

"Then you may proceed."

"Thank you. Mrs. Wilson, do you know a man who goes by the name of John Doe?"

"I object," the D.A. shouted angrily. "The defense has again clearly embarked upon some ill-conceived fishing expedition. If there really is somebody named John Doe, it's obviously some pseudonym. In any case John Doe, whoever that may, or may not be, is not on trial, the defendants are. This line of questioning has absolutely nothing whatsoever to do with the matter now before this court."

"Miss Daniels?"

"Your Honor, it is the intention of the defense not only to show that there were others who had greater motive than the defendants in this case, but to exonerate the defendants, and, hopefully to disclose the actual murderer of Miss Murdock in this courtroom today."

An audible murmur of anticipation throughout the courtroom was followed by the judge's ruling.

"Mr. Roberts?"

"Your Honor, if the defense actually intends to disclose the `true murderer of murderers' in court today," the D.A. answered sarcastically, casting a condescending glance toward the defense stand, "then by all means, do let Miss Daniels continue." He returned to the prosecution's table and whispered to the assistant D.A., "I'm in so far over my head that I don't have any idea where this is going, or any kind of strategy anymore, at all. The best I can do is to keep objecting, but that's about like being stuck in your car on the railroad tracks and yelling `stop' at a runaway freight train bearing down on you at 70 miles an hour. I've totally lost control of this trial. At this point we're just along for the ride."

"You may answer the question," Mrs. Wilson.

“Yes, he’s my boyfriend.”

“Is John Doe some sort of nickname?”

“No, it is his legal name. He had it changed legally to John Doe.”

“And why did he do that?”

“Objection. The question calls for a conclusion.”

“Sustained.”

“In your opinion then Mrs. Wilson,” Daniels continued, “and solely as a matter of your personal conjecture, why do you think he had his name legally changed?”

“He told me…”

“You are not permitted to state what he told you, Mrs. Wilson. I’m asking you why, in your opinion, you think he had his name changed?”

“He was a `high yellow,’ you know, of mixed race, half black and half white, the result of a hook-up at the Newport Jazz Festival. He was born in France, but then put in some Catholic orphanage somewhere up north, in Massachusetts, I think, and raised there, until he somehow found out who his parents are, or were. He knew he wasn’t wanted by anybody, and didn’t belong anywhere. In my opinion, that’s why he changed his name. I think it was sort of a formal way to tell the world to go to hell.”

“Your Honor, the prosecution asks that the court bring an end to this entire line of questioning once and for all. It’s but another of the well-known attempts of the defense to detour the jury by diverting its attention away from the actual facts which concern this case.”

“Miss Daniels the court has been extremely lenient in allowing the defense to stray so far afield, and only because this is a murder trial, but its patience is rapidly waning. I’m going to insist that you tie all of this together quickly or I shall be forced to sustain Mr. Roberts’ objections.”

“Your Honor, the defense understands and acknowledges the court’s concerns, but in the interests of providing the defendants fair and thorough representation, humbly requests the court's further, but brief indulgence."

"The defense may continue," Judge Brock ruled, as an obviously irritated district attorney again took his seat.

"Who were his parents?" Daniels asked the witness.

His father was the late jazz saxophone player Omega Santi…"

"And? Please continue Mrs. Wilson."

"And his mother," she paused, "was the dead woman, that Miss Murdock." The statement from the witness was met with a stunned silence, rapidly followed by a loud and audible gasp throughout the courtroom.

"Order! I want order in this court," Judge Brock shouted, striking his gavel repeatedly.

"Objection!" Roberts shouted as he jumped to his feet. "This is absurd. The decedent had no offspring, and this entire line on the part of the defense is not only an attempt to divert the course of justice, but to defame the decedent."

"Overruled. I want to see where this is leading."

"You stated earlier you thought that your boyfriend, your companion John Doe, had been murdered. Why do you think that, Mrs. Wilson?"

"He told me that he was going to Halcyon with a friend of his to do some work for somebody. He wouldn't tell me exactly where he was going or what he was going to do, which meant that he was probably involved in something illegal. He had some bad friends, and he knew that I didn't like any of them. I wouldn't let him bring anybody to the apartment. He'd tried to straighten up, but they just kept pulling him back into their web."

"And when was this?"

"It was August 6, last year."

"How is it that you happen to remember that date?"

"It was the last time I saw him alive. That's why I remember it.

He took off with that low-life so-called friend of his Deon Washington, he said, to go do some work for somebody in Halcyon, and he never came back. They was killed in some car wreck, burned alive. They was run off the road into a tree. I know it wasn't no accident, I don't care what the paper said. John Doe owed some people money in Jackson, and said they was after him, but that if he did this job for that man over in Halcyon, then he'd be able to pay him back, the man he owed the money to in Jackson. It was all about it in the Jackson paper the next day. They identified Deon Washington as one of the two people killed in the burnt-up car by his dental records from some prison he'd been at, but not John Doe. I knew it was him though, John, since I knew that's where he was going, and who with. They said the other dead man remained unidentified, but I knew it was John. It had to be."

"Why didn't you come forward with that information if you knew that he'd died?"

"Three reasons. In the first place, John Doe owed that man in Jackson $20,000."

"Wait, what man?"

"I don't know," she said looking at Jay Steiler and then turning away quickly, "just some man in Jackson."

"Is that man in this courtroom today?"

"I wouldn't know whoever it was, if I saw him," the witness answered, carefully avoiding looking at Jay Steiler who beheld her with an icy stare.

"Well, continue if you will Mrs. Wilson."

"Since the money wasn't paid, on account of the car accident, I knew they'd be coming after me next…to collect his debt. That's the way it works. I figured that John got what he'd been courtin' all his life. You can't make a good deal with bad people. I told him that time after time, but he wouldn't never listen to me. I loved him, but he got himself killed, and that was his fault, and not mine. I just didn't want to be next. The less said about all of it, the better. So that's number one. Number two is, I don't owe the police nothing. They ain't ever done anything but cause me trouble my whole life. Why would I want to help them?"

"And the third reason?"

"I got $5,000 from John the afternoon of the day he died. He said it was a down payment for the work he and Deon Washington were going to do on the night they was killed."

"And what work was that?"

"I told you, I didn't know what he was doing then, and I don't want to know now. He's dead and gone, and there ain't nothing going to bring him back. All I know is that he was getting paid $20,000 and that the $5,000 he gave me was the down payment, and that he was supposed to be getting the rest as soon as the job was done. His part was $20,000, and that no account jailbird Deon Washington was getting $20,000 too, so whatever they was doing, or about to do, was something not only illegal, but wrong, and I didn't want to know nothing about it. That money was supposed to get him out of whatever trouble he was in, once and for all, but it turned up getting him killed."

"Was that a lot of money for the type of work he did, Mrs. Wilson?"

"Objection, calls for a conclusion."

"I withdraw the question. Mrs. Wilson, do you know who had hired him to do this work on the night he was killed?"

"It was that man over there…over here in Halcyon he did yard work for, Mr. Mark…He called him Mr. Mark, but his last name was, Delagate, or something like that, yes, it was Mark Delegate."

"Do you mean Mark Delgado?"

"Yes, that's it. Mark Delgado, that man sitting over there."

"And how do you know that?"

"He told me. John told me."

"Objection, Your Honor. Hearsay."

"Sustained."

"Let me rephrase the question Mrs. Wilson."

"Don't bother doing that. John gave me $4,500 in cash and a check from Mark Delegate, I mean Delgado, made out to him for $500, the very day he died.

"And that $5,000 was for work John Doe was doing for Mr. Delgado, is that right, Mrs. Wilson?"

"Objection. Defense is leading the witness. This is also hearsay, Your Honor."

"Sustained."

"No further questions Your Honor."

"Mr. Roberts?"

"No questions, Your Honor."

"The witness may step down."

"Demonbreun," Solomon instructed, "follow Mrs. Wilson out of the courtroom and find out what happened to that check. Go now, I don't want you to have to track her down at her aunt's house all the way upin Tupelo. Let's do this now."

"Got it," the detective said as he rose and quickly followed the previous witness out of the courtroom.

"The defense calls Jay Steiler."

Jay Steiler walked silently to the witness stand, was sworn in and took his seat. He was tall, more than six feet, immaculately groomed, and impeccably dressed. He could have easily been mistaken for a banker, or a high-end car salesman, except for an all-pervasive air of menace, of impending violence, which seemed to surround him. He was someone you'd rather not have thinking about you. Solomon recognized him for what he was and wasn't intimidated. "Mr. Steiler, I understand that you're a businessman. Would you please tell the court what businesses you currently own and operate?"

"I own the Big Wheel, a night club in Jackson, the Booby Hatch, a strip joint in south Jackson, and I'm part of a corporation which owns several of the Dreamboat, riverboat casinos along the Mississippi River, from Coahoma County down to and including Black County."

"It sounds like you are a busy man."

"I am."

"Well, then in addition to these business interests would it also be safe to say that you are a loan shark?"

"Safe?" he laughed. "I wouldn't recommend asking me that question in that manner outside of this courtroom...but to answer you, I do let some of my friends borrow money from time to time, provided I know them well, and feel that they're likely to repay me. I like to help people."

"Mr. Steiler, are you acquainted with a man named John Doe? Is he a friend of yours?"

"We weren't...I mean, aren't, but yes."

"Did you ever `help' him? Does he owe you money?"

"He did."

"So, he paid you what he owed?"

"No, the debt was considered uncollectable and written off."

"And why is that?"

"He seems to have disappeared."

"Is he dead?"

"I wouldn't know."

"How much does, did he owe you?"

"I can't recall."

"Well, Mr. Steiler, was it closer to $5.00 or $20,000?"

"Closer to 20 Gs."

"Do you usually write off large debts?"

"No, not as a rule, but things happen. I established a rule for myself a long time ago. If I let a friend borrow money, I personally consider the money to be a gift. I never say that of course, because I want to be repaid, but if someone can't, or doesn't repay me, I don't sit and stew about it, I let it go. I don't let him borrow any more money, of course, but I don't get angry about it. In that way, my life is serene and tranquil as opposed to me being upset."

"What a bunch of crap," Lucien Dale whispered to Nikki Daniels. "He's probably had more people killed than Idi Amin."

"One more thing," Jay Steiler continued, "in relation to your last question. My sainted mother told me, God rest her soul, that the best way to get rid of someone you don't like is to lend him some money, not enough that it causes you any hardship, but just enough so he'll avoid you. Maybe I should lend you $20. Mr. Solomon."

"That's amusing, Mr. Steiler, but you don't seem like someone I would want to owe money to. Now I'll ask you, is there anyone else in this courtroom who now owes you money, Mr. Steiler?"

"Objection."

"Your honor, if it please the court, this is a hostile witness."

"Overruled. Answer the question."

"Mr. Steiler, I'll ask you again. Is there anyone in this courtroom at present who owes you money?"

"No."

"Is Mark Delgado a friend of yours, Mr. Steiler, that is, have you ever `helped' him? Has he ever owed you money?"

"I may have advanced him a little money, since we're friends, I can't really remember."

"Well, Mr. Steiler, would you consider $600 thousand a little money?"

"No, of course not, however, what does that have to do with anything?"

"Isn't it true that Mr. Delgado owed you gambling debts in excess of that amount?"

"He might have owed me some money at some point, but I can't recollect a specific amount."

"But he paid you what he owed you, is that right?"

"Your Honor, the prosecution must again object. This blatant but pointless and futile attempt to involve Mark Delgado in some sort of questionable financial loan business has nothing whatsoever to do with the matterbefore this court at present. Mr. Delgado is not on trial here, and Mr. Steiler is a legitimate businessman who operates his casinos under the very strict guidelines of the Mississippi Gaming Commission. I ask that you please instruct the defense to stay on course."

"Mr. Solomon?"

"Your Honor, the prosecution opened this line of inquiry by stipulating robbery as one of the motivating factors in the murder of the decedent, Miss Murdock. The defense is merely seeking to establish that there were others beside the defendants, who also had a legitimate motive for robbery."

"Mr. Roberts, since the prosecution opened this door, I'm going to allow Mr. Solomon to step through it. Objection overruled. The witness may answer the question."

"Yes, Mr. Delgado paid me the money I loaned him."

"When did he repay you Mr. Steiler?"

"I don't remember, exactly. Last fall, sometime."

"Would it have been in September or October?"

"I can't recall, but probably around then."

"It was on October 14, isn't that right?"

"I really don't know."

"Your Honor, I introduce this bank record showing that Mark Delgado withdrew $637 thousand as defense exhibit number 7 on October 14, last year. Now Mr. Steiler, would that be the date your loan was repaid?"

"I really can't recall."

"But the loan was repaid?"

"Yes, the loan was repaid, and his credit is good."

"But isn't it true Mr. Steiler that you had to actually threaten Mr. Delgado in order to collect the money he owed you?"

"Mr. Solomon, I think that you've been watching too many movies, living in Hollywood, and all."

"Answer the question!"

"No. That isn't how I operate. I wouldn't risk my casino business over any loan, not for any amount, not for anybody," he bristled. "I've worked hard all of my life. I came from nothing and worked hard. I've had to jump through every kind of hoop the gaming commission threw in front of me. I'm clean as a whistle."

"That's nice, and I congratulate you on your success, but you are stating that Mr. Delgado owed you more than half a million dollars and that it was paid in full at one time?"

"No, I didn't say that at all, it's you who said that. I said that I don't recall an exact amount. I don't remember."

"Your witness, Mr. Roberts."

"No questions Your Honor," the D.A. replied, then turned to his co-counsel and whispered, almost apologetically, "How can I cross examine this witness? There's nothing whatsoever to connect him in any way with either of the defendants. As far as I know, they're totally unknown to each other."

Tchoupitoulas reentered the courtroom through the door at the rear and approached Solomon. "Excuse me again, Your Honor," he shouted as he approached the defense table and whispered, "Mrs. Wilson…she had the check from Mark Delgado in her purse, thinking somebody might have asked for it in court" the detective said, as Co-counsel Dale and Daniels moved close to listen to him. "I've got it right here," he said, handing it to Solomon. "It was made out to John Doe, and he's dead. She doesn't have any legal authority to cash it, so she gave it to me. What's next?"

"I don't know. Good work Demonbreun, I mean it. You're almost worth the high fees you and Pommerly extract from me. You know I don't like to take chances, especially this close to the finish line. This will take us over the top."

"Mr. Solomon, before you call your next witness, court will recess briefly. Court will resume in fifteen minutes."

"Yes, Your Honor."

"Does this check mean what I think it means?" Daniels asked.

"Yes, it means that Delgado hired those two to make sure we didn't represent Toma and Dautery, but I can't prove it. All I have is a check from him to a dead man who happened to be his on and off again yardman.Delgado could credibly state that the check to John Doe was for general clean up, or labor on the property, hell, or anything else, for that matter. He can easily explain a check for $500. If the check had been for $5,000, that would have been a different matter. He wouldn't have been able to explain that at all, but since he paid John Doe that other $4,500 in cash, there's no way to connect John Doe with Mark Delgado, beyond the fact that Doe was sometimes his yardman."

"While Delgado didn't succeed in getting us off the case," Daniels added. "It certainly worked out well for him anyway, even with the new will. With Murdock's son, John Doe out of the way, Delgado still ends up with everything, even if we win an acquittal for Toma and Dautery."

"I have no doubt that a DNA test could have substantiated the relationship between Jeannie Murdock and John Doe, and it's doubtful he'd be exhumed, but yes, with Doe dead, Delgado becomes the sole heir after all."

"Now, I can't help but wonder if those two were trying to kill us, or just scare us off," Nikki Daniels speculated. "Maybe they weren't really trying to kill us, after all. I'm no gun expert, but even I know that it's hard to miss somebody at point blank range with a 12-gauge shotgun, even in a moving car."

"If Tom hadn't reacted so quickly, I doubt we'd be here talking about it today."

"I imagine that Delgado merely wanted to scare you two into dropping the case and returning to Los Angeles," Lucien Dale conluded.

"No I don't think so. Let's return to Mrs. Wilson's testimony. Delgado wouldn't have been willing to spend $40,000 merely to frighten us into leaving, especially given his reputation as a skinflint, who wouldn't, as Pommerly phrased it, `spend a dime to see an ant eat a bale of hay.' He could've easily persuaded Doe that it was in both of their best interests to scare us off, and it wouldn't have cost him anything. Murder, however, was another matter entirely. Doe would've wanted to be paid for that, and paid well. If Delgado had been willing to spend $40,000, it was for more than merely scaring us off. He wanted us off the case permanently, by any means necessary. He wanted us dead.

"Delgado would've had to structure a deal with John Doe at some point," Solomon continued, "given that Doe was Murdock's closest and direct relative. Considering Doe's criminal proclivities, I doubt that it would've been easy. But on the other hand, Delgado is a powerful figure in Halcyon and Doe knew it. Doe was afraid of Delgado's political connections and probably thought that Delgado could make a phone call, possibly to someone in the police department here or even in Jackson, and have some charge fabricated against Doe that would stick. Maybe Delgado had offered Doe some of the inheritance to just sit back and shut up. Delgado knew the contents of the original will, and how much Jeannie Murdock was actually worth, John Doe did not. After the deal was done, Delgado could have paid Doe whatever he wanted, and that would have been that. Doe would have been glad to get anything."

"You're assuming that Delgado knew that John Doe was Jeannie Murdock's son, and I'm not so sure that he did."

"That may be, but the reason that Delgado had that will probated so quickly was that he owed Jay Steiler a lot of money and Steiler wasn't going to let it go, or wait. I have no doubt that Delgado was threatened and forced to move much faster in regard to the will than he would have otherwise."

"How do you figure Steiler got his hooks into Delgado?" Daniels asked.

"Delgado probably was tagged by one of the casino's floor managers as a big spender, more specifically, a big loser.He was introduced to Steiler, and subsequently invited to a private game. This would appeal to Delgado's inflated sense of his own self-importance in that he would be receiving the attention he felt entitled to, given his high birth and inherent nobility. He'd developed a gambling addiction but wouldn't want to be seen, or even present in the company of polyester clad mid-westerners, or anyone else he felt didn't live up to his own sense of self-importance."

"Then, Steiler let him win enough to interest him in continuing to play what would soon become a consistently losing game. Delgado, inflated with his own sense of high intelligence and self-worth was an easy mark for someone like Steiler," Dale concluded.

"In any event, it couldn't have worked out better for Delgado, but that still begs the question, who killed Jeannie Murdock?"

"It could have been John Doe," Nikki Daniels ventured.

"No, your friend Pommerly was right," Lucien Dale observed. "No black man ever kills his own mother, especially in the south. It wouldn't happen. The black family unit is primarily matriarchal in structure."

"That may be, but not necessarily in this instance. Jeannie Murdock had not acknowledged that she even had a son, legitimate or otherwise, and wouldn't have, ever, especially one of mixed race, not here, not in Halcyon, not anywhere in the deep-south. There was no familial bond of affection between them, nothing whatsoever, which would've given Doe any sense of loyalty to Miss Murdock. She no doubt treated him like a low-end domestic worker, and when she gave him money, it was probably in that capacity, and probably in cash. He resented her enough that he actually went to the trouble to legally change his name. He had no sense of loyalty to her at all. I imagine that Doe actually hated her."

"Perhaps so. I imagine that he did hate Miss Murdock, and in terms of the murder, he knew the house, Murdock's daily routine, when Delgado usually arrived and left, and when the maid came and went."

"And Miss Murdock would have likely opened the door to him."

"The bottom line is that who killed her and why is really not our problem, but in terms of my personal desires in this matter," Solomon ventured, "apart from exonerating the defendants, I'm satisfied that the persons involved in the attempt on our lives last fall received the justice they deserved in some sort of strange karmic twist of fate. You know that I'm personally opposed to the death penalty under any circumstances, but in this instance, it was imposed by a higher power. Who am I to question what was evidently an example of `cosmic justice'? In any event, I think we can wrap this up tomorrow. This trial is costing us money. The prosecution has failed completely to prove guilt beyond a reasonable doubt. I'm ready to get back to L.A. It's hot as hell down here, and there's nothing to do."

"I probably know the answer to this question already," Daniels hesitated, "but do we plan to call either of the defendants as witnesses? You didn't put them on the witness list and haven't mentioned them."

"No, we don't. Toma is basically incompetent, and Roberts would confuse him to the extent that he would confess to having burned the White House during the War of 1812. And Olivia Dautery wouldn't do either of them any good on the witness stand given her overt hostility, actual hatred of the justice system, and her contempt for any form of authority. She understandably considers this entire trial to be a waste of her time and the taxpayers' money, and has no hesitation in saying so. Her testimony in their behalf would be detrimental to their defense…no, I'd never put either of them on the witness stand."

"Well, you can't blame her," Daniels spoke in Dautery's defense.

"No, I can't, and I don't," Solomon half laughed. "It was her righteous indignation that initially convinced me that the two of them were innocent in the first place, not that we wouldn't have taken their case anyway. If we only represented innocent clients, we'd starve to death. But Toma and Dautery had been minding their own business, and were literally snatched from their home in the dead of night, and railroaded into trial, in an action reminiscent of the raids upon innocent citizenry at the hands of carpetbaggers during that terrible second era of northern aggression, known as reconstruction," Solomon pontificated, smiling and winking at Lucien Dale. "You see, Mr. Dale, I do know my history. But no, Nikki, she would…all she'd do is potentially irritate some members of the jury."

"Court is now in session. All rise. You may be seated."

"Your Honor, may I approach?" Solomon asked, as D.A. Bill Roberts stood quickly and followed the defense attorney to the bench. "I've literally just received a more recent and valid will prepared under the direction of the decedent, Miss Murdock, which supersedes that which has already been probated."

"Let me see that."

"It's a valid document," the judge said, passing it to the district attorney, who stood in stunned silence for a moment as he perused the single page document, before returning it to the judge.

"Miss Murdock did not have a son. Surely you can't give

credence to the rambling testimony of defense witness Mrs. Wilson. This is insane," the district attorney objected. "And who is this John Doe you keep harping on? Where does he fit into this picture anywhere? This doesn't make any sense at all."

"I would like to introduce this will as defense exhibit number 12, Your Honor."

"No, no. I must object. Your Honor, while this may well be a valid document, it's an issue for a civil court to address. If the decedent had a son, and it proves through DNA testing to be this mysterious and missing John Doe after all, it still has nothing whatsoever to do with the matter before the court at present."

"It has everything to do with the matter before the court," Solomon argued. "It goes straight to motive."

"No, Your Honor, Mr. Solomon hasn't gone `straight to' anything yet, let alone motive. He has more `loco-motives' than a freight train, and this ploy is nothing more than one more attempt to delay this trial and confuse the jury even further."

"Mr. Solomon?"

"Your Honor, since this is a murder trial, and the defense is providing its services pro bono, which include transportation, lodging and food, as well as associated miscellaneous expenses, absolutely the last thing any member of my team wants to do is prolong or delay this trial in any way. I humbly ask the indulgence of the court in order to serve the cause of justice."

"You may present your evidence, Mr. Solomon. The purpose of this trial is to reach a just verdict. Note this as defense exhibit 12," Judge Brock said, handing it to the woman seated at his right. "Call your next witness."

"The defense calls Arthur Tanner to the stand."

After the witness was sworn in and seated, Solomon addressed the witness. "Please state your full name for the court."

"Henry Arthur Tanner."

"Now Mr. Tanner, I submit this document, this will, dated February 4 of last year, for your examination. It has your signature as well as the signatures of three witnesses, and a notary. As Miss Murdock's attorney, did you prepare this document?"

"Yes, and no. I wasn't her attorney, per se, although I am an attorney. Miss Murdock had already taken an earlier, existing will, and made a few changes on her own, some substitutions, which she wanted me to examine and make certain they were legal. I looked them over quickly, since that's what she wanted, and they appeared to be acceptable from a legal standpoint, so, I had my secretary retype the singlepage document while she waited, which was what Miss Murdock wanted. It was witnessed, signed, and notarized in my office. She paid me for my services and left."

"Do you have a copy of this will?" Solomon asked.

"No, she took the original with her, didn't want multiple copies, and insisted that the typed version be erased from the office computer hard drive while she was in my office. I was sworn to secrecy, and promised her that I would not mention her visit, or that I'd ever even met her. She was...well, she struck me as peculiar, eccentric...actually. She already knew precisely what she wanted when she walked through the front door. Of course I knew who she was, but I'd never met her before that day, and I didn't see her again."

"So, she paid you and left, is that right?"

"Yes, she paid me in cash, left with the new will, and that was the first, and last time I saw her."

"Any questions Mr. Roberts? The witness may step down."

"The defense calls Mark Delgado."

"I object, Your Honor," Bill Roberts shouted, as he again rose from his seat at the prosecution's table. "Mr. Delgado is a witness for the prosecution, and Mr. Solomon had ample opportunity to question him during regular cross examination. This is highly irregular."

"Mr. Solomon, I'm inclined to agree with the district attorney. Mr. Delgado is not on trial, and you've already had an opportunity to cross examine him. The court has granted you…"

"Your Honor, this new evidence goes directly to the heart of this trial. It clearly establishes the real motive for this murder, and proves beyond doubt that what the prosecution has claimed as the defendants' primary motive, robbery, has no bearing on this case at all as far as it pertains to the defendants."

"Then you may proceed Mr. Solomon," the judge stated, as the dejected and disheartened district attorney took his seat.

"Hell, I give up," he whispered to the assistant D.A. "He keeps changing the game in play, introducing new witnesses and documents without notice. I can't believe that Judge Brock is letting him get away with this. He must be starstruck by Solomon's flashy Hollywood image."

"Well, Bill, you once told me, and I quote: `The prosecution has to provide the defense everything, and the defense doesn't have to give us jack shit.'"

"Mr. Delgado, you were acquainted with the man named John Doe, were you not?"

"Objection. Your Honor, here he goes again off on some tangent with this John Doe. I ask the court to put a stop to this charade once and for all."

"Overruled. The witness may answer the question."

"No, I wasn't, not at all." Delgado replied disdainfully. "I have no knowledge of, nor am I acquainted with anyone named John Doe. No, wait... Miss Murdock had an on and off yardman who came by upon occasion to do some minor work for me, more or less on loan from her. That might have been his name, but I'm not sure."

"So you don't know anyone named John Doe other than as the decedent's sometimes yardman. Is that what you're telling the court,

Mr. Delgado?"

"That is precisely what I said."

"So you've never had any personal dealings with him at all apart from having seen him solely upon occasion at Miss Murdock's? Is that your testimony?"

"He may have cut my yard once or twice when my regular yardman, Chantelle's husband was out of town, and I think he repaired a section of my front porch railing several years ago, but that's the extent of it. No wait, he replaced the small columns on my back porch last fall."

"So you don't know him apart from his work as a yard or maintenance man?"

"No, I don't."

"So Mr. Delgado, it therefore follows that you've never met him or had any commerce with him anywhere other than in Halcyon, is that correct?"

"That's right," Delgado answered with disdain.

"Mr. Delgado, I'll ask you again. Have you ever met Mr. Doe or had any interaction with him anywhere other than in Halcyon?"

"I've already answered your question."

"Your honor, I'd like to introduce this photograph of this witness Mark Delgado, John Doe, and another man taken last August 4 in the parking lot of the Town & Country Steak House in Jackson, as defense exhibit number 13, and ask that it be published for the jury. It was taken by a security camera in the restaurant's parking lot. I ask the court to note the date and time code at the lower right of the image. The address of the restaurant is clearly visible, and painted upon the side of the building. The other man is the late Deon Washington, the man identified by the police, and just a moment ago, by defense witness Mrs. Nancy Wilson, as one of the men who sought to kill myself, Miss Daniels, and the district attorney's brother on the night of August 6, last year. Now, Mr. Delgado, I ask you again, what is your relationship with John Doe?"

"There was no relationship between myself and John Doe, but I do happen to remember that particular occasion, now that you mention it. I chanced to run into the man you refer to as John Doe, and a friend of his at the Town & Country Restaurant when I happened to be in Jackson on business."

"Can you explain this photograph?"

"No I can't. It has nothing to do with me."

"Members of the jury, I call your attention to this photograph of Mr. Delgado, John Doe, and Deon Washington. Again, note the camera's time code and the date in the lower right corner of the image. Mr. Wiltz, please display this image on the screen for the court and jury. Deon Washington was identified by police through dental records, as one of the men who attempted to kill me and two of my associates, on the night of August 6, last year. Now, Mr. Delgado, isn't it true that you met the two men at that restaurant specifically for the purpose of concocting a plan to permanently remove me and my associate Nikki Daniels from this case by arranging our assassination?"

"That's absurd. I may have arranged to have the railing on my back porch repaired when I chanced to run into John Doe. I can't remember, but as I mentioned, he'd done lawn and maintenance work for me before, although, as I testified, infrequently."

"Isn't it true that you hired him and his associate to intercept us on the way back from Jackson on the night of August 6 of last year? Wasn't it on this occasion, when this photograph was taken, that you made arrangements with Doe and his associate Deon Washington to kill us and make it appear to have been a robbery that went awry?"

"Absolutely not," Delgado answered calmly. "It's no secret that I don't particularly like the defendants personally, and that I do believe that they were responsible for murdering my Jeannie, but it makes no difference to me who represents them in the matter before the court at present."

"On the contrary, I think it makes a great deal of difference to you, Mr. Delgado. You've deliberately sought to, and have succeeded in implicating the defendants in the murder of the decedent, knowing full well that they were in no way involved. In fact, the prosecution's case against Miss Dautery and Mr. Toma was built entirely upon information provided by you, wasn't it, Mr. Delgado?"

"The police asked me questions about the ongoing enmity between the defendants and Miss Murdock, and I answered them honestly. The district attorney'sown brother told this court of Miss Murdock's fear of them. The district attorney and the grand jury are responsible for the charges against them, not me."

"I couldn't help but wonder why," Solomon speculated loudly as he approached the jury box, "why Miss Murdock's maid, Hattie Livingston, was so vehement in her refusal to answer questions regarding details of that doctored photo of the decedent that had been found under the rug at Miss Murdock's house on the night of the murder. It had her fingerprints all over it. Everybody assumed that she'd done it, and why? Because she's black. It never occurred to anyone that a white person could have, or would have produced some Voodoo amulet or talisman. And yet, she was fully willing to be unjustly jailed for contempt of court and perjury rather than admit she'd had anything to do with turning that photograph into some sort of hoo doo designed to injure Miss Murdock. Why? To answer that question, I reviewed her testimony before this court. She'd been asked if she'd altered the photo and she'd answered honestly and simply. `No.' She felt that was sufficient. She was unwilling to have her reputation as an upstanding Christian woman damaged by admitting to having done something she hadn't done. In other words, she was willing to be falsely accused and to go to jail if need be, rather than to lie to this court. Everyone assumed that since a Voodoo amulet or talisman had been found, and that since Mrs. Livingston was black, that she must have placed it there. She was not willing to let the matter rest, and neither was I. Mr. Delgado, you were the one who altered that photograph were you not?"

"Of course not. That's absurd. I don't know anything about that type of thing. That's the sole province of the black underclass."

"On the contrary, Mr. Delgado. Wasn't it you who altered the image of Miss Murdock, placed it beneath the rug, and on the night of the murder, pulled it out just enough that the police photographer or some other investigator couldn't miss it? Wasn't it you, Mr. Delgado, who'd sought to make it appear that Mrs. Hattie Livingston had done this?"

"Please, Your Honor. I object most strenuously to this entire line of questioning. Again, Mr. Delgado is not on trial. If he'd been a suspect at anytime, he'd be on trial now, and not the defendants. This attempt to somehow blame him for placing some photo in the house of the decedent is offensive not only to Mr. Delgado, but to the court as well. It doesn't matter who put the altered photograph of Miss Murdock under the rug, or anywhere else, since the cause of death was gunshot wounds, not some picture. Mr. Delgado has displayed the patience of Job as Mr. Solomon has practically accused him of Conspiracy to Commit Murder, Attempted Murder, and other equally pernicious personal actions which are absolutely baseless."

"Sustained. Mr. Solomon, I'm going to agree with Mr. Roberts in this instance. You're going to have to pursue another line of questioning with this witness."

"Yes, Your Honor. Mr. Delgado, you have recently sold or otherwise disposed of the majority of your investments, including large blocks of shares in British Petroleum, General Dynamics, ATT, and other large corporations, as well as divested yourself of what were substantial real estate holdings..."

"So what?" Delgado asked, cutting Solomon off before he could ask his question. Even though the judge had shut down Solomon's attack, the defense attorney was not prepared to let go of the witness just yet. Delgado's calm, cool air of detachment was starting to crack around the edges, not enough to be discernible to the jury, but enough to further embolden Solomon.

"Isn't it true, Mr. Delgado, that you were systematically disposing of everything you could sell in order to pay your enormous and ongoing gambling debts?"

"Objection!" the district attorney shouted angrily, but Solomon continued before the judge had time to rule on the objection.

"Isn't it true, Mr. Delgado, that you would have been financially bereft in short order if not for Miss Murdock's murder, if not for her will? Isn't that why you had the will probated so quickly? You're the only person alive who benefitted from her death. You inherited more than $15 million, as well as her house, her property, the insurance payment for her jewelry, in fact, everything she owned."

"Sustained."

"Yes, Your Honor. Now, Mr. Delgado, when you found out that Miss Murdock had an illegitimate child, a son, how did you react to that information?"

"If it's true, which I sincerely doubt, I knew nothing about the matter until today in court."

Solomon hesitated, and then walked over and picked up the new will. He examined it thoughtfully for a moment, then folded it quietly and wrapped his fingers around it. "No, Mr. Delgado," the lawyer said calmly, "I believe that you knew about John Doe before today, didn't you? I think Miss Murdock told you about him, told you about her illegitimate son, the man known as John Doe. I imagine she then told you that she'd been more or less silently supporting him for years, over in Jackson, where he lived."

"She did nothing of the kind," Delgado bristled. "You're insane."

"This, members of the jury," Solomon stated loudly, waving the will back and forth in his hand, "this was the real motive for the murder, not the avenging of a couple of dead goats, as the prosecution would have you believe. It was this new will which would've deprived Mark Delgado of half of Miss Murdock's estate, millions of dollars, money which Mr. Delgado considered to rightfully belong to him."

"Objection."

"Overruled. Mr. Roberts, you introduced robbery as motive, Mr. Solomon is free to pursue the subject."

"The world was closing in on you, wasn't it Mr. Delgado? Mr. Steiler was pressing you for a large sum of money, for repayment of a series of critically overdue gambling debts, money that you didn't have, and couldn't easily get. And Mr. Steiler isn't the sort of man who likes to wait, is he? You were just about at the end of your rope, desperate to come up with more than half a million dollars, and quickly. You'd already sold off your remaining assets to fuel your insatiable gambling addiction, only now there was nothing left to sell, no further options, no way to raise more money. Time was running out for you. What killed Miss Murdock wasn't the defendants' retaliation over three goats. Miss Murdock's fatal mistake was telling you she intended to bequeath half of her large estate to John Doe, someone you considered to be nothing more than a deadbeat, a mere yardman, a man with criminal tendencies, someone beneath your contempt....a black man..." Solomon said, drawing out the word for its effect on a predominantly black jury. "A member of the black underclass, as you referred to them a moment ago. Isn't that right Mr. Delgado?"

"Your Honor!" Delgado shouted as he rose from his seat in the witness stand, "I'm not on trial," he protested angrily. "I insist that you rein in this so-called lawyer. I want him charged with public slander. My name and reputation are above reproach. I've never received as much as a parking ticket, ever."

"Mr. Delgado, this is my court and I will not allow you to interrupt its proceedings. Take your seat."

"You probably reacted calmly, to this most unwelcome news, prodding Miss Murdock for details," Solomon continued. "Since you were the only person she trusted completely, I imagine she told you that her existing will, the one which you already had, the one which had been in place for years, the one which left you everything, was about to be changed. She foolishly imagined you'd have no problem with it, that you would understand, and that it wouldn't matter to you one way or the other, since you were already rich. Calling upon her trust of you, exploiting that trust, you questioned her, and found out that she had a copy of the original will on hand, the one prepared by her attorney, Mr. Light, and that she had substituted her desired changes within the text herself, but otherwise maintaining the same legal language of the original will, the original of which was in her lock box, and a copy of which was with her lawyer's office. Mr. Light, she told you, had no knowledge of the new will she was planning. She handed you the copy with her notations, cutting you out of half of her fortune, and asked you to read it, to look over it and see that it was in order, before she had Mr. Light revise it, just like she did with everything before she signed it. You read it and told her that it looked ok, but you immediately realized that it would cost you more than eight million dollars. For some reason she thought you wouldn't mind.

"You knew her well enough to know that arguing with her would be futile. You asked her if her lawyer, Mr. Light, was aware of her plans, making certain you'd heard her correctly. `No', she told you she wanted to run this by you first. She'd get it changed, signed, and notarized after you'd read it over and approved it, she said. She just wanted you to make sure it looked all right to you.

"Your mind raced as she put the will back into her lock box, the place where she kept all of her valuable jewelry, and replaced thebox under the bed, and suddenly everything came into focus. There was an immediate answer to all of your problems, wasn't there Mr. Delgado? All you had to do was act. Everything was already in place."

"Objection!" the district attorney shouted, as Delgado sought to regain his slipping composure. "Again, Your Honor, Mr. Delgado is not on trial. Would you please ask the defense to remain focused on the matter at hand? This fishing expedition of Mr. Solomon's is a blatant attempt to confuse and bewilder the jury by seeking to confound them with matters which are not in evidence, and not germane to these proceedings."

"Overruled, Mr. Roberts."

"A new will must never see the light of day," Solomon continued, "and above all, it must never be signed, witnessed, or notarized. Ever. At that point you moved quickly as your mind raced, retrieving the .32 caliber pistol from the drawer of the mahogany sideboard where you knew she kept it loaded and ready, out of fear of her neighbors. Isn't that so, Mr. Delgado?"

"Objection!" the district attorney shouted.

"Overruled. Continue Mr. Solomon."

"Then you turned and shot her where she sat, in her chair, in her ownhouse. You took the rosewood box containing her valuable jewelry, and the rough draft of her new will, making sure it would never be seen or signed. You hid them somewhere in your car, knowing that you'd never be a suspect, and that neither your car, your person, nor your residence would be searched, ever, no matter what. Your aristocratic pedigree would place you beyond suspicion and above the law. After all, weren't you a direct descendent of the Spanish nobleman who sold the city of Halcyon the very land upon which the city was erected? No, you'd never be a suspect. You could destroy that will later, the copy she'd made notations upon in her own hand, the one she showed to you for your approval.

"Everybody in Halcyon knew Miss Murdock was rich, and lived alone, so it was a perfect plan. It would look like a robbery. You wiped the murder weapon, and Miss Murdock's .45 clean of fingerprints, hid them in your car. Then you carried and dumped her body close toCypress Hill in an attempt to frame her neighbors, the defendants. Then you called the police. Later, youplaced both guns in the defendants' house, Cypress Hill, just inside the door where they would appear to have been quickly hidden, but were certain to be found. The doors to Cypress Hill were unlocked and open, and you'd been in that house many times and knew your way around.

"When the police arrived at Eldorado on the night of the murder, you acted very concerned about finding Miss Murdock, while attempting to offhandedly steer blame toward Toma and Dautery. And you lingered at the crime scene, casually smoking your expensive English cigarettes, and fooling everybody, or so you thought...but just because justice is blindfolded, Mr. Delgado, doesn't mean she's blind. What goes on in the darkness eventually comes to light. You sir, are the real murderer, are you not, Mr. Delgado? Wasn't it you who killed Miss Murdock?"

Delgado had fidgeted and squirmed as he sat in the witness box, attempting to appear calm and detached, but barely able to conceal his mounting rage as Solomon insulted him publicly. If he could just manage to retain his composure a little bit longer, Solomon's false and absurd accusations would blow over him like a hot wind, and pass by, leaving him none the worse for the experience. But nobody had ever spoken to him like this, and, at length, Solomon's verbal onslaught proved too much. Pushed beyond his endurance, Delgado finally reacted angrily, and explosively, just as Solomon had hoped, had expected he would.

"God damn you sir!" Delgado shouted loudly as he quickly stood and jumped from the witness stand in an attempt to attack the defense attorney. "Nobody talks to me like that! Nobody!"

"Order!" Judge Brock shouted, banging his gavel repeatedly against its stand as the courtroom erupted. "Bailiffs! Restrain Mr. Delgado and remove him from my courtroom until he calms down. This a court of law, not a circus sideshow. And you, Mr. Solomon, you're out of order. You're absolutely out of order. I demand order in this court!" Judge Brock shouted over the din.

"The defense rests, Your Honor," Solomon shouted loudly, before the judge had time to reprimand him in front of the jury, "and I again ask the court for a directed verdict in this case, in that the prosecution has failed to present sufficient evidence against the two defendants to convict them." Solomon made his point and then quickly took his seat, not waiting for the judge's response.

"Your request is denied," the judge answered after order had been restored in the courtroom. "Are you prepared for your closing statement at this time, Mr. Solomon?"

"Yes, Your Honor, the defense is ready."

"As it's nearly 5:00 o'clock, we're going to adjourn for the day. Again," he said, turning toward the jury, "you're not to discuss this case with anyone, and not among yourselves. The defense will present its closing arguments first, tomorrow morning. That presentation will be followed by the prosecution's closing statements. After that you will receive your instructions, and will then begin your deliberations as to the guilt or innocence of these defendants. Court will reconvene at 9:00 a.m. tomorrow morning."

22.

A Jury of One's Peers

Tom Roberts stood in the hall outside the courtroom the next morning, awaiting the beginning of court, his phone held against his ear. "Yeah, that's it," he said. "Things moved much faster than I thought they would. Closing arguments are next, then jury deliberation, and then I'm out of here. Mark Solomon is giving me a ride back home…back to L.A. on his jet, as soon as the verdict is delivered."

"You mean you're leaving today?" Leah asked, an obvious trace of sadness in her voice. "So I won't see you again?"

"No, I guess not, at least not this trip. Solomon told me to have my bags packed and ready." He sensed the disappointment in her voice and didn't want to leave it at that. "I'm glad we had some time together," he continued, "and that I've finally achieved some sense of a resolution. That's something I could only have done by coming back here, by seeing you again. Halcyon will always be a part of who I am, just as you are, but the truth is, I'm not the same person as I was ten years ago when I left town with my tail between my legs in that beat-up old Cadillac convertible. I love my life in L.A. now, and I couldn't even make a living here. Life takes us where it will, whether we want it to or not. Court is starting. I've got to go now. I hope things work out for you here, Leah. I'm sure they will. You're still young and beautiful, as always."

"But I still love you," she said.

"Me too, Leah, but I've got to go."

"All rise, court is now in session. Be seated."

"Mr. Solomon," the judge asked, "are you ready?"

"Yes, Your Honor. Thank you," the defense attorney replied as he rose from the table and approached the jury. "Members of the jury, first of all I want to thank you on behalf of myself, and my co-counsel Nikki Daniels, and your own Lucien Dale. We've enjoyed our stay in your beautiful city. The southern hospitality which you are so noted for is no exaggeration. Sadly, what brought us here in the first place is not your beautiful city, the wonderful people we've met here, or your gracious manners, but an erroneous charge of Felony Murder against two of your neighbors, Bill Toma and Olivia Dautery. The fact of the matter is that they are innocent of all charges.

"Despite the absolute lack of any evidence against them at all, the district attorney, Mr. Roberts has persistently sought to convince you that they're murderers. Why would Mr. Roberts have done that if they weren't guilty? Quite simply, Mr. Roberts has a job to do. He isn't a bad man, he'sjust wrong. Somebody did kill Miss Murdock, that's something we all agree upon, but it wasn't either of the defendants. If they're guilty of anything, it's of being somewhat peculiar, of being individuals, and that is not a crime in Halcyon, Mississippi or anywhere else in America. They may have neglected the maintenance of their house, Cypress Hill, and they may have let animals stray from their property upon occasion, but sometimes life, and circumstances can be cruel. They, like so many in this era, have simply fallen on hard times.

"The prosecution has the burden of proving beyond reasonable doubt that the defendants did knowingly and intentionally murder Miss Murdock in the commission of a robbery. The district attorney would have you believe that these two of your neighbors were cunning, ruthless, cold-blooded killers, criminal masterminds who formulated an elaborately detailed plot to rob and murder their neighbor.

"The fact is, the prosecution has completely failed to prove anything of the sort. The prosecution has sought to establish robbery, specifically valuable jewelry, as the motive for the slaying of Miss Murdock, and yet a thorough search of the defendants' house, Cypress Hill, turned up nothing other than the jewelry of Miss Dautery, all of which had been handed down for generations. Photographs of Miss Dautery's mother and grandmother, and even further back, satisfied the police that all of the jewelry found at Cypress Hill belonged to Miss Dautery. None of the jewelry allegedly missing from Miss Murdock's house was found at Cypress Hill, and still hasn't been found, anywhere. Did these criminal masterminds, these internationally famous cat burglars fence the allegedly stolen jewelry in Amsterdam, London? The Far East? No. Neither of them have left Black County since the night they were awakened from their slumber and abducted by the police from the sanctity of their own home, and falsely charged with robbery and murder. Miss Dautery doesn't even wear jewelry. Personally, I doubt that the missing jewelry will ever turn up. My guess is that it's at the bottom of the Mississippi River, halfway to New Orleans by now, since the insurance money has already been paid. So, if robbery was the actual motive as stated by the prosecution, and we now find that it wasn't, after all, then what was the real motive?

"Well, Miss Murdock shot three of their goats. There's your compelling motive right there, but is it? Really? Olivia Dautery was understandably angry about the cold-blooded murder of her goats, because she loved her animals, as many of us do our own, but this was hardly a motive for cold-blooded murder. She knew in her own mind that her goats had wandered over there, and that she was in the wrong for letting them wander, she just couldn't afford to fence that much land.

"So, if it wasn't the international jewel heist, as the prosecution claimed, then it must have certainly been a cold-blooded revenge killing over some goats. But if you don't think that revenge for goat killing is a sufficient motive for the murder of Jeannie Murdock, then it must have been something else. Perhaps you might accept the premise that Miss Murdock's stealing Olivia Dautery's fiancé thirty years ago might work. Maybe you'll fall for that. The fact is that there is no real motive for the defendants to have killed Miss Murdock, none at all, and they didn't. The defendants were doing all right financially as the result of opening their house to visitors. Their taxes were paid, and they were getting by. As a result of money from tourists, they'd had the house cleaned up and some repairs made. They weren't rich, but they were doing all right. The fact is that there weren't many motives, as the prosecution would have you believe, there weren't any motives. These people are absolutely innocent.

"Mr. Delgado testified that the decedent, Miss Murdock always locked her door, and yet when he arrived, he said, the door was unlocked. He's the only person other than the decedent and her maid who is known to have had a key, so who unlocked the door? The maid didn't open the door. She was at a tent revival on the night of the murder. It wasn't the defendants. They didn't have a key, didn't like Miss Murdock, and wouldn't have come over, especially at night. And Miss Murdock wouldn't have opened the door to either Toma or Dautery anyway, not because she hated or feared them, but simply because she just didn't like them.

"Now, Mr. Delgado had stated that goats from Cypress Hill had destroyed Miss Murdock's expensive car, but the truth was that she had allowed the registration to expire several years earlier because the car no longer worked. Mr. Delgado speculated that the motive for the murder was the robbery of her jewelry, and yet it was he who was paid $1.25 million by the insurance company, not the defendants. Mr. Delgado also inherited more than $15 million from the decedent, as well as her house, Eldorado. Mr. Delgado had excessive and ongoing gambling debts and withdrew more than half a million dollars from his bank account in one day, at one time, presumably to pay Mr. Steiler. If anyone had a motive to kill Miss Murdock, it certainly wasn't the defendants. The truth is that Mr. Delgado is the only person at all who benefitted from Miss Murdock's death, certainly not either of the defendants.

"The fact of the matter is that the prosecution's entire case is built upon nothing but the testimony of the one person, the one and only person who benefitted from Miss Murdock's murder. Under the circumstances he just can't be considered a credible witness. But Mark Delgado isn't on trial in this court, the defendants are.

"Now, let's look at police procedure on the night of the murder. The police arrived, questioned Mr. Delgado, the only person at the scene of the crime, but didn't examine his clothes for bloodstains, and didn't conduct a gunshot residue test. They didn't search him for evidence, they didn't search or examine his car. They didn't search his house. The bloodhounds that were supposed to have arrived never made it because their handler was in a motoring accident on the way to the scene of the crime. They never arrived, period. The district attorney's brother, Tom Roberts was allowed at the crime scene, a violation of standard procedure. Mr. Delgado was allowed to smoke at the scene, in the murder room. A search party mob was allowed to trample willy-nilly all through the woods in almost total darkness, between and around Cypress Hill and Eldorado, thoroughly destroying any useable evidence. Everybody from Chief Bowman on down had already privately concluded that Miss Murdock was already dead given the presence of blood at her house. They said so on the witness stand. It should've been treated as a criminal investigation to start with, a murder investigation. Professional crime scene investigators should have immediately been brought in from Jackson, given the inexperience of everybody involved in this investigation. Prosecution witness Sgt. Davis, the officer who found Miss Murdock's body, testified that he'd never discovered a body prior to having found Miss Murdock's. In other words, he had no idea how to process a crime scene. It's doubtful in the extreme that either, or both of the defendants carried Miss Murdock's body 327 feet, and they certainly wouldn't have carried her in the direction of their own house. None of this makes any sense.

"Now, let's talk about the murder weapon. The prosecution has sought to make a big issue about the murder weapon having been found at the defendants' house on the night of the murder. The murder weapon, a .32 caliber pistol was indeed found at the defendant's house, along with a .45 caliber pistol, but neither weapon had either of the defendant's fingerprints anywhere on it. It's obvious that the weapons were placed there, planted in the house by the murderer. It would certainly have been easy enough to do, given that the weapons were found downstairs, close to the front door, a door which was never locked. In fact, none of the seven doors from the first floor to the outside of Cypress Hill were ever locked. And does it make any sense to you that the defendants would hide the murder weapon in their own house, almost in plain sight, and yet actually go to the trouble to wipe away their own fingerprints? Of course not, and yet this is exactly what the prosecution would have you believe. The fact is that there is no connection between either of the guns and either of the defendants. None whatsoever. The district attorney's own brother, Tom Roberts, could not identify the .45 caliber pistol produced by the police as having been the weapon showed to him by the decedent despite his apparent knowledge of guns. All he could say is that `it looks like it.' The prosecution sought to prove that the .32 caliber murder weapon had been seen by one of the policemen, Lt. Thompson who'd answered a disturbance call at Cypress Hill, but all he could say about the pistol in Olivia Dautery's possession is that it was shiny. He said in that regard, and I quote his words verbatim, "I cannot positively identify this particular revolver, as the same gun that I saw in Miss Dautery's possession." Any pistol would have appeared shiny in the bright afternoon sun more than thirty feet away.

"The prosecution also asked Lt. Thompson about his two visits to Cypress Hill to investigate gunshots. Miss Dautery told Lt. Thompson that she'd been shooting in the general direction of trespassers. What the prosecution had conveniently failed to mention to the court, however, is that Miss Dautery had previously filed multiple police reports regarding trespassers before she finally took matters into her own hands, shooting not at anyone in particular, but merely in their general direction, seeking to frighten them off. The prosecution also failed to mention complaints about rowdy teenagers drinking beer, racing cars, and playing loud music, gathering on the defendants' property, complaints which had also been filed by other neighbors across the way on the Gale Lane side. On neither occasion when Lt. Thompson responded to reports of gunfire at Cypress Hill, did he issue Miss Dautery a citation. Why? Because he testified under oath that he didn't consider her to be a threat to himself or anyone else. Those were his words.

"In conclusion, the prosecution's entire case is based solely on the testimony of Mr. Mark Delgado, the only person who benefitted from Miss Murdock's murder. He is hardly an impartial or reliable witness, and certainly his testimony and questionable behavior are insufficient to convict two of your own neighbors of murder, in the total absence of any corroborating evidence. In a headlong rush to judgment, critical mistakes were made by the police, not only in terms of securing the crime scene, but with the entire investigation. Crucial evidence that could've convicted the actual killer or killers was not gathered, was destroyed or simply ignored by a police department inexperienced in such matters. These errors of omission and commission on their part were not intentional, they're just inexperienced, and not used to conducting murder investigations. When you, in your deliberations, consider the absence of motive, and total lack of evidence, presented against these two neighbors, members of your own community, you will conclude, as I have, that they are innocent.

"We all seek justice in this courtroom today, and we of the defense sincerely hope that the true killer or killers of Miss Murdock will, in due course, be found and brought to justice, but that's not in your power or ours either. The only justice that can be achieved in this courtroom today, right here, and right now, is up to you. It is within your power to acquit these two innocent fellow citizens of the false and unsubstantiated charges against them, and to allow them to reenter your good graces and your fellowship as the good neighbors they've always been. Thank you."

"Mr. Roberts?"

"Members of the jury, I'll be brief. The citizens of Black County thank you for taking valuable time away from your work and families to serve your community as jurors. Jury duty is always a sacrifice, and yet an impartial consideration of facts is at the very core of our judicial system. Let's get down to the facts, because that is what this trial is based upon. A member of our community, one of your neighbors, has been murdered in her own home. That is a fact. Many of us have upon occasion had disagreements with some of our own neighbors. These are usually just misunderstandings, and seldom go beyond that. This was an exception that went terribly wrong, culminating in the robbery and murder of Miss Murdock by the two defendants. There had been a continuing and well documented history of hostility and enmity between the dead woman and her so-called neighbors. Miss Murdock had complained to the police about trespassing animals from the defendants' house, Cypress Hill, on several occasions, but to no avail. Mr. Delgado had personally interceded between the two sides, speaking directly to the defendants, but again, to no avail. At length, hostilities escalated between them to the extent that the decedent, Miss Murdock, finally had to take matters into her own hands in order to simply protect her property. As a matter of consequence, she killed three of the defendants' marauding goats. Another matter of record, another fact. Killing one of the goats should've been enough, and it would have been for anyone else, but not for the defendants. Instead of apologizing and tethering, or in some other way restraining their animals, instead of being sorry for the damage their animals had caused the defendant, damages which were well documented and costly, the defendants became even more combative and actively sought to upset Miss Murdock further, rejoicing at the continued destruction of the victim's garden and shrubbery. The defendants then threatened 'to blow the decedent's head off,' as you heard in testimony. Miss Murdock was genuinely afraid of the defendants, that they would either burn her house down or kill her. She feared for her very life. It appears that Miss Murdock's fears were certainly justified for she was indeed gunned down in cold blood in her own home, her body then carried by the defendants toward their lair where they intended to butcher and dispose of her in the same way that they butchered hogs and cattle on the premises. But moving her body had been more than they'd bargained for, however, so they left the body where they'd dropped it, retraced their steps back to the side of the driveway at Eldorado, and then under cover of an extremely dark night hugged the shadows, walking down the main road until they reached their house again, then clumsily hiding the murder weapon and Miss Murdock's .45 which they had removed from the house along with the missing box of jewelry, which they'd stashed and would come back for later. They had the motive, the means, and the opportunity.

"Mr. Solomon has said that robbery was not the motive, but Mr. Delgado testified that the jewelry box was missing from Miss

Murdock's house, and it is. The fact is, there were multiple motives going back more than thirty years to the time that the decedent Jeannie Murdock had brazenly stolen Olivia Dautery's fiancé, taken him with her back to Newport, Rhode Island, toyed with him for a few weeks, and then thrown him aside. It had been a lark for the decedent, but this was the man Olivia Dautery was to marry, the love of her life. Miss Dautery's fiancé killed himself over the matter. The emotional damage done to her by Jeannie Murdock could not be repaired, could not be undone, and more importantly, could never be forgiven. And Olivia Dautery never married. Some things are unforgiveable, and this was one of them. Then, it seemed, insult was added to injury. As Miss Murdock's wealth increased, the fortunes of the defendants waned.

"And Miss Murdock's closest associate, Mark Delgado, bought the defendants' house, Cypress Hill at auction on the public square right out from under them for unpaid taxes, certainly in collusion with Miss Murdock, and with the intention of throwing Dautery and Toma onto the street. Surely, if ever there were genuine reasons for hatred, real motives for killing someone, the defendants had them.

"And Miss Murdock had very good reason to fear for her life. She'd been threatened with violence by someone known to be a skilled marksman, someone with a violent temper, and a history of being visited by the police in response to complaints from neighbors about gunfire emanating from Cypress Hill. Olivia Dautery felt herself to be above the law and had nothing but contempt for any form of authority. She had absolutely no respect for anyone else's feelings, property rights, or even personal safety. She and Bill Toma took care of the problem of Miss Murdock once and for all, using robbery as a cover for their overriding, all-consuming purpose, the removal of Miss Murdock forever. The only problem was that in their arrogance, and convinced of their own invincibility, they lacked the foresight to conceal their crime, and that's why they're here before you today, facing the serious charges placed upon them by the state of Mississippi. They weren't charged on a mere whim, as Mr. Solomon would have you believe, but were indicted by a duly constituted Grand Jury.

"Mr. Solomon is a rich and famous Hollywood attorney, I'm not rich or famous, I'm just a local man, a public servant, one of you. Mr. Solomon will be on his expensive private jet and back in some fancy California restaurant as soon as you reach your verdict, none the worse for the experience, but we live here. We cannot allow one of our fellow citizens to be murdered in her own home without consequence, and watch as the killers go free and walk among us. The defense has intentionally sought to confuse and confound you by diverting the focus of this trial away from the actual facts. Mr. Solomon has introduced persons as witnesses who have absolutely nothing to do with the matter at hand. Early in the presentation of his defense, he sought to implicate Miss Murdock's maid, Hattie, as the murderer through some sort of Voodoo. When that didn't work, he attacked Mr. Delgado, and yet it's common knowledge that Mark Delgado was Miss Murdock's closest, and basically only friend. That he benefitted from her will is to be expected. They were life long friends. Despite Mr. Soloman'songoing attempts to bewilder you, the facts are clear and indisputable.

"In a few minutes Judge Brock will give you instructions for your deliberations. Basically, the state wants you to simply consider the facts presented to you in an objective and impartial manner. I know that when you do, you will conclude that the defendants are guilty of all charges. Thank you again for your service."

For the next half an hour the judge gave instructions to the jury in excruciating detail and though this was Tom Roberts' first murder trial, he didn't have to be experienced to note that the judge lost the attention of two thirds of the jury after the first ten minutes, yet still he continued. Finally, after more than half an hour, the jury was escorted out of the courtroom and court was recessed. Tom approached Mark Solomon and said, “What happens next?”

“We wait around for the verdict. I doubt that this will take long, no more than a half hour or so. If it’s longer than that I’ll be surprised. We’re all going over to the bar at the Moro, why don’t you come with us. They’ll call us when a verdict comes in.”

“Come on, Tom,” Nikki Daniels beckoned him.

“You don’t have to ask me twice.”

“All three of the defense attorneys were assailed by reporters with microphones and flashing cameras the instant they stepped through the courtroom doors. “Any comment Mr. Solomon?” shouted a reporter from some station in Milwaukee. “I think it went well,” he answered, “but we’ll have to wait and see. No further comments, please, just let us through.”

At the hotel bar Tom ordered a Coors Light, and asked the defense team how they thought the jury would rule. Solomon was very edgy and appeared nervous. “Don’t worry about him,” Daniels laughed, “he’s like that during every jury deliberation no matter how strong our case is.”

“I can’t help it,” Solomon answered, “too many things can go wrong.There are always too many variables, and you never know how any jury will rule, ever. Anybody who thinks he knows any jury is delusional. You have to address them on their level, in terms that they understand, and that isn’t easy.”

“You mean you have to talk down to them?”

“Sometimes, but that’s not what I mean. This jury, for example, considers me an outsider. That’s the bottom line. Eloquence and a grandiose manner merely emphasize, heighten, the fact that we have little in common. I can’t pretend to be one of them, a down-home kind of guy. They know better than that, and would react negatively. There’s an unconscious resistance to people we don’t like, and this is especially true with any jury. There always exists some sort of mass, or group consciousness within any jury which is greater than the sum of its individual members. You have to find that common denominator and strike there, and that's difficult, because it's largely unconscious, at least from their perspective. They don't like me because they don't know me. The bad thing is that if they knew me, they wouldn't like me either," he laughed nervously, "so I'm trying to punt out of the end zone. In other words, I'm at a disadvantage right out of the starting gate. Your brother, on the other hand, is well known to them. He has a reputation of protecting honest, hard-working people from predatory criminals. He also has the home court advantage. He's a Halcyon native, not an outsider, like me."

"But you presented a compelling case for the defense," Tom laughed, "I don't get it. What are you worried about?"

"Well, thanks for your vote of confidence, Tom, but your brother kept to the issues, while I was forced to step outside the comfort zone of the jury. The law says that it's up to the state to prove the guilt of the defendants, and the defendants don't have to prove anything. Technically, a defendant is not required to even mount a defense at all, but every lawyer knows that's pure horseshit. You'd better have a defense, and that defense had better not be sitting around waiting to see what happens. I don't care what the law says, a defense attorney had better be proving his client's innocence, or he's through, and so is his client. As always, in court as anywhere else, the best defense is a good offense.

"I'm convinced that those two are innocent. They had nothing to do with that woman's murder," Solomon fretted, as Nikki Daniels gently ran her fingertips across Tom Roberts' thigh beneath the table.

After around 40 minutes Solomon's phone rang. "The jury has reached a verdict, let's go. Put the drinks on my bill," he said hurriedly to the waitress on the way through the door, "we've got to go."

The courtroom was packed with reporters when the defense team arrived, and Tom noticed an increased police presence with more than a dozen uniformed guards and nearly that many plainclothesmen on hand, all with very visible pistols strapped to their waists or resting at the ready in shoulder holsters. It took nearly ten minutes from the time that they arrived before court was called to order.

"I understand that the jury have reached a verdict," Judge Brock stated as he addressed the jury foreman. "The defendants will stand as the verdict is published. What is your verdict?"

"On the charge of Aggravated Robbery, we the jury find the defendants not guilty. On the charge of First Degree Murder, we the jury find the defendants not guilty. On the charge of Felony Murder, we the jury find the defendants not guilty."

"Are each of these unanimous verdicts?" the judge asked.

"They are, Your Honor."

"The jury is dismissed. The defendants are free to go. Court is adjourned."

23.

Ex Post Facto

It took Solomon, Nikki Daniels, and Lucien Dale twenty minutes to cut through the press which had gathered in the corridor and on the courthouse steps. Solomon was all smiles as he talked to and with reporters from the worldwide news media about how difficult the trial had been and what a formidable adversary the Black County district attorney Bill Roberts had proven to be.

At some length, after having dispensed with the media, the prosecution, the defense team, and Tom Roberts adjourned to Queen's Court Tavern for drinks and a post-trial get together.

"The state sought to establish that the motive for Miss Murdock's murder was robbery," Solomon observed, "and yet, we'd discovered that the defendants were financially solvent, and that they'd profited during the twice annual pilgrimages, in addition to opening their house almost daily to the public for paid tours. The annual property taxes had been paid and were current at Cypress Hill. The gas, water, phone, and electricity were and are all current. In other words, if robbery had been a motive, as you maintained Bill, it would scarcely have been a motive for the defendants. They were by no means rich, and won't be, unless they get some kind of big book and, or movie deal out of this, and they might, but they were on the way up."

"Yes, but there was a robbery."

"No, Delgado said that there'd been a robbery. I eventually suspected that the robbery story was an attempt to divert attention away from the underlying motive, which was really murder."

"I wonder what happened to all of that expensive jewelry," Nikki Daniels speculated wistfully.

"It might turn up later, but I doubt it."

"Me too," Tom Roberts laughed. "Mark Delgado considered it played and paid, as we say in L.A., but I'm surprised that he didn't plant some of it at Cypress Hill."

"I'm sure he thought about it, but he'd received the money from the insurance company, so he benefitted doubly in that regard, helping divert suspicion from himself, while getting paid full value by the insurance company. To him the jewelry was just an extra problem, something else to be dealt with. I imagine all that jewelry was dumped off the bridge into the Mississippi River, and is well on its way to New Orleans by now, or buried in three feet of silt."

"I'd always thought robbery had been the real motive," the district attorney speculated, "that, and a genuine, longstanding hatred for the decedent. Cypress Hill was literally falling down. Usually, when a grand house is deteriorating, it's the result of lack of money."

"While that's often the case, I don't necessarily equate eccentricity with poverty," Solomon offered. "Some people simply don't want to be bothered with having to deal with repairmen and other people who they don't know coming into their home. They value their privacy more than nearly anything else. In fact, as Katherine Harrington of the *New Orleans Sun* observed, `privacy is the new standard of luxury in the 21st century.' Besides, Delgado's own house, Oakmont, was falling down."

"Yes, but if that's so, how do Toma and Dautery deal with the public every day, with those strangers coming into their house?" Tom Roberts asked.

"From what I know of the defendants, they probably consider that they're entertaining guests rather than having people they didn't want, working in their house, snooping, and probably stealing. Toma sings and plays piano for them. Olivia Dautery reads excerpts from magazine articles she'd written long ago, and quotes some of her own poetry. They're treated as minor celebrities by their visitors."

"Yes, they are celebrities," Daniels agreed. "I imagine they enjoy the attention. And now, they'll be free to discuss their murder trial as well. It'll be good for business. It makes them seem even more interesting."

"But what about the maid?" Tom Roberts asked. "That whole incident was strange, to say the least."

"Hattie Livingston, Miss Murdock's maid had, I thought at the time,attempted to murder Miss Murdock through the use of some sort of Voodoo or hoodoo," Solomon stated frankly. "According to Pommerly's investigations, it was believed by many in the black community that the amulet, the altered photograph of the decedent, was the real reason for Miss Murdock's death. The .32 revolver was merely an accessory, the means by which the murder was carried out, and not its underlying cause. Technically, I thought at the time, she should've been charged with attempted murder at the very least, not that it would have stuck, but that it would've further diverted attention from the defendants."

"You actually thought that she had doctored that photograph?" the district attorney asked. "Didn't you?"

"Yes, of course I did, didn't you? That's why I went after her so hard on that subject."

"Yes. I thought that she did it too, and you were about to nail her to the wall on the second day of her testimony, but then suddenly dropped the whole issue like a hot brick. What made you change your mind so quickly? It threw me off guard."

"I just realized that she must've been telling the truth. She was willing to spend the night in jail and to face perjury and contempt of court charges rather than recant her testimony. Again, why? I concluded that she was innocent."

“But if she hadn’t doctored that photo then why was she so hostile on the witness stand?”

“She was hostile because I’d basically portrayed her in court as a liar, when she’d actually been telling the truth the whole time. No wonder she reacted angrily.”

“So who altered the photograph? In court you implied that Delgado had done it.”

“Delgado did. I can’t prove it of course, but I’m sure of it. He’d altered that photograph and placed it where it was certain to be found,” Solomon answered, “not that it matters now, at least in terms of this trial.”

“But if he’d wanted to frame Dautery and Toma, what would he have gained by seeking to implicate Miss Murdock’s maid?” Tom Roberts asked.

“I believe it was his desire to simultaneously divert attention from himself on as many fronts as possible. He didn’t care who the police arrested and charged, as long as it wasn’t him, and his strategy worked, just as he’d intended.”

“What made you begin to suspect Delgado? I still don’t get what made you turn your attention to him,” the district attorney asked.

“Well, Bill, I already knew the two defendants were innocent, and felt like we could get an acquittal anyway, based upon both your...the prosecution’s lack of evidence, as well as any really compelling motive.”

“Yes, but this isn’t Los Angeles. You could’ve always lost in a Mississippi court, and the defendants found guilty anyway. My worst-case scenario as the district attorney is exactly what happened. Toma and Dautery were set free, and there is no hard evidence to connect anybody else to Miss Murdock’s murder.”

“Basically, you’d built your case solely on the testimony of Mr. Delgado, the only person who’d truly benefitted from Miss Murdock’s death. He had the most to gain financially, in excess of

$15 million. That's a lot of money by anyone's standards. He wasn't tested for gunpowder residue. He wasn't searched. His car wasn't impounded and examined. It was all too clean."

"Well, I admit," the district attorney observed, "it never occurred to me, or to any of us, that Delgado could've had any involvement at all. It was a serious mistake on my part. Chief Bowman was in charge of the investigation, and I let him run with it. He never suspected Delgado either, not even remotely. I sure didn't. None of us did. Delgado's family history is still taught in Halcyon history classes. Everybody on our team dropped the ball. As the one who reported the crime, and the first person on the scene, Delgado should've been given the same treatment as anyone else would have received under similar circumstances. I guess we were all awed and overwhelmed by his family history, and his pompous, aristocratic attitude…I don't know. We've all learned our lesson. But still, what made you suspect him?"

"At first I didn't. The police seldom make mistakes, despite the way they're sometimes portrayed on film. I attributed the fact that all of you had given him a pass to your personal knowledge of him. This is your town. If you didn't consider him a suspect, I assumed there was no reason for us to do so either. Then, I began to think that perhaps Delgado might've had something to do with the attempt on our lives on the way back from Jackson last August, but I didn't really know why. It was more of a hunch than anything else.

"For me, I guess, it all goes back to that will," Solomon continued. "There was no reason that it should've been probated so quickly. It usually takes over a year anywhere, even under the best circumstances. Mr. Dale said things of that nature move faster in a small town, and they probably do, especially among members of the upper class, but the overriding question for me was `why?' Why would someone supposedly very rich be so anxious to get his hands on that money? Money that was already coming to him anyway?

There had to be something more pressing, more urgent than just closing the books and putting the matter to rest. It didn't seem logical, especially in view of the fact that Mr. Delgado and the decedent had supposedly been so close. It also struck me as odd that he appeared so undisturbed by the murder of his closest, and from what I could tell, only friend, and lifetime lover. What was considered by the prosecution to be the emotionless manner of an aloof patrician, seemed to me to be more one of cold-bloodedness, than aristocratic indifference. There should've been some period of mourning on Delgado's part, however contrived, some something, but there wasn't. My eloquent co-counsel, your Mr. Dale, here, was able to contact the lawyer who'd drawn up her original will, Don Light, who confirmed to him what I'd suspected, that it was Delgado, and not Light, Murdock's attorney, who was in a hurry to probate that original will. But again, why?

"Like I said, I already knew the two defendants were innocent, and felt like we could get an acquittal anyway, based on the prosecution's lack of evidence and of any real motive. There were no other suspects, and the murder and its investigation would've been dropped after the defendants' acquittal, having been determined to have been perpetrated by a person or persons unknown. Behind the scenes, I'd instructed Demonbreun Tchoupitoulas to find out anything and everything he could about Delgado. His discoveries told a tale of squandered inheritance, current debt, and looming financial ruin. Delgado wasn't broke yet, but would've been soon enough, given his penchant for gambling, and he was in debt way over his head at the time of the murder.

"Those elaborate casinos aren't built upon the winnings of their patrons, but upon their losses. Delgado was addicted to gambling. It was the one vice to which he succumbed, and in his case, one vice was enough. But as Demonbreun discovered, it wasn't the tables or the slot machines that were his undoing, it was the rigged back room games, those only open to the high rollers, and unknown to the general public. The stakes are higher and the games dirtier. Credit is extended, and winnings and losses unreported, and untaxed, which isn't the case in any legal operation.

"Delgado's real motive for the murder was that new will, although I didn't know there was one at the time. When I was handed that copy of the second, more recent will, all of the loose ends suddenly came together, I mean immediately, almost like a flash of lightning. Suddenly everything made sense. Miss Murdock had mistakenly shown Delgado the new will she was working on, one which would've cost him nearly $8 million. It seemed that she had some conscience after all, and her son, John Doe, was a bastardchild in the truest sense of the word. She felt that she could never make up for having treated him with such contempt, but she also knew that she could never have been a mother to him under any circumstances. It wasn't in her nature, and furthermore, given the mores of the era in this part of the country, at the time of his birth, impossible as well. She'd given him money from time to time with the understanding that he was never to come to her house or to present himself in any capacity other than that of her yardman. She knew that he'd become a petty criminal, a gambler, and a wastrel, and I imagine she felt largely responsible for his condition. At length, and consumed by guilt, she'd decided to cut him in for half of everything she owned. She hadn't been a mother to him, and she could never make up for that, but she could at least make him rich. That was within her power.

"While Mark Delgado was the only person she trusted completely, she'd already had the new will prepared by a lawyer she probably got out of the phone book, just in case Delgado didn't approve. She was a strong-willed woman by all accounts, and had already made up her mind, and had in fact already had a new will prepared. Her own lawyer, Don Light, knew nothing about the new will. This was all under the radar. She made the fatal mistake of telling Delgado that she was making a new will, disclosed to him its contents, and then compounded the error by stating that she was working on it herself. As far as he knew, there was no new will, just the one which he undoubtedly took from her house on that night, the one she'd been revising in her own hand. As far as Delgado knew, the original will was still in force. He couldn't let her make a new will, so he killed her. It was really that simple. That was the true reason for her murder. It was the spontaneous act of a desperate man, and not something he'd planned for months. It was something which had to be stopped at that very moment."

"But if Miss Murdock had been so secretive about everything, why would she have even mentioned it to Delgado at all?"

"She trusted him completely. We can only speculate as to what she actually told him regarding the new will which left her son half of everything, or why, but there's no way Delgado would have killed her unless she had, for whatever reason, led him to believe that there was only one copy of that will, the one she was working on. I concluded that she would've had to have told him something along those lines. If Delgado had thought for one minute that her lawyer, Don Light, had a new will, or that there was a new will already fully executed in her safe deposit box at her bank, she'd still be alive today."

"Yes, but nobody knew there was another, newer will, until Delgado's maid found it while cleaning up Miss Murdock's house and gave it to Pommerly," Tom Roberts speculated.

"That's right. Delgado would have burned that house down and everything in it rather than have a second, newer will located. As it turned out though, he killed her for nothing. Since her son John Doe subsequently died in the car wreck, Delgado would have inherited everything anyway."

"So he really didn't know that John Doe was her illegitimate son?"

"No, Delgado thought John Doe was merely a yardman with criminal tendencies. He had no idea until she told him about Doe, and about the new will, the night she was murdered."

"I'd like to have seen his face when she laid that on him," Tom Roberts laughed. "Delgado really almost got away with it. He had the perfect alibi. He was known by all to visit Miss Murdock's house nearly every day. He had keys to her house. He knew where everything was hidden. That his fingerprints were all over the house was expected, and therefore raised no red flags with the police. He had what he absolutely believed to be the only copy of the new will in progress in his pocket when he called the police to report her disappearance. The rich are frequently flawed but seldom stupid. Things went exactly as planned for Delgado."

"The defendants, on the other hand," the district attorney argued, "were known to have threatened the decedent. Olivia Dautery was considered to be hotheaded and overtly hostile. She looked crazy, and was known by the police to have shot at trespassers before. It was the perfect cover for Delgado."

Tom Roberts looked puzzled. "Yes, but there still would've been the problem of her son, John Doe who certainly could've come forward to claim some, if not all, of Murdock's estate."

"Yes, and no. Who would have believed any claim he might have made on her estate, had he lived? This is still Mississippi, and it appears that any guilt, or blackmail money he might have received from Miss Murdock was paid in cash, since there were no bank records or other documents linking her to him. She was careful to make certain that no paper trail existed between the two of them. Everybody considered him to be her yardman," Solomon suggested, "and nothing more."

"But a DNA test would have clearly substantiated his claim."

"Like I said, who would have believed Doe? It would've been

hard for him to ever get a hearing, given his lengthy criminal record."

"Yeah, you're right. It was a safer bet for Doe to wait and try to extort some money from Delgado, after Miss Murdock's death. At least he'd end up with something, and probably a large amount at that. Who knows what Delgado might have promised him, if anything? There was certainly enough money available that Delgado could've made it good for him. Toma and Dautery were charged with the murder, so everything was working for Delgado."

"That is," interrupted the district attorney, "until you and your crew descended upon our quiet town in a cloud of media frenzy. Delgado was probably afraid that you'd eventually conclude that the defendants reallywere innocent, at which time you'd start looking elsewhere. He hired those two to kill you, Mark, because he knew that if you were out of the way, once and for all, Toma and Dautery would have probably been found guilty, and the matter would've been dropped. Delgado would have been in the clear, with all that money, since he was the most obvious person to inherit her holdings anyway. He would've been completely above suspicion. He hired John Doe and his accomplice Deon Washington to dispose of you, and probably knew that Doe had been the unidentified man in the car who'd been killed during the botched attempt. So much the better.

"When the assassination attempt backfired, and Doe and the other man died in the subsequent crash, it proved to be a mixed blessing for Delgado. With Doe dead, there was nobody left who could've had any claim on the estate. Given Doe's character, it's possible that he would've attempted to blackmail Delgado sooner or later, no matter what he'd been paid. On the other hand, since they'd been unsuccessful in killing you Mark, that still left you in charge of the defense team.

"That was the other half of the mixed blessing. Maybe, Delgado figured the assassination attempt would scare you enough that you'd pack up, go back to L.A. and forget all about it. At the very least, nobody in his wildest dreams would've ever connected Delgado with the attempt on your life."

"Yeah, although you still headed the defense team," Lucien Dale speculated, "you could always lose in a Mississippi court, and the defendants be found guilty anyway. In the worst-case scenario, even if Toma and Dautery were set free, there was still nothing connecting Delgado to Miss Murdock's murder. He was literally beyond suspicion. He was considered to be the decedent's best friend, and he was perceived to be, and had been, really rich. He had no motive. Furthermore, that first will leaving him everything was more than ten years old. It wasn't something that had been drawn up hastily three weeks before the murder. There was nothing suspicious about it."

"You have to appreciate the irony," Daniels noted, "that John Doe, a man who would've stood to have inherited $8 million that Delgado regarded as his, rode to his death as part of a plan Delgado had hatched. I'm certain that John Doe had no knowledge of the second will, or even the first will, for that matter."

"So Delgado killed Miss Murdock for nothing after all," Dale observed.

"Since John Doe had a criminal record already and known bad association, why didn't Delgado just kill him or have him killed, and leave Miss Murdock alone? That would've seemed to have been a more prudent course of action. John Doe would most likely have been considered to be just another thug who got what he had coming to him."

Solomon scratched his eyebrow and then answered Lucien Dale. "As Sherlock Holmes observed, 'Crime is common, logic is rare.' The world was closing in on Delgado. He needed a large sum of money immediately. Miss Murdock might have lived indefinitely.

And again, all he knew of John Doe was that he was a sometimes yardman with criminal tendencies. He had no idea Doe was Murdock's son. The new will was the final straw. That the co-heir died as the result of actions Delgado had initiated is the synchronistic icing on the cake of supreme irony. And besides, Delgado didn't move in circles where he could just ask around among his friends and easily find someone to do a hired killing for him."

"But you didn't actually know that Delgado had hired Doe to assassinate you? You couldn't have. You were just bluffing him weren't you?"

"Yes, it was pure speculation on my part," Solomon concurred. "Only someone who had something to gain directly from us being removed from the case would've cared one way or the other, except for the defendants, who were in jail at the time, which of course eliminated them. Besides, we were here to help them. When the terms of Miss Murdock's original will became known to me, it was clear that Delgado was the only person who stood to gain from our removal. That made me curious. That curiosity prompted me to call Tchoupitoulas and Pommerly, both of whom, as I've mentioned, subsequently discovered a long and ongoing trail of high stakes gambling losses by Delgado. He'd been really rich for a long time, but started gambling when his mother died. It seemed that she'd controlled the purse strings his entire life. When she died, he suddenly had all of that money at his disposal, and basically went wild. By the time Tchoupitoulas and Pommerly began investigating him, he'd quietly sold his plantation, and all the other real estate he'd inherited, and was basically down to stems and seeds. Most of his property was outside of the state so nobody here knew about it."

"Where did you get that picture of Delgado, John Doe, and Deon Washington at the Town & Country Restaurant in Jackson?" Tom Roberts asked, "It proved that Delgado had been lying."

"It was an image taken from one of the security cameras in the parking lot, courtesy of Demonbreun P. Tchoupitoulas."

"That was an amazing piece of detective work, to come up with that image, but I still don't understand what the motive was for her murder," Tom Roberts continued, "Delgado would have ended up with everything sooner or later. All he had to do was wait."

"Again," Solomon asserted, "He couldn't wait. He was almost broke, and heavily in debt to someone who wasn't going to wait."

"Then why didn't he just ask Miss Murdock for the money to cover his losses? She would probably have given him whatever he wanted, if he'd asked her. She was rich, and he was almost the only person she actually liked."

"Who's to say that he didn't? He might have, and she could've turned him down," Solomon speculated. "Or she might have given him money repeatedly and finally cut him off. She didn't seem to me to be the type of person to countenance such a blatant and frivolous waste of money. In any event, we'll never know.

"She probably would've given him what he needed to fix his house, or for anything else she considered to be legitimate. But she wasn't the type to support his gambling, and from all accounts, wouldn't have. He couldn't ask her for anything without risking that she'd find out about his passion for gambling, and penchant for losing, in which case she would have certainly disinherited him altogether. She wouldn't have left her family fortune to someone she considered to be a spendthrift, but Bill, as the Black County district attorney, what are you going to do about Delgado, now that I've basically exposed him in public as the murderer?" Solomon asked.

"I don't know that there's anything I can do. Because of bad police work, there's nothing connecting him to the crime. That $500 check to John Doe doesn't prove anything. It could've been for yard work, or maintenance on his house. Doe is dead and so is his cohort Deon Washington, so neither of them can testify against him, not that they would have anyway, that is, if they were still alive. Sadly, I can't relive that night and do what should've been done in the first place. I don't have enough hard evidence to even file charges against him. I know that a grand jury wouldn't indict him. He's home free and he knows it. Do you have any ideas?"

"No I don't, I'm sorry to say," Solomon observed. "I don't think that there's anything you can do under the circumstances, but I wouldn't feel too badly about it. Every criminal attorney has something along those lines somewhere in his past. I know I do, and I'm not proud of it, but hopefully we learn from our mistakes. None of us are perfect."

"At least the defendants weren't unjustly convicted. That's the only bright spot I can find in this whole case," the district attorney confessed. "I guess I was blinded by my inability to get beyond Delgado's reputation as a rich aristocrat, and all that implies, but I'd known him all of my life, and I really believed that Toma and Dautery were guilty.So did the grand jury. I wasn't the only person who thought so. Well, I was wrong, and I hate to admit it. I got my ass whipped, but I appreciate your work, nonetheless. This crime would've remained unsolved forever if not for you, and justice is what the state sought, what we all sought. I would've never suspected Delgado...ever."

"Again, don't feel too badly about it," Solomon replied. "Your case was logical, and well considered, given the evidence at hand. I guess I've been more exposed to the darker elements of the human personality over a longer period of time than you have, so perhaps I automatically peer more deeply into the darkness, looking for possibilities that most people wouldn't be likely to consider. In the circles in which I travel, or should I say traffic, those I'm involved with legally are usually rich and greedy, ego-driven sociopaths, with a blatant disregard for anyone and everything which doesn't feed their insatiable narcissistic need for their own self-approval. They're literally capable of anything, and easily reconcile the cruelest, most horrible deeds with their own high opinions of themselves. It doesn't matter what they do, it's always somebody else's fault. Hell, just ask your brother. Ask Tom."

"Wait a minute," Tom Roberts interrupted, scarcely able to believe what he'd just heard, "it sounds like neither one of you are going to take any kind of action against Mark Delgado. It sounds like you're literally letting him get away with murder."

"There isn't anything either of us can do," Solomon replied. "That's just the way it is. Our legal system isn't perfect, sometimes guilty people fall through the cracks, and sometimes the innocent are unjustly punished, but it's still the best legal system on earth. Delgado did get away with murder, and all of the money. It really was the perfect crime. He'll never be charged with anything."

"He's right, Tom," the district attorney agreed, "that's just the way it is, and there's nothing either one of us, or anybody else can do about it. I do have one lingering question though, which makes no sense to me at all."

"And what's that?"

"Mark, how is it that someone of your stature is friends with my brother, a mailman? That's not to diminish the significance of mailmen in general, or Tom specifically, but still…I just don't get it."

Tom Roberts and Mark Solomon looked sheepishly at each other and then at Nikki Daniels, and the three of them burst out laughing. "Maybe someday Tom will tell you all about it."

EPILOGUE

Tom Roberts returned to Halcyon five years later for his mother's funeral and found little changed in the town as a whole. Some things had changed though. His lost love, Leah, had remarried, and had a daughter. He saw her at the funeral, wished her well, and was happy for them. Time really does heal all wounds, after all. Mark Delgado, now rich again with Jeannie Murdock's money, had stopped gambling, ceased his reclusive lifestyle, and seemed none the worse for the entire incident. If some of the town folk thought him guilty of murder, he was apparently unconcerned. Delgado's house Oakmont, had been fully restored. Delgado also bought several very expensive cars, and traveled extensively. Within another year, he was dead, felled by a heart attack somewhere in Spain. His possessions as well as those he'd inherited from Jeannie Murdock were sold at public auction at Oakmont, conducted by Crescent Estate Auction Company of New Orleans.

Toma and Dautery had died within a short time of each other, their once sensational trial largely forgotten. Theironce grand house was razed, and its contents auctioned, with nothing remaining there other than a street named Cypress Hill.

Scott Faragher

About the author: Scott Faragher spent 20 years on and off as exclusive agent or agency, for Jerry Lee Lewis, Waylon Jennings, Jessi Colter, Tompall Glaser, Dr. Hook, David Allan Coe, George Jones, Tammy Wynette, Ray Price, Johnny

Rodriguez, Johnny Paycheck, Louise, Mandrell, Barbara Mandrell, and others, including Merle Haggard, The Statler Brothers, Don Williams, Ronnie Milsap, Brenda Lee, Carl Perkins, etc. He set the Marlboro Tour, the longest running, most lucrative corporate sponsorship in the history of country music at the time. He was president of In Concert International, representing Mickey Gilley, Lou Rawls, James Brown, Fats Domino, John Anderson, and numerous Jamaican reggae acts, etc. as well as former manager of Billy Ray Cyrus and Ray Price. He maintained offices in Los Angeles and Nashville.

His first book, `Music City Babylon, Inside the World of Country' Music' (1992) chronicled his wild life behind the scenes. As a result of its success he did `Entertainment Tonight', PBS `Word on Words,' and many others, and has been reviewed by everyone from *Kirkus*, and *Publishers Weekly*, to the *Houston Chronicle*, and *Chicago Tribune, Nashville Tennessean, Atlanta Journal, etc.* Since then he's written about subjects of personal interest which include mountain biking, music, art, architecture, antiques and vintage cars. He currently splits his time between homes outside of Nashville, Holly Springs, and Natchez, Mississippi.

His books so far:

Music City Babylon, Inside the World of Country Music. Birch Lane Press, New York, 1992

The Branson, Missouri Scrapbook. Citadel, New York, 1994

The Complete Guide to Riverboat Gambling. Citadel, New York, 1995

Making It In Country Music. Citadel, New York, 1996

Nashville, Gateway to the South. Cumberland House, Nashville, 1998

Chattanooga, Best of the Lookout City. Milton Publishing, Chattanooga, 2001

New Orleans in Vintage Postcards (Images of America). Arcadia Publishing, Charleston, SC. 1999

Nashville in Vintage Postcards (Images of America). Arcadia Publishing, Charleston, SC. 1999

Memphis in Vintage Postcards (Images of America). Arcadia Publishing, Charleston, 2000

Beer Signs for the Collector. Schiffer Publishing, Atglen, PA. 2001

Cameras for Collectors. Schiffer Publishing, Atglen, PA. 2001.

The Peabody Hotel. Arcadia Publishing, Charleston SC. 2002

The New South. (Contributing Author) Insight Guides, London 2004

Porsche, The Ultimate Guide. KP Books, Iola, Wisc. 2005

The Hammond Organ. Privately published, 2009

The Hammond Organ. Backbeat Books (Hal Leonard Books) 2011

The Arlington Resort Hotel & Spa. DeathcatMedia, Nashville, 2017

The Peabody, the South's Grand Hotel. DeathcatMedia, Nashville 2019

Pigeon Drop. DeathcatMedia, Nashville 2021-2023

Car Crazy ! (A Lifelong Obsession). DeathcatMedia, Nashville 2021-2022

Glenn Ferguson, A Life of Public Service. DeathcatMedia, Nashville 2023

God as I Understand Him. DeathcatMedia, Nashville 2018-2026

Destination Unknown. DeathCatmedia, Nashville, 2017-2026

For further information on these books as well as reviews, pictures, and upcoming books, check out **deathcatmedia.com**

Made in the USA
Monee, IL
04 November 2026

67384878R00216